THE DUAL STATE

THE DUAL STATE

A CONTRIBUTION
TO THE THEORY OF DICTATORSHIP

ERNST FRAENKEL

TRANSLATED FROM THE GERMAN BY
E. A. SHILS, IN COLLABORATION WITH
EDITH LOWENSTEIN AND KLAUS KNORR

OXFORD UNIVERSITY PRESS
NEW YORK   LONDON   TORONTO

PREFACE

THE CONDITIONS under which this book was conceived and written deserve a brief comment. The book is the product of the paradoxical isolation enforced upon those who lived and carried on their work in the Germany of National-Socialism although they were opposed to this regime. The purpose of the author was to describe the basic principles of the legal and constitutional developments of the Third Reich. His activity as a practising attorney in Berlin from 1933-38 provided the close and continuous contact with the legal system of National-Socialism necessary to check and recheck his generalizations by confronting them with the reality of practice.

In writing this book the author had at his disposal all the National-Socialist sources pertinent to his subject, including all the significant decisions published in the different German law reviews. Unfortunately it was impossible for him to take account of material unavailable in Germany, such as the writings of the German emigrés and many other publications outside Germany. Essentially the manuscript was completed before the author left Germany.

The course of this work was fraught with many difficulties. Its publication would have been impossible without the generous assistance of a number of friends.

For financial assistance, the author gratefully acknowledges his indebtedness to:

The American Guild for German Cultural Freedom; the Graduate Faculty of Political and Social Science organized by the New School for Social Research; the International Institute of Social Research; Professor Alfred E. Cohn, New York; Dr. Fritz Karsen, New York; and Dr. Frederick Pollock, New York.

The manuscript has been read and many valuable suggestions have been offered by Professor Arthur Feiler, New School of Social Research, New York; Professor C. J. Friedrich, Harvard

University; Professor Waldemar Gurian, University of Notre
Dame; Professor Friedrich Kessler, University of Chicago; Professor Wolfgang Kraus, Smith College; Professor Oskar Lange,
University of Chicago; Dr. N. C. Leites, University of Chicago;
Dr. Franz Neumann, New York; Professor Max Rheinstein, University of Chicago; Professor David Riesman, University of Buf-
falo; and Professor Albert Salomon, New School of Social Research, New York.

The author is especially grateful to Dr. Gerhard Meyer of the
University of Chicago, for his kind permission to use his unpub-
lished manuscript on the economic system of the Third Reich.

I wish to express my gratitude to Mr. E. A. Shils of the University of Chicago who so generously made his time and skill
available for the onerous task at hand.

Mr. J. Bryan Allin checked the whole manuscript for points
needing clarification for the American reader unfamiliar with the
German legal tradition. Mr. Allin, with Messrs. A. Bell and I.
Pool, very kindly helped the author to adapt the book for this
purpose, each with one of the chapters. Mr. Bell also assisted the
author in including certain sections added to take account of
later developments. The author would like here to express his
gratitude for this assistance.

In order that the nature of the book should remain unchanged,
it was decided to take account only of the National-Socialist publications and decisions concerned. It should be understood that
the book treats of the legal and constitutional development only
to the outbreak of the present war.

I should like to thank Mr. George Rothschild, graduate student
of the Law School of the University of Chicago, for helping to
prepare the manuscript for publication.

The author is grateful to the following publishers for permission to quote from copyright works:

G. P. Putnam's Sons: A. J. Carlyle, *A History of Medieval
Political Theory in the West, Vol. I;* D. Appleton Century
Company: Raymond Gettell, *History of American Political
Thought;* The Macmillan Company: Charles H. McIlwain, *The*

Growth of Political Thought in the West; J. R. Tanner, *Constitutional Documents of the Reign of James I;* John Neville Figgis, *Studies of Political Thought from Gerson to Grotius;* International Publishers Inc.: Frederick Engels, *The Housing Question;* Karl Marx, *Critique of the Gotha Programme;* Charles H. Kerr & Co.: Karl Marx, *Capital,* Vols. I & III, ib., *The Eighteenth Brumaire of Louis Bonaparte;* Harcourt, Brace & Co.: R. H. Tawney, *Religion and the Rise of Capitalism.*

It is unfortunate that I am forced to omit acknowledgment here of a most important help received in the production of this book. The conceptions contained here were greatly influenced by the author's discussions with a number of his friends who are at present residing in Germany and must consequently remain unnamed.

Chicago, June 15, 1940.

TABLE OF CONTENTS

PART II

THE LEGAL THEORY OF THE DUAL STATE

CONTENTS

INTRODUCTION

'TOTALITARIAN' is a word of many meanings too often inadequately defined. In this treatise we have tried to isolate one important characteristic of the totalitarian state in Germany, and by studying this fundamental aspect of the National-Socialist regime we hope to make clearer the legal reality of the Third Reich.

We have not attempted an exhaustive picture of the whole of the emerging legal system; rather we have sought to analyze the two states, the 'Prerogative State' and the 'Normative State,' as we shall call them, which co-exist in National-Socialist Germany. By the Prerogative State we mean that governmental system which exercises unlimited arbitrariness and violence unchecked by any legal guarantees, and by the Normative State an administrative body endowed with elaborate powers for safeguarding the legal order as expressed in statutes, decisions of the courts, and activities of the administrative agencies. We shall try to find the meaning of these simultaneous states through an analysis of the decisions of the German administrative, civil and criminal courts, at the same time attempting to indicate the line of division between the two. Since this problem has not yet been considered by theorists it will be necessary to quote the original sources themselves *in extenso*. In studying the development of judicial practice as it is embodied in decisions, we learn that there is a constant friction between the traditional judicial bodies which represent the Normative State and the instruments of dictatorship, the agents of the Prerogative State. By the beginning of 1936 the resistance of the traditional law-enforcing bodies was weakened; thus the decisions of the courts are an impressive illustration of the progress of political radicalism in Germany.

The first part of this book is exclusively devoted to a description of the existing legal order. A second theoretical part attempts to prove that because of the parallel functioning of the traditional procedure and of a method of making decisions by considering only the peculiar circumstances of the individual case, the legal

tradition of the West has been radically changed. In this section
we venture to explain the juridical 'dualism' which characterizes
the entire system of private and public law in contemporary Germany. In the third and concluding section we confront the legal
system and legal theory with the legal reality of the Dual State.
In this critical, sociological part we indicate the relationship of
contemporary German capitalism to the functioning of the Normative State and of the Prerogative State. We shall inquire whether
the legal situation characterized as the Dual State is not the necessary consequence of a certain stage of crisis for the directing elements of capitalistic society. Perhaps it can be shown that they
have lost confidence in rationality and have taken refuge in irrationality, at a time when it would seem that rationality is needed
more than ever as a regulatory force within the capitalistic structure.

To demonstrate this it is necessary to do more than compile a
list of cases in constitutional law which do not confirm to the Rule
of Law. The National-Socialist state is remarkable not only for
its supreme arbitrary powers but also for the way in which it has
succeeded in combining arbitrary powers with a capitalistic economic organization. One of the basic propositions of Max Weber's
works is that a rational legal system is indispensable for the operation of a capitalistic economic order. The German reformist labor
movement took this proposition for granted. But we must then
resolve the paradox of a capitalistic order continuing within a
system under which there is no possibility of rationally calculating
social chances. Rational calculation is not consistent with the rule
of arbitrary police power which is characteristic of the Third
Reich.

It may be argued, both by those who are sympathetic with and
by those who are opposed to National-Socialism, that the problem of the Dual State has no fundamental or permanent significance, that it is merely a transitory phenomenon. To those who
think the Prerogative State transitory we point to the records of
judicial proceedings in the Third Reich, which show that it is
gaining rather than losing importance. And we would remind

those who think that the Normative State has already disappeared or that, if it exists, it is a mere remnant of the old state and therefore doomed to oblivion, that a nation of 80 million people can be controlled by a plan only if certain definite rules exist and are enforced according to which the relations between the state and its members, as well as the relations between the citizens themselves, are regulated. These problems will be dealt with in the third part of the book.

It must be clearly understood that when we speak of the Dual State we do not refer to the co-existence of the state bureaucracy and the party bureaucracy. We do not place great importance on this new feature of German constitutional law. Although National-Socialist literature often discusses the problem and although this book will refer to it occasionally, an attempt to find the exact legal distinction between the two would be futile. State and party are increasingly becoming identical, the dual organizational form is maintained merely for historical and political reasons.

In a speech at Weimar in July 1936, Hitler himself defined the line of demarcation between state and party. He asserted that government and legislation should be the task of the party, administration the task of the state. Obviously this statement has little value as a juridical explanation. Neither in legislation nor in administration is it possible to distinguish the activities of the state and the party; not even the administrative activities are a monopoly of the state. When we speak of the state therefore we are using the term in its broader sense, i.e., as the entire bureaucratic and public machine consisting of the state in the narrower sense and of the party with its auxiliary organizations. Whether this amalgamation of state and party is useful for the analysis of legal social phenomena remains to be seen. In order to facilitate the analysis of a more significant distinction within this system of the Third Reich, the author feels justified in neglecting one of lesser importance. Both the party and the state in its narrower sense function within the scope of the Normative State and the Prerogative State. Preoccupation with the superficial distinction between party and state tends to efface the more significant distinction between the Normative State and the Prerogative State.

The fact that National-Socialist jurisprudence gives such emphasis to the state — party problem is an encouragement to the author and provides him with an indirect justification for his undertaking, inasmuch as a favorite device of National-Socialist jurisprudence is to obscure the real significance of certain issues by a clamorous insistence on the importance of incidental ones.

The book is restricted to a discussion of National-Socialist Germany. Although a comparative study of dictatorships would be extremely enlightening, it has not been possible for this author. This book is a first-hand description of the National-Socialist legal system, seen from the point of view of an anti-National-Socialist participating observer. First-hand experience in the National-Socialist juridical system, as well as a study of National-Socialist literature, have had a part in its construction. A discussion of similar problems in other dictatorships would require that the author be as familiar with their situation as he is with that of the Third Reich. Knowledge of the fact that the German dictatorship thrives by veiling its true face discourages us from judging other dictatorships by their words rather than by their deeds, to which we have no adequate access.

A superficial view of the German dictatorship might be impressed either by its arbitrariness or by its efficiency based on order. It is the thesis of this book that the National-Socialist dictatorship is characterized by the combination of these two elements.

THE LEGAL SYSTEM OF THE DUAL STATE

Do you believe that a state in which the decisions of the courts can have no validity, but can be reversed and nullified by particular persons, would subsist rather than perish?

SOCRATES

CHAPTER I

THE PREROGATIVE STATE

1. THE ORIGIN OF THE PREROGATIVE STATE

MARTIAL LAW provides the constitution of the Third Reich. The constitutional charter of the Third Reich is the Emergency Decree of February 28, 1933.[1]

On the basis of this decree the political sphere[2] of German public life has been removed from the jurisdiction of the general law. Administrative and general courts aided in the achievement of this condition. The guiding basic principle of political administration is not justice; law is applied in the light of 'the circumstances of the individual case,' the purpose being achievement of a political aim.

The political sphere is a vacuum as far as law is concerned. Of course it contains a certain element of factual order and predictability but only in so far as there is a certain regularity and predictability in the behavior of officials. There is, however, no legal regulation of the official bodies. The political sphere in the Third Reich is governed neither by objective nor by subjective law, neither by legal guarantees nor jurisdictional qualifications. There are no legal rules governing the political sphere. It is regulated by arbitrary measures (*Massnahmen*), in which the dominant officials exercise their discretionary prerogatives. Hence the expression 'Prerogative State' (*Massnahmenstaat*).

In the following pages an attempt will be made to show in detail the systematic growth of the absolute dictatorship of National-Socialism which has arisen on the basis of the 'Emergency Decree for the Defense against Communism.' Supplementing this Emer-

gency Decree against acts of violence endangering the state, the
law of March 24, 1933 gave National-Socialism unlimited legislative power. The official legend which the Third Reich seeks to
propagate maintains that the National-Socialist state is founded on
valid laws, issued by the legally appointed Hitler Cabinet and
passed by the legally elected Reichstag. It would be futile to deny
the significance of this legislation in the transformation of the
German legal order. A study of this legislation and its influence
on the activity of the courts presents a clear picture of the existing German legal order in so far as it can be said to exist. But it
should be remembered that on the statute books after February
28, 1933, can be found almost no legislation referring to the part
of political and social life, which we have labelled 'political
sphere,' now outside the sphere of ordinary law. Legislation regarding politics would be futile inasmuch as legal declarations in
this field are not considered binding.

The National-Socialist legend of the 'legal revolution' is contra-
dicted by the reality of the illegal *coup d'état*.[3] The events leading
up to the Decree of February 28, 1933 are known generally and
need not be repeated here. What is significant, however, is that
the *coup d'état* consists neither in the Reichstag fire of February
27, 1933, nor in the Emergency Decree of February 28, 1933, but
rather in the execution of this decree itself. Three acts of President Hindenburg between January 30 and March 24, 1933, helped
National-Socialism into the saddle: the appointment of Hitler to
the post of Reichs-Chancellor, the proclamation of civil siege by
issuing the Reichstag Fire Decree and the signing of the Enabling
Law of March 24, 1933. Two of these acts could scarcely have
been avoided, but the third was entirely voluntary. The appointment of Hitler, the leader of the strongest party, to the post of
Reichs-Chancellor was in conformity with the Weimar Constitution; historically, the proclamation of a state of 'civil' instead of
military siege subsequent to the Reichstag fire was the decisive
act of Hindenburg's career. It was the necessary consequence of
the instigated *coup d'état* (based on the Reichstag Fire Decree),
when Hindenburg signed the law of March 24, 1933, and thus
sounded his own death knell.

Endowed with all the powers required by a state of siege, the National-Socialists were able to transform the constitutional and temporary dictatorship (intended to restore public order) into an unconstitutional and permanent dictatorship and to provide the framework of the National-Socialist state with unlimited powers. The National-Socialist *coup d'état* resulted from the arbitrary application of the Emergency Decree of February 28, 1933, which made a mandatory dictatorship absolute.[4] The extension and maintenance of this absolute dictatorship is the task of the Prerogative State.

In contrast to the earlier Prussian law which contained provisions only for military martial law, the Weimar Constitution conferred on the President the power to decide whether 'measures necessary for the re-establishment of public safety and order' were to be enforced by civil or military authorities. In conjunction with the tremendous power accorded to the 'executive authority' by the decree-issuing potentialities of Art. 48 of the Weimar Constitution, the decision whether the National-Socialist ministers or the conservative *Reichswehr* generals should be given the responsibility of restoring public order had most weighty implications. The failure of von Papen, Hugenberg and Blomberg to perceive the critical importance of this question was decisive in settling their political fates. Of course it is idle to speculate concerning unrealized possibilities; nevertheless one thing may be said with certainty: on February 28, 1933, the fighting power of the National-Socialist Storm Troopers was negligible in comparison with the power of the police and the *Reichswehr*. But when Hitler was enabled to add to the strength of Storm Troopers the decree power of martial law, the Reichstag fire became a sound political investment.

No doubt, the National-Socialist *coup d'état* of 1933 was, at least technically, facilitated by the executive and judicial practice of the Weimar Republic. Long before Hitler's dictatorship, the courts had held that questions as to the necessity and expediency of martial law were not subject to review by the courts.[5] The German law never recognized the principle of English law, expressed in the following decision:

'A somewhat startling argument was addressed to us by Mr. Serjeant Hanna, that it was not competent for this Court to decide whether a state of war existed or not and that we were bound to accept the statement of Sir Nevil Macready in this respect as binding upon the Court. This contention is absolutely opposed to our judgment in Allen's case (1921) ... and is destitute of authority, and we desire to state, in the clearest possible language that this Court has the power and the duty to decide whether a state of war exists which justifies the application of martial law.'[6]

The traditions of the monarchic period, when the declaration of martial law was the privilege of the government and was independent of the jurisdiction of the courts, carried over into the Weimar Republic. The German courts, possessing no guiding traditions in questions of constitutional law, never succeeded in establishing a claim to jurisdiction in these particularly crucial cases.

However, the National-Socialists would probably have been successful even had such constitutional-judicial safeguards existed. The absence of a legal tradition analogous to the Anglo-American tradition enabled them, however, to render lip service to the laws, a procedure found useful during the transitional period, when the army and the officialdom were not entirely dependable.

2. THE ALLOCATION AND DELIMITATION OF JURISDICTIONS

a. GENERAL REGULATION OF JURISDICTION

Absolute dictatorial power is exercised by the Leader and Chancellor either personally or through his subordinate authorities. His sole decision determines how this power shall be wielded. The steps taken by Hitler on June 30, 1934,[7] therefore needed no special justification. His powers were derived from the new German 'constitution' and analogous actions may be taken at any time. The measures taken on June 30, 1934, may differ in quantity but not in content from like measures taken on other occasions. The law passed by the government on July 2, 1934, expressly legalizing the steps taken on June 30, is of declaratory significance only. To issue such laws now would be superfluous, since the developments of the past years have entirely clarified the 'constitutional' situation. The sovereign power of the Leader and Chancellor to act unhampered by restrictions is now thoroughly legalized. With few exceptions the Leader and Chancellor exercises absolute dictatorial powers through political authorities. No delimitation of jurisdictions is provided for. Political officials may be instruments of the state or the party. The jurisdiction of party and state officials is not subjected to general regulations and in practice is flexible. According to the theory formulated by the outstanding National-Socialist constitutional lawyer Reinhard Hoehn, the party makes assignments to the Secret Police. One of the heads of the Prussian Secret State Police (*Gestapo*), Heydrich, advances the following theory: All Black Shirts (*SS*), whether civil servants or not, must cooperate. The results of their espionage activities will be utilized by those Black Shirts with civil service standing.[8] According to a view accepted by a considerable number of laymen as well as officials, the supreme task of the German Labor Front is to act as the agent of the Secret Police within industrial enterprises. Whenever jurisdiction between state and party is delimited it is by unofficial orders inaccessible to the outsider. They can be changed at any time by the Leader and Chancellor, as demonstrated at the Nürnberg Party Congress of 1935, where Hitler proclaimed that he would delegate the solution of the Jewish question, under certain conditions, exclusively to party authorities.

In order to justify the fact that in these pages no distinction is made between the state and the party as executive powers, we quote some decisions which may amply illustrate the impossibility of such a distinction.

I. A decision of the Court of Appeals of Karlsruhe dealt with the confiscation of trade union property by the Prosecuting Attorney of Berlin. When the Court questioned the Chief Prosecuting Attorney as to whether the confiscation was still in force he replied that he could answer this question only after consultation with the legal department of the German Labor Front.[9]

II. A Reich Press Leader was appointed by a party order of January 19, 1934. He was to exert 'every influence' and had authority to 'take all steps necessary for the fulfillment of his tasks.' Thus authorized by the party, the Reich Press Leader ousted the editor-in-chief of a newspaper, although this man was under irrevocable contract until 1940. An action by the editor for payment of his salary was dismissed. The Court held that the order of January 19, 1934, was an order of the Leader which, although not issued in the correct form provided by the Enabling Law of March 24, 1933, must be considered binding for all the state, party and private officials affected by the decree and that 'the objections made by the plaintiff against the validity of this order ignored the close, confidential relationship between the Leader and his followers, which is the basis for the unlimited power given to the government in the field of legislation.' [10] The Leader's order of January 19, 1934, was therefore considered to be within the scope of this power. Whether this obviously illogical argument by which the general power of the party leader is derived from the general power granted to the government of the state is deliberate, or whether it is a mere lack of understanding, is irrelevant. The result, however, is that, according to the court, 'even if the position of Press Leader is a party function . . . the decree of the Leader endowed him with certain governmental functions. There are no valid objections to the delegation of governmental functions to important party authorities. . . .' [11]

The validity of the decisions of the Reich Press Leader was not questioned by the Hamburg Appellate Court, which decided that 'such decisions must be accepted by the Court even if they seem inequitable.' [12]

III. In contrast to this rather supine capitulation of the judiciary, we find an admirable frankness in a decision of the District Labor Court of Berlin. It concerns an order which had been signed by Hitler and which had never been officially published. According to this Court 'the Leader of the Movement is at the same time the Leader of the Nation. It is up to him to decide whether he is acting in one function or the other. . . . To us it is sufficient that the name Adolf Hitler is affixed to the order.' [13]

b. THE STATE POLICE

Outstanding among the executive branches of the absolute dictatorship is the Secret State Police (*Gestapo*). This body has always been and still is organized in accordance with state law. In Prussia, the functions of the *Gestapo* are regulated by three statutes. The Office of the Secret Police was established in April 1933. The Secret State Police was transformed into a special police force in November 1933. The general powers of the *Gestapo* were finally defined by the Prussian statute of February 10, 1936, which revoked the earlier statutes.[14]

Section 7 of the law of February 10, 1936, besides correcting a printing error (which will be discussed below), and announcing some organizational regulations, contains a provision of substantive law concerning the examination by administrative courts of decrees in matters relating to the *Gestapo*.

Following the Prussian example, the other German states enacted statutes building up Secret State Police systems. In some German states, where the jurisdiction of the administrative courts is regulated by a general clause, every decree issued by an administrative authority was made subject to review by administrative courts. In other states, the courts review the act if the situation is enumerated in the statute regulating the jurisdiction of the administrative courts. Prussia, in the pre-Hitler-period, adhered to the latter method, but required review of police orders in so far as they were explicitly enumerated in the relevant statute. The extent to which changes have occurred in the principles governing the acts of the *Gestapo* in Prussia and other states will be examined below.[15]

3. THE ABOLITION OF THE RULE OF LAW

a. HISTORICAL INTRODUCTION

Since February 28, 1933, Germany has been under martial law. Martial law as such does not necessarily clash with the rule of civil law. Martial law, as it has developed in the constitutional history of the nineteenth and early twentieth centuries, supplements the Rule of Law. At times when the Rule of Law is endangered or disturbed, martial law is invoked to restore the constitutional order necessary for the existence of the Rule of Law. If we consider the situation which led to the proclamation of a state of martial law as a negation of the Rule of Law, it can be stated that a constitutional martial law situation is a 'negation of a negation,' whose purpose is the restoration of the (positive) rule of law.

The constitutional invocation of the martial law requires that (1) the civil rule of law be threatened or infringed; (2) martial law be declared with the intention of restoring the Rule of Law at the earliest possible date, and (3) martial law remain in force only until the Rule of Law is restored.

The National-Socialist *coup d'état* consisted in the fact that the National-Socialists, as the dominant party in the government, (1) did not prevent but rather caused the infringement of the Rule of Law, (2) abused the state of martial law which they had fraudulently promoted in order to abolish the Constitution, and (3) now maintain a state of martial law despite their assurances that Germany, in the midst of a world corrupt with inner strife, is an 'island of peace.' On the 'island of peace' there is a continuous state of martial law. This method was not invented by the Nazis; such tendencies have frequently appeared in modern history. More than thirty years ago, Figgis characterized such methods as Machiavellian:

'Every nation would allow that there are emergencies in which it is the right and the duty of a government to proclaim a state of siege and authorize the suppression of the common rules of remedy by the rapid methods of martial law. Now what Machiavelli did, or what his followers have been doing ever since, is to elevate this principle into the normal rule for statesmen's actions. When his books are made into a system they must result in a perpetual suspension of the Habeas Corpus Acts of the whole human race. It is not the removal of restraints under extraordinary emergencies that is the fallacy of Machiavelli, it is the erection of this removal into an ordinary and everyday rule of action.' [16]

But not only in political theory but also in practical life these methods were utilized. In 1633 (three hundred years before the Reichstag fire), Wallenstein realized that martial law was a particularly useful instrument for the suspension and also for the abolition of the existing legal order.

Carl Schmitt, not without approbation, quotes the following passage of a letter of Wallenstein: 'I hope with all my heart that the gentry will be difficult, since this would cause them the loss of all their privileges.' [17] As early as 1921 Carl Schmitt pointed out the parallel between the privileges of the gentry and the Bill of Rights enjoyed by citizens living under the civil Rule of Law.

It is interesting that in the early seventeenth century, contemporaneous with Wallenstein, an attempt was made in England to create the impression of an emergency in order to provide a legitimate excuse of absolute tyranny. While Parliament was suspended, Charles I tried to raise ship money by asserting that peace was threatened by 'certain thieves, pirates, and robbers of the sea, as well as Turks, enemies of the Christian name. . . .' (First ship money writ, 1634 [18])

His success, however, was short lived and the claim made by Charles I to override the law on a 'fancied emergency' was defeated in the revolution.[19] The Anglo-Saxon world has since then been wary of 'fancied emergencies.' [20]

The absence of a similar tradition in Germany has had the most weighty consequences for its constitutional history. For a short period, during the March Revolution of 1848 and the reaction following it, there was a certain wariness of the dangers connected with the abuse of martial law. Mittermaier, the most famous liberal German jurist of this period, said: 'A revolt, caused, favored, or provoked by a ruse of the government party itself may easily serve it as a pretext for suspension of the law. An exaggerated fear, which sees the threatening specter of anarchy everywhere, may induce the political party (possibly in good faith) to suppress the alleged rebellion by emergency decree.' [21]

Consequently, in view of this danger, he says that 'we must never use emergency laws as a pretext in order to continue violence beyond the immediate need of warding off a threatened attack.' [22] The experience of the unsuccessful revolution of 1848 caused Mittermaier to be apprehensive of the political dangers of martial law. A Bavarian legal scholar of this period, Ruthardt, painted a vivid picture of the condition characteristic of a state of martial law. He explains that 'war is regulated and restrained by war itself; but when it is over, when the *Te Deum laudamus* is mixed with *Vae victis*, when revenge and hatred are let loose, all laws are suspended or the victor uses them for his own purposes.' [23]

Attempts to use a temporary emergency as a stepping-stone to the establishment of an absolute dictatorship had been made in Germany long before 1933 and were foreseen by Max Weber even as early as in the Hohenzollern epoch.[24]

Even National-Socialists occasionally admit that the Reichstag fire came at an opportune time and that the ensuing temporary dictatorship was a welcome occasion for the abolition of the civil Rule of Law. The mouthpieces of National-Socialism themselves state that the threat of Communism was merely the excuse for the breaking of the old laws. Hamel, a Nazi expert in police law and Professor of Constitutional Law at the University of Cologne, says that 'the fight against Communism merely gave the National-Socialist state the opportunity to break down barriers which now must be regarded as senseless.' [25] The same attitude is expressed in Hamel's statement that protective custody is not merely incidental to the revolution, disappearing upon the return to normal conditions or being absorbed by the general penal law.[26] The fiction that protective custody is a necessary means of dealing with the enemies of the state long since has been abandoned. It is now recognized to be what it actually was in the beginning, a means of preserving the absolute power of the National-Socialist Party, i.e., of establishing an absolute dictatorship. As this author writes: 'If the education, the formation of a nationalistic point of view is the proper task of the state, the means of education and especially the most effective means, arrest, must be at the disposal of the police.' [27] Therefore it is not surprising for Hamel to assert that 'protective custody is a feature of a truly political state which is purged of all traces of liberalism.' [28] From such statements we may conclude that the concentration camp is not only an essential component in the functioning of the National-Socialist state, but also an indication of the enduring character of the sovereign National-Socialist dictatorship.

An even more frank expression is to be found in the decision of a special court in Hamburg. While discussing Art. 48 (the dictatorial article of the Weimar Constitution) which is found satisfactory to National-Socialism, the court pointed out that 'the destruction of this constitution has been one of the outstanding goals of National-Socialism for many years. It is only natural, that, when finally victorious, it has used its power to overthrow that constitution.' [29]

The ideal type of all *coups d'état* attempting to establish a Caesaristic, formal plebiscitarian dictatorship, is to be found in *The Eighteenth Brumaire of Louis Napoleon* (December 2, 1851). In this book Karl Marx made a classic formulation of the procedure used by this type of dictatorship when he said that Bonaparte, 'while seeming to identify his own person with the cause of order, rather identifies the cause of order with his own person.' [30]

The legend of the legal revolution is built around Adolf Hitler's identification of his person with public 'order'; the history of the illegal *coup d'état* is characterized by the identification of 'order' with Hitler's person. This attempt to veil the true character of the martial law dictatorship by legalistic tricks was brought about by the means of plebiscitary democracy. 'The cloak of plebiscitary democracy is, however, very broad and covers a great deal,' [31] as Carl Schmitt said in 1932. It covers the Prerogative State as well as the Normative State, and only intensive investigation can uncover the real forms which are hidden beneath it.[32]

The consequences in the Prerogative State of identifying 'order' with the person of Adolf Hitler will be studied from the official documents of the Third Reich. We shall take particular note of the German administrative, civil, and criminal court decisions bearing on problems of the Prerogative State. In the Third Reich there are no decisions on constitutional questions as such. The courts touch on them only in so far as their discussion is necessary, to enable them to deal with other problems. Nevertheless the decisions furnish a fairly comprehensive picture of the 'constitutional law' of the Third Reich.

b. THE DISSOLUTION OF THE RULE OF LAW AS REFLECTED IN THE DECISIONS OF THE COURTS

1. The Abolition of Constitutional Restraints

During the first years of the National-Socialist regime, the decisions of the courts revealed many attempts to preserve at least theoretically the supremacy of law in the Third Reich. This is indicated, for instance, by the endeavor of the Supreme Court (*Reichsgericht*), to consider the Reichstag Fire Decree (*Brand-Verordnung*) as effective for only a limited time.

A decision of October 22, 1934, considered expropriation proceedings. This involved discussing whether the protection of property, as guaranteed by Art. 153 of the Weimar Constitution, was affected by the Decree of February 28, 1933. It was held that '§ 1 of the decree suspended the constitutional guarantee of property (Art. 153 of the Weimar Constitution) until further notice . . . since the relevant section of the decree clearly declares the suspension of Art. 153 with the limitation that the new regulation be valid only until further notice be given.' [33]

It was this emphasis on the temporary character of the decree that aroused the critical comment of Professor Huber, the occupant of the Chair of Constitutional Law at the University of Kiel. Professor Huber declares that 'contemporary legislation has used the formal procedures of the Weimar Constitution for reasons of public order and safety (legality), but this does not mean that this legislation is based on the substance of the Weimar Constitution or that it derives its legitimacy therefrom.' [34]

Of greater importance is the question whether the Reichstag Fire Decree, which is based on Art. 48 of the Weimar Constitution, suspends those basic rights which this very Constitution declares inviolable and not to be suspended by emergency measures under Art. 48.

This problem became rather acute in connection with the dissolution of the German branch of Jehovah's Witnesses, *Ernste Bibelforscher* as they are called in Germany. This dissolution was justified by the Decree of February 28, 1933. Jehovah's Witnesses based their claim on Art. 137 of the Weimar Constitution, which guaranteed freedom of worship and belief, and they pointed out that the right guaranteed in Art. 137 is one of the fundamental rights which could not be suspended under Art. 48 of the Weimar Constitution. Their contention was sustained, and they were acquitted by the Special Court of Darmstadt.[35] This decision, however, represents a rather isolated phenomenon. The courts have sought to circumvent this constitutional restriction by a great variety of arguments. In a decision of the District Court of Dresden, the court interpreted the decree of the Minister of the Interior, which dissolved the association of Jehovah's Witnesses, as a constitutional amendment voiding Art. 137 of the Constitution. According to the view of the court, 'the Constitution is amendable by administrative decrees and similar measures.'[36] Thus, in the decision of the Dresden Court, the prohibition of the Police Minister (based on the Emergency Decree) was interpreted as a legislative action based on the Enabling Law.

Although the *Reichsgericht*, in a decision of September 24, 1935, accepted the validity of Art. 137, it did not interpret it as including the unrestricted freedom of religious association. 'Granted the validity of Art. 137,' said the court, 'its correct application does not prevent the suppression of a religious association if the activities of that association are incompatible with public order.'[37] This decision puts even the so-called fundamental rights at the disposition of the police power. Religious freedom is thereby reduced to the category of rights dependent on the discretion of the authorities.

This decision of September 24, 1935 still has recognized certain fundamental rights. But in a later case, both the *Reichsgericht* and the Prussian Supreme Administrative Court (*Oberverwaltungsgericht*) went a step further in their curtailment of fundamental rights.[38] They abolished the right of the civil servant to examine his official records. The court held: 'Art. 129, section 3, sentence

3 of the Weimar Constitution entitles the civil servant to examine his official record. This provision is in contradiction to the National-Socialist conception of the relationship between civil servant and state, and, without special legislation, is therefore no longer in force. The leadership principle does not admit the questioning and criticism of the rulings of his superiors by the civil servant.' [39] Thus, we can safely state that constitutional restraints on the sovereign dictatorship have been disregarded.

2. The Abolition of other Legal Restraints

In their enforcement of the Decree of February 28, 1933, the police are neither bound by the provisions of the Constitution nor by any other law. The Prussian Supreme Court (Kammergericht) in a decision of May 31, 1935, held that 'the Prussian Executive Decree (Durchführungsverordnung) of March 3, 1933,[40] leaves no doubt that Par. 1 of the Decree of February 28, 1933, . . . removes all federal and state restraints on the power of the police to whatever extent is required for the execution of the aims promulgated in the decree. The question of appropriateness and necessity is not subject to appeal.' [41] We shall show that this decision of the Prussian Supreme Court (Kammergericht) foreshadowed the conclusion at which the majority of the courts arrived only after long and involved developments.

A reluctance to acknowledge a legally unrestrained police as a consequence of dictatorship was evinced by the Supreme Labor Court (Reichsarbeitsgericht). Creating the conception of 'self-defense of the state,' it dismissed the action of an employee of the Soviet Trade Delegation who had been discharged by a commissar appointed by the police. The court recognized the commissar's right to discharge employees with the following rationalization:

'It is doubtful whether the police power under normal condition entitles the Prussian Minister of the Interior to endow a State Commissar with such broad powers. However, even if the appointment could not be upheld under the Decree of February

28, 1933, it might be justified with reference to the necessities of the self-defense of the state. . . . In the first half of the year of 1933 the situation of the National-Socialist state could not be regarded as secure. As long as the Communist threat lasted, the state of insecurity continued and necessitated the extension of police powers beyond their regular limits.' [42]

It is not accidental that the court uses the past tense in its justification of the law of the self-defense of the state. It seems to have desired to indicate that the emergency had ended by the time this decision was rendered, thus reopening the period of normal conditions. In like manner the decision of the *Reichsgericht* had opened the way for the re-establishment of the rule of the law (see p. 14).

This trend, however, did not persist. It had originated with the assumption of the preamble of the February 28, 1933, Decree, that the sole motive of the law was the overthrowing of Communism. Hamel declares this interpretation of the Decree of February 28, 1933, to be erroneous. 'It would be a mistake,' he writes, 'to assume that the authorities are freed of liberal fetters only in their fight against Communism. Liberal restraints are not just suspended by the laws for the fighting of Communism; they are abolished without reservation.' [43] This view has been followed by a great number of the higher courts. The Special Court of Hamburg (*Sondergericht*), in a decision regarding Jehovah's Witnesses, holds that the decree was issued after the Reichstag fire in a major emergency and with great haste and that it was 'directed against dangers threatening the state not only from Communist but from any other sources as well.' [44] The theory, however, that the special mention of the Communists is an editorial error cannot be reasonably upheld.

To justify its application to churches, sects, anti-vaccinationists and Boy Scouts, the Prussian Supreme Court (*Kammergericht*) created the theory of the indirect Communist danger. A decision of December 8, 1935, of the criminal division of the Prussian Supreme Court reversed a decision of the Municipal Court of Hagen (Westfalen) and acquitted the defendants who were members of a Catholic youth organization. The defendants had participated in hiking trips and athletic contests. The complaint stated that by so doing they had violated an ordinance issued by the District President (*Regierungspräsident*) which was based on the Decree of February 28, 1933. The decision declared that the goal of National-Socialism was the realization of the ideal 'ethnic community' (*Volksgemeinschaft*) and the elimination of all conflicts and tensions. For that reason, manifestations of religious differences, aside from church activities in the narrowest sense, met with the disapproval of National-Socialism, or, in the words of the *Kammergericht*: 'This type of accentuation of existing cleavages bears in itself the germ of the disintegration of the German people. Such disruption will only aid the spread of Communist aims.' [45]

The fact that the defendants were directly opposed to 'Atheistic Communism' did not safeguard them from punishment for 'indirect Communist activities,' because according to the court 'the public expression of a private opinion will all too easily serve only to encourage persons who believe in or who sympathize with Communism or who are politically undecided. This encouragement will lead such persons to form and diffuse the opinion that the National-Socialist state is not supported by the entirety of the people.' [46] This theory of the indirect war on Communism permits the extirpation of any movement which in the slightest sense can be construed as supporting Communism.

In a decision of March 5, 1935, the Prussian Supreme Court (*Kammergericht*) reversed a decision of the lower court and condemned a minister of the Confessional Church for violating an ordinance (issued by the chief of police) prohibiting 'demagogic polemics in the church conflict' (the Confessional Church is the part of the Protestant Church which stands—at least in religious questions—in opposition to the regime). This ordinance was based on the Reichstag Fire Decree. The minister had distributed to the parents of his Sunday School students a letter criticizing the 'German Christians' (the section of the official Protestant Church which sympathizes with National-Socialism). In deciding this case, a connection between the church struggle existing inside the Church between both these groups and Communistic violence was established as follows:

'It is sufficient for the application of the decree that an indirect danger to the state is created by an expression of disaffection with the new order. Such disaffection provides fertile soil for the re-emergence of Communist activities.' [47]

The participation of National-Socialism in the church struggle and the abuse of the anti-Communist decree for the persecution of the Confessional Church was justified by the contention that 'such criticism naturally provokes dissatisfaction . . . especially since the inimical attitude of Communism towards the church might acquire new hope and strength from this situation.' [48]

It is not surprising that the theory of the indirect war on Communism has been used as the basis for a prohibition of the anti-vaccinationists, as was expressly recognized by a decision of the *Reichsgericht* of August 6, 1936.[49] Here again there is a historical parallel mentioned by Carl Schmitt in his discussion of Wallenstein's legal position: 'The right of expropriation is allowed only against rebels and enemies. But in every revolution it has been the rule to brand political opponents as enemies of the fatherland and so to justify completely depriving them of legal protection and property.' [50] The courts have since adopted this theory with little hesitation.

The Administrative Court of Württemberg, in a decision of September 9, 1936, dealing with the *Innere Mission* (Missionary Work of the Protestant Church), dropped all pretence of a connection between police actions (based on the Reichstag Fire Decree) and the anti-Communist campaign. It bluntly declared that 'the decree was not intended exclusively as a protection from the threat of Communism but from any danger to public safety and order regardless of its source.' [51] This decision emphasized a legal condition which had already been foreshadowed by the District Court of Berlin when, on November 1, 1933, this court declared in a decision, unique at that time, that 'all attacks upon public safety and order are to be regarded as Communistic in a broader sense.' [52]

No discrimination was made among the various opponents of National-Socialism. They were all labelled as Communists. Martial law was applied equally against all opponents of the present regime. Through the application of martial law, the National-Socialists obtained a monopoly of power and have maintained it through continuous use.

3. The Abolition of Restraints on the Police Power

The wider application of the Decree of February 28, 1933, to include all non-National-Socialists can only be explained if it is assumed that 'the preamble of the decree expresses only its motive and not its substance.'[53] Whether the police authorities may act upon the decree only as a defensive measure or in all cases which they decide within its scope also depends upon the interpretation of the preamble.

The crucial question is whether the usual limitation of the police power should be observed in the application of the Reichstag Fire Decree.[54] At first the Prussian Supreme Administrative Court (Oberverwaltungsgericht) attempted to uphold these restraints on dictatorial power. In consistency with its past traditions, the court declared on January 10, 1935, that 'the Decree of February 28, 1933, did not extend the police power beyond its fundamental scope. . . . A police order exceeding these limits, unless based on an explicit law, violates § 1 of the Prussian Police Administrative Law (Polizeiverwaltungsgesetz) which has thus far been valid. Such a police order would therefore be void.' [55] Had this opinion been followed in later decisions the use of state terrorism to accomplish the Gleichschaltung of the whole of German society would have been impossible. Accordingly, it is not very surprising that on March 3, 1933, a Prussian ministerial order declared: 'The police are permitted to exceed the restrictions of their power specified in § 14 and § 41 of the Prussian Police Administrative Law.'[56] This was the beginning of a crucial conflict between the executive power and the judiciary.

Although the Reichsgericht supported the Supreme Administrative Court,[57] the Gestapo disregarded its decisions. A leading official of the Gestapo, Ministerialrat Eickhoff, characterized the

Gestapo as a 'general staff, responsible for the defense measures as well as the equally necessary offensive measures against all the enemies of the state.'[58]

Before showing how further developments in this matter culminated in a victory for the police, we must return to the decision of the Württemberg Administrative Court of September 9, 1936. A private association devoted to the care of children applied for a modification of its charter by a transfer of its property to the *Innere Mission*. The County Magistrate (*Landrat*) objected to this, arguing that the property should go to the National-Socialist Welfare Organization (NSV) which 'bestows its charities on all citizens equally'.[59] Objections were filed against this decision but they were overruled by the Ministry of the Interior in Württemberg on grounds drawn from § 1 of the Decree of February 28, 1933. The association then appealed to the Administrative Court, arguing that 'the proposed change in the charter cannot be considered a danger to the state nor can it be claimed that the application of the decree would constitute an action in self-defense of the state. The decision of the County Magistrate was motivated not by the intention to defend the state from a threatened attack but by the desire to expropriate the association.'[60] The complaint of the child welfare association was dismissed. The association was said to have erred in its interpretation of the law, having conceived the aim and scope of the Decree of February 28, 1933, too narrowly. The decision reads: 'The protection of public order and safety carries with it the preservation of the wealth of the ethnic community. If the decree had been framed with the intention of allowing not general but only specified infringements on the restraints which have been previously in effect, such would have been expressly stated in § 1 of the decree.'[61]

It was indeed unmistakably stated in the preamble. It would be wrong to suppose that the National-Socialist legal doctrine generally pays no attention to the preamble of statutes. Whether it heeds them depends on 'the nature of the individual case.' In interpreting the 'constitutional' document of the Third Reich (the Decree of February 28, 1933), the introductory phrases are ignored. Nevertheless when other governments use similar methods,

National-Socialist writers vehemently express their contempt.

Thus Swoboda, the National-Socialist Professor of Law at the German University of Prague, assails this method of interpretation but only with regard to the Czecho-Slovak Constitution. After he stated that during the 20 years of the Czecho-Slovakian Republic, the dominant attitude of pure positivism had prevailed and that during that time the preambles to statutes were considered mere rhetoric he emphasized: 'This, in the eyes of the National-Socialists, branded both the constitution and its interpretation as insincere and dishonest. National-Socialism, of course, is alien to so irresponsible a method.'[62]

But the National-Socialist authorities not only disregard the preamble of the Decree of February 28, 1933; they also interpret the decree directly opposed to its significance. The decision of the Administrative Court of Württemberg indicates that a fundamental shift in the setting of the problem has occurred. The Decree of February 28, 1933, broadly interpreted, took cognizance of the problems involved in the relationship between individual and state. With the increasing mingling of party and state functions, the conflict between individual liberty and state coercion yielded its pre-eminent position to the problem of the relationship between corporate competition and party monopoly. In order to obtain spoils for party organizations and party finances the National-Socialist Party has, through the use of the Prerogative State, managed to abolish competing organizations.

A decision of the Administrative Court of Baden shows that even the pretense of concealing this tendency has ceased. In a small town in Baden, a conflict had arisen between the Protestant women's organization and the local Red Cross organization, which was under National-Socialist leadership. Apparently, personal quarrels lay at the bottom of the feud. This quarrel became to a degree historically significant when the government tried to deprive the religious organization of its function of caring for the ill, a privilege regarded by the church as its own for almost two thousand years. The police solved the problem by banning the religious association on the basis of the Decree of February 28, 1933, and the court affirmed the action of the police.[63]

No attempt was made to establish a connection between the dissolution of the nursing association and the anti-Communist decree. The National-Socialist antagonism toward competing organizations is clearly evident in the decision. The court asserts that 'it is demonstrated that an association founded under the pretense of church interests was visibly injuring the local unit of the Red Cross.'[64] Therefore the court decided that this fact in itself was sufficient grounds for the prohibition.

'Since the Minister of the Interior declares that the admitted competition between the two organizations is a disadvantage to important concerns of the state . . . it is not within the domain of the court to refuse to acknowledge the decision of the political leadership.'[65] These decisions have, at least in the cases of Württemberg and Baden, abolished all traditional restrictions on the police power.

If free access to the courts had still been permitted in Germany, the child welfare and the nursing associations might have been able to appeal the decision on grounds of an arbitrary application of justice. If the legal literature on this question is indicative of judicial opinion, however, it is doubtful whether such a hearing could have been obtained.[66]

When the restrictions on the police power were abolished, the question of 'indispensability' fell into discard. The police need no longer show that any action undertaken by them is indispensable to the attainment of their purpose. Only when we view the discontinuance of the 'indispensability' clause as a consequence of the dissolution of the Police Law can we appreciate the significance of the decision of the Appellate Court (*Oberlandesgericht*) of Braunschweig of May 29, 1935. In that case the closing of a publishing house belonging to the *Wachtturm* Bible Tract Society was justified by the consideration that 'as a defense measure against Communist violence which endangers the state it may be expedient to prohibit associations the officers of which may even unintentionally provide shelter for Communist sympathizers.'[67] The decision states nothing as to whether the police should have first asked the officials of the sect for the expulsion of 'Communist sympathizers.' The police are accorded complete discretionary power in all questions involving the harboring of Communists. Their actions are not subject to the control of the courts.

4. The Abolition of Judicial Review

a. *Introductory Remarks.* Before we discuss the right of the courts to review the acts of the police, a few introductory remarks are pertinent. Legal review of acts of the police is possible only if legal norms exist which the police must respect. This is only true, however, as long as the normal legal order prevails. In the German legal system, as well as in the Anglo-American, the opposite is true under martial law. The derivation of the Prerogative State from martial law should facilitate an understanding of the co-existence of legal order and lawlessness to the Anglo-Saxon reader. The state of 'siege' is unknown to English law as a legal institution in it. Martial law is a type of self-defense of the state against disturbances of the public peace. In case of actual war (the existence of which has to be determined by the courts), the acts of martial law, which are to be regarded as self-defense, are outside the jurisdiction of the legal system. According to a statement of Chief Justice Cockburn, 'Martial law, when applied to the civilian, is no law at all, but a shadowy, uncertain, precarious something depending entirely on the conscience, or rather, on the despotic and arbitrary rule of those who administer it.'[68] The Prerogative State is thus defined as a continuous siege. Since martial law is a part of every constitution, the extent to which it is subject to control is decisive.

American law also emphasizes the proposition that the activity of the state under conditions of martial law is not legal activity in the proper sense, as Field said in *ex parte* Milligan:

'People imagine, when they hear the expression "martial law", that there is a system of law known by that name, which can upon occasion be substituted for the ordinary system; and there is a prevalent notion that under certain circumstances a military commander may, by issuing a proclamation, displace one system, the civil law, and substitute another, the martial. . . . Let us call the thing by its right name; it is not martial law, but martial rule.'[69] In recognizing that a state of permanent martial rule obtains in

Germany today, it must also be appreciated that the opposite of the legal order of the rule of law is the lawlessness and arbitrariness of the Prerogative State.

Martial law, according to Carl Schmitt, 'is characterized by its practically unlimited authority, i.e., the suspension of the entire hitherto prevailing legal order. It is characterized by the fact that the state continues to exist while the legal order is inoperative. This situation cannot be branded as anarchy or chaos. An order in the juristic sense still exists even though it is not a legal order. This existence of the state is accorded priority over the continued application of legal norms. The decisions of the state are freed from normative restrictions. The state becomes absolute in the literal sense of the word. In an emergency situation the state suspends the existing legal system in response to the so-called "higher law of self-preservation".'[70]

Schmitt's theory has been adopted by the *Gestapo*. Dr. Best, legal adviser to the *Gestapo* writes:

'The task of combatting all movements dangerous to the state implies the power of using all necessary means, provided they are not in conflict with the law. Such conflicts with the law, however, are no longer possible since all restrictions have been removed following the Decree of February 28, 1933, and the triumph of National-Socialist legal and political theory.'[71]

These open statements of the most prominent authors of National-Socialist constitutional theory find their expression in the decisions of the courts only in connection with the problems of judicial review. Thus the question whether the decrees of the dictatorial power are subject to judicial review illustrates again how a question of substantive law may be concealed behind procedural issues.

b. *Review by Administrative Courts.* The Prussian Supreme Administrative Court (*Oberverwaltungsgericht*) was at one time of the opinion that even in the Third Reich dictatorial measures were subject to judicial review. Thus, in a decision of October 25, 1934, this court claimed the unqualified right of judicial review on the ground that 'the fact that the decree was within the sphere of authority of the so-called "political police," does not deprive the affected persons of the right of appeal.' [72] But by May 2, 1935, the court retreated from this stand. [73] The second law regarding the jurisdiction of the Gestapo (Gesetz über die Geheime Staatspolizei, November 30, 1933) [74] offered an occasion to differentiate between acts of the state police and acts of the ordinary police. The court argued that the State Police (Stapo) and the Gestapo were a special police and that no particular law providing for the judicial review of its actions existed. For this reason, the Supreme Administrative Court (Oberverwaltungsgericht) on the basis of the principle of enumerated powers, denied the right of judicial review. Acts of the ordinary police, however, even when performed in the service of the Gestapo, remained subject to judicial review. [75]

On March 19, 1936, a case came before the Prussian Supreme Administrative Court (Oberverwaltungsgericht) concerning the legality of the expulsion of a missionary from a certain district. The expulsion order was issued by a district magistrate and was justified by a reference to the church conflict. This involved the general question whether the police were justified in compelling people to leave their residences. A short time previously, the Prussian Supreme Administrative Court (Oberverwaltungsgericht) had passed on the validity of the order of the District President of Sigmaringen to expel German subjects of foreign race (in this case gypsies) from a certain district. The court held that 'the police may not expel members of the German Reich from their permanent or temporary residence for reasons other than those specifically enumerated in the Law Regulating the Right of Movement (Freizügigkeitsgesetz). [76] The police order requiring the plaintiff to leave the municipality of St. is declared void.' [77]

According to general administrative law, the steps taken against the missionary would have been pronounced invalid. The police are not empowered to issue orders which are clearly forbidden by law. Nevertheless the missionary's appeal was dismissed on the grounds that the law of February 10, 1936, concerning the Gestapo (Gesetz über die Geheime Staatspolizei), [78] which had meanwhile been passed, prohibited a review. The Supreme Administrative Court of Prussia (*Oberverwaltungsgericht*) refused to review the case because the magistrate had acted within 'the sphere of authority allotted to the Secret Police.' [79] § 7 of the Law of February 10, 1936, stated that orders *and* affairs within the jurisdiction of the *Gestapo* are not subject to the review of the Administrative Courts. A 'printer's error' [80] had turned the 'and' into an 'in.' Since the magistrate's order for the expulsion of the missionary was, in the opinion of the Supreme Administrative Court, an order which 'was obviously intended to contribute to the foreign and domestic security of the State,' [81] it treated the police measure of the magistrate as an order 'in' affairs within the jurisdiction of the *Gestapo*.

The *Völkische Beobachter* (March 1, 1936) had violently assaulted the 'reactionary' attitude of the Prussian Supreme Administrative Court and the latter finally capitulated on March 19, 1936, in the foregoing case of the missionary. The last vestige of the Rule of Law in Germany was abolished by exploiting a printer's error. This is typical of the cynical contempt for law which prevails among the power-intoxicated clique now dominating Germany. By refusing to dismiss an absolutely illegal police order, the Supreme Administrative Court gave the police a blank check for the performance of every type of illegal action.[82]

The Supreme Administrative Court left itself a loophole by saying that it was not of decisive importance whether the order was outside the sphere of the *Gestapo* or apparently within it, though not substantially so. In a decision of November 10, 1938, the Prussian Supreme Administrative Court (*Oberverwaltungsgericht*) clarified the principles of judicial review. The theory that orders of the *Gestapo* are not subject to review is interpreted in such a way that the following acts are exempt from state administrative review: (1) all direct acts of the *Gestapo*; (2) all acts of the ordinary police pursuant upon *special* orders of the *Gestapo*; (3) all acts of the ordinary police pursuant upon *general* orders of the *Gestapo*; (4) all acts of the ordinary police which fall within the jurisdiction of the *Gestapo*. Review is limited to those instances when, in cases 2 and 3, the ordinary police have transcended the orders of the *Gestapo*, and in case 4, when the

ordinary police took the prerogative of the *Gestapo*.[83] The significance of the decision cited above lies in the acknowledgment of
the *Gestapo's* power to transfer entire spheres of life from the jurisdiction of the Normative State to the Prerogative State (case 3).
If, as in the above decision, the *Gestapo* decide that the promoting
of sharpshooting lies in the province of the 'German Defense Association,' the owner of a shooting gallery has no resort against
the banning of a rifle match, even if the ban was the result of
'personal antagonism between him and the shooting association.'[84]

The use of the Decree of February 28, 1933, (which was intended to suppress political opposition) as a decree for dealing with
competing organizations that threaten to infringe on monopolies is
characteristic of recent developments. How this distinction between 'political' and 'non-political' cases works in practice may
be illustrated by the fact that the courts cannot interfere with the
confiscation of a papal encyclical, whereas the seizure of 'six dream
books, two sets of fortune-teller cards and two copies of an astro-
logical periodical entitled *Kosmisches Tagebuch der Gesellschaft
für astrologische Propaganda* may give rise to administrative proceeding,'[85] because obviously these are not of political significance.

With the decision of March 19, 1936, when it refused to uphold its autonomy in political cases, the Prussian Administrative
Court passed into the ranks of those who had previously denounced it.[86]

c. *Review in Civil Procedure*. The law of February 10, 1936,[87]
placed actions of the *Gestapo* outside the reviewing authority of
the administrative courts. Does the law apply equally to ordinary
courts? A certain attorney brought suit for damages caused by
disbarment following unjustified suspicions that he had been engaged in Communist activities.[88] It was held that the *Reichsgericht*
could not re-examine 'decisions which on account of their political
character are not adapted to review by ordinary courts.'[89]

On the other hand, a later decision of the *Reichsgericht* held
that the statute making the state liable for any damage caused by
an unlawful act of its servants [90] is valid regardless of whether the

unlawful acts are political or non-political. Disregarding its previous decision, the court claimed that 'the mere facts that the act of state in question was of a more or less political significance does not necessitate a restriction.' [91] The phrasing of this decision indicates that the *Reichsgericht* intentionally dissented from the doctrine that political questions are outside the jurisdiction of the court. For 'even the legislation of the Third Reich . . . did not limit the application of Art. 131 of the Constitution to non-political acts of the state.' [92]

The contradiction between the two decisions dealing with almost identical cases might conceivably be interpreted as a return of the courts to the Rule of Law after having approached the very threshold of legal anarchy. In reality, however, the second decision does not involve a return to the Rule of Law. On the contrary, it directly leads toward the Dual State.

During the period elapsing between the two decisions, an important innovation was introduced in the form of § 147 of the Civil Servants' Law [93] which reintroduced the so-called *Konflikt* into the German legal system. *Konflikt* entitles the supreme administrative authority in actions for damages against the state to substitute the Supreme Administrative Court for the civil court which would ordinarily have jurisdiction. The Supreme Administrative Court, then, represents the court of last appeal as far as the claimant is concerned.[94] The consequence of this seemingly unimportant innovation is that the rule of the Supreme Administrative Court not to review actions of the *Gestapo* is extended to civil law cases concerning damage suits against the state. This preserves the integrity of the principle that political actions are not subject to review in so far as the administrative authorities through the application of § 147 of the Civil Servants' Law have withdrawn the case in question from the jurisdiction of the ordinary courts. It also leaves the way open for the courts to assert the rule of the Normative State (in substantive matters) within the jurisdiction allotted to them. In damage suits against the state the supreme administrative authority, by using its judicial discretion in applying the *Konflikt* procedure, decides whether legal norms or the refusal of judicial review will govern future litigation. The final word rests with the political authorities. *Konflikt* is the technical instrument which draws the line between government by law (the Normative State) and government by individual decree (the Prerogative State).

§ 147 of the Civil Servants' Law gave permanent form to a provision which had been in force as a special decree during the transition between democracy and dictatorship. During this period the Adjustment of the Civil Claims Law (issued December 13, 1934)[95] entitled the Minister of the Interior to interrupt judicial proceedings and refer the case to the administrative authority provided claims arising from the National-Socialist revolution were involved. The administrative authority was not bound by the legal code, but made its decisions according to 'equitable considerations.' This was held necessary in order to prevent the Normative State from cancelling the gains of the *coup d'état*. The way in which this statute works becomes clear in a decision of the *Reichsgericht* delivered on September 7, 1937, which reveals at the same time the true methods of the 'legal revolution.' At the outset of the National-Socialist revolution, the mayor of Eutin was removed from office. Originally the authorities wished to institute proceedings against him for malfeasance in office under the legal provisions of the Normative State. But this plan was soon dropped, and they pursued the course prescribed by the Prerogative State. The mayor was placed under protective arrest on July 24, 1933. Negotiations between his counsel and the government representative resulted in a written statement (August 4, 1933) in which the mayor waived his salary—as well as all other claims—and obligated himself to pay 3,000 marks to the government for the damage he was alleged to have inflicted on the reputation of Eutin, although German law does not recognize restitution for moral damages in cases such as the foregoing. In this case, the state ordered protective custody and threatened internment in a concentration camp in order to prevail upon one of its citizens to waive his lawful claims against it. Furthermore it induced him to make payments for which there was not the slightest legal justification. (The legal term for such conduct of course is robbery and extortion.) The highest official in the county (*Regierungsprä-*

sident) and the newly appointed mayor of Eutin, once their booty
was secured, became generous. The *Reichsgericht* records that
'the government and the mayor of the city of Eutin declare that
the state and the city are now willing to regard the matter as
closed. They have no intention of taking any actions which might
cause difficulties for the plaintiff. The plaintiff is hereby dismissed
from protective custody.' [96] This procedure, however, was apparently not entirely satisfactory to the National-Socialist officials,
and to preclude any expression of doubt concerning their conduct
they offered the following explanation: 'The plaintiff and his
counsel declare that all their statements and agreements were made
of their own free will and that no duress of any kind was exercised.' [97]

This decision has an epilogue. The plaintiff, after the first storm
of the National-Socialist revolution had subsided, tried to withdraw his waiver on the ground of duress. Since the Minister of
the Interior, on the basis of the Adjustment Law of December 13,
1934, declared that the case was within his jurisdiction, his appeal
was not heard. The courts refused to hear the complaint and it
was dismissed forthwith. The slightest legal control over its
authoritarian decisions is viewed by the National-Socialist Prerogative State as a greater evil than the perpetuation of injustice.

d. *Review in Penal Procedure.* Theoretically, political acts are
still subject to judicial review in the sphere of penal law. In practice, however, this power of review is meaningless, as was demonstrated by a decision of the Bavarian Supreme Court (*Oberlandesgericht* München) of November 4, 1937. The Reichsminister
of the Interior issued an order (based on the Reichstag Fire
Decree) penalizing any minister announcing from the pulpit the
names of those members of his congregation who had resigned
from the Church. A minister who had been accused of violating
this order argued that the decree was invalid.

The purpose of the Decree of February 28, 1933 was the defense of the state against Communist violence. Is it conceivable
that the prohibition of the public announcement of the names of

persons who had withdrawn their church membership promoted rather than diminished Communist propaganda? And how does it represent 'positive Christianity' — according to Art. 24 of the Nazi platform one of the aims of the National-Socialist Party — to prevent a minister's fulfilling his ecclesiastical obligation of counteracting the anti-religious movement?

The declaration in favor of 'positive Christianity' in the National-Socialist Party program was merely a political maneuver. The more radical members of the party had long broken with the church and turned to Neo-Paganism. But since formal resignations from church membership might engender unrest among those sections of the population which are still attached to the church, a method of combining the furtherance of church resignations while still maintaining the pretense of 'positive Christianity' was found through the invocation of the Reichstag Fire Decree.

This decree was thus used to prohibit the announcement of resignations from church-membership, and the Supreme Court of Munich found a close relationship between the prevention of Communist violence and the prohibition of the announcement of church resignations: accordingly it declared valid the order of the Minister of the Interior. It then rationalized its decision by claiming that the preamble is not a legal part of the decree. It holds that the decree 'applies to all sorts of situations and hence any measure is admissible which is necessary for the restoration of public safety and order, no matter what the source of the threat.'[98] Nor did the court hesitate to invoke the Weimar Constitution in order to create a connection between a long-established practise of the church and a danger to public safety. The National-Socialist state, though it has boasted time and again that it has abolished the Weimar Constitution, and although it has suspended all the civil rights specified in the second part of this constitution, has none the less asserted, through one of the highest German courts, that 'announcement of church resignations from the pulpit, although not a legal threat to the freedom of worship and conscience as guaranteed by the constitution, is in practise a restriction of that freedom. . . . It might also cause resentment and dissatisfaction with a state which permits such pressure on freedom of religion in direct contradiction with the constitution, and might thereby easily endanger public safety and order.' [99]

A casual reading of this argument does not reveal its significance. According to this decision it is not the Third Reich which exerts pressure on the freedom of worship and conscience, nor is it the National-Socialist Party: it is rather the clergy itself. Hence, in order to protect the rights which the National-Socialist Party has destroyed, action is taken against the clergy. In order to justify these acts of the Prerogative State, the courts designate the police authorities as guardians of the Weimar Constitution with its civil liberties provisions. The exploitation of 'this forcibly extended interpretation of the concept of "defence against danger" bears within itself the essence of fictiousness,' a reproach against the judiciary made by none other than one of the highest leaders of the *Gestapo*, Dr. Best.[100] This decision indicates that the last vestige of judicial review, namely the right to review administrative acts, which was at least theoretically preserved in penal law, is reduced to a 'mere fiction' in the Prerogative State. Dr. Best suggests therefore that the right of judicial review be abolished in penal procedure as well. It is highly probable that the 'Law concerning the Secret State Police' will be extended to include penal cases. The 'Principles of a German Penal Code' formulated by Minister Hans Frank paved the way for their inclusion when he wrote: 'The extent to which this principle is to be extended in the future to the consideration of all crimes with a political motive or of political significance is a decision for the Leader alone to make.' [101]

5. The Party as an Instrument of the Prerogative State

Decisions of a political nature are made not only by state authorities but also by party authorities.

The District Labor Court (*Landesarbeitsgericht*) of Gleiwitz, in handling the complaint of an employee dismissed for alleged political unreliability, was confronted with the review of a political decision rendered by a party authority. The employer based the dismissal upon a memorandum of the District Leader of the

National-Socialist Party, but the employee was unsuccessful in his attempt to dispute the correctness of the memorandum. According to this court 'the evaluation of a person's political character is the exclusive prerogative of the District Leadership of the National-Socialist Party. The District Leadership alone is responsible for this task and the courts have neither the right nor the duty of review.' [102]

This view, in theory at least, has not been confirmed by the decision of the Supreme Labor Court (*Reichsarbeitsgericht*). In a parallel case of April 14, 1937, the Supreme Labor Court argued that the memorandum of the District Leader of the party did not relieve the court of its duty of independent consideration. On the other hand the court emphasized, however, that the question of the *legal* status of a decision of a party authority should be clearly distinguished from the question of the *actual* influence of the District Leader. The court recognized that 'unfounded charges and even an unjustified suspicion coming from influential quarters may carry enough weight to constitute a major cause for dismissal.' [103] It is superfluous to point out that in reality the opinion of the District Leader is decisive.[104]

The relationship between the National-Socialist Party and the courts can be clearly perceived in the Supreme Labor Court's (*Reichsarbeitsgericht*) decision of February 10, 1937. This involved the case of an employee of the Storm Troopers (SA) who had been dismissed from his position. The dismissed employee sued the SA for the salary to which he was entitled under the law providing for previous dismissal notice. Appealing to Adolf Hitler's Pronouncement at the Nürnberg Party Congress of 1935, that 'the Party controls the State,' the SA refused to acknowledge its subordination to the courts. The Supreme Labor Court thereupon had to decide whether the National-Socialist Party enjoyed immunities from the law of the land analogous to those of accredited diplomats representing foreign powers. To this contention the court gave a negative answer. It referred to an earlier decision of the Appellate Court of Stettin [105] and declared that 'although it has been pointed out that the Party as such is superior to the State, this does not exclude the principle that in its relations to

the individuals it is subject to the general rules of public life.'
And therefore the court concluded that 'the application of legal
principles to the party's relations with individuals is not affected
by the position of the Party in the State.' [106]

This decision is basic to the propositions set forth in the present book. A *general* exemption of the National-Socialist Party from
the jurisdiction of the courts would be a denial of the Normative
State.

The ruling of the Supreme Labor Court that the party is subject to certain laws, however, does not prevent it from exercising
the sovereign powers in the Prerogative State. From the principle
that political acts of the party are acts of sovereignty, it follows
that acts of party officials, in so far as they are within the scope of
their political authority, are beyond the jurisdiction of the courts.
This doctrine was at first developed by Carl Schmitt, who pointed
out that 'disputes between individuals and party officials cannot be
submitted to the courts, since these conflicts generally deal with
questions which are to be settled outside the sphere of judicial
authority.' [107]

The following case illustrates the practical consequences of
these theories: an Aryan merchant of Wuppertal applied for an
injunction against the son of one of his competitors who had
damaged his business by spreading rumors to the effect that he was
Jewish. The lower court decided for the plaintiff. The defendant
then appealed the case, changing his defense by emphasizing that
he was a leading officer in the National-Socialist Artisan Guild
(*N.S.–Hago*). The Appellate Court of Düsseldorf (*Oberlandesgericht*) reversed the decision in favor of the defendant. The
court decided that the defendant held public office (*N.S.–Hago*)
and that he had to be dealt with as a public official and that the
diffusion of the philosophy of the party (including anti-Semitic
propaganda) was therefore strictly in his line of duty. Said the
court: 'An official act is not changed by the fact that an error
has been committed or that it constitutes an abuse of official
orders. The legality or appropriateness of such political acts cannot be made to depend on the judgment of the courts.' [108] The
complaint was dismissed on grounds based on claims which, by

virtue of their political character, are outside the jurisdiction of the courts.

This line of argument was also used in one of the decisions of the *Reichsgericht*. An injunction was demanded against a mayor who had spread false allegations as to the parentage of the plaintiff by asserting that he was an illegitimate child, actually the son of a Jewish horse-dealer who had employed the plaintiff's mother as a kitchen maid. In spite of the fact that the plaintiff could prove that the mayor had made the statements in the presence of both party officials and outsiders, the *Reichsgericht* overruled the lower courts and refused to grant an injunction, holding that 'the official position of the defendant and the contents of his allegation, which are of great concern to the party (i.e. non-Aryan descent), raise the presumption, in the absence of contrary evidence, that the defendant was acting in his official capacity.' The plaintiff's allegation that the defendant's motives were personal in character did not influence the decision. 'An official act,' said the court, 'does not fall within the jurisdiction of ordinary courts merely because it arose from unjustifiable motives.' [109]

A decision of the *Kompetenzgerichtshof* shows, however, that even National-Socialists doubt that the denial of the jurisdiction of the courts was justified in the case we have just discussed. At a meeting of the Winter Relief Organization a National-Socialist official charged that a certain business man had not given his contribution. The business man applied for an injunction. He was successful in the lower courts. But before the matter came before the Appellate Court of Königsberg the governor of the province of East Prussia applied *Konflikt*, (cf. p. 29) contending that this was a political question and therefore within the jurisdiction of the Leader. The Court in Charge of Questions of Jurisdiction (*Kompetenzgerichtshof*) denied its jurisdiction in this matter on technical grounds (June 27, 1936).[110] It cannot be denied, however, that the East Prussia president's claim that political questions may be decided only in the light of political considerations and only by political authorities is entirely consistent with the development. In the near future we may expect the establishment of a rule for party authorities on the same order as § 147 of the Law concerning Civil Servants (*Deutsches Beamtengesetz*).[111] That is, while generally recognizing law, it will withdraw the political acts of the party from the jurisdiction of the Normative State and turn their regulation over to the Prerogative State.

6. Politics as the Aim of the Prerogative State

One of the major problems of the legal theory of dictatorship is that of determining the dividing line between political and non-political acts. The courts have tried to confine the Prerogative State to the purely political sphere, and in so doing have been faced with the necessity of giving a practicable form to this distinction.

It is a rather grotesque aspect of recent German legal developments that the general legal principles of the Normative State are applied in proceedings against gypsies, while in parallel cases access to the courts has been denied on the ground that 'political' considerations were involved. Thus several gypsies were once taken into protective custody by the police on the ground that their presence caused disturbances among the population. The Supreme Administrative Court of Prussia (*Oberverwaltungsgericht*) annulled the order, arguing that 'the fact that the population of St. considers the mere presence of gypsies a molestation potentially giving rise to aggressive defensive actions on the part of the populace does not mean that the gypsies constitute a menace to public order and safety.... The police were therefore not entitled to proceed against the gypsies.' [112]

These principles were of no avail, however, to Koeppen, Director of the *Reichsbank*, when he was taken into protective custody because of a popular demonstration against him. His crime consisted in executing an eviction order against a tenant who had failed to pay his rent. The *Angriff*, Dr. Goebbels' paper in Berlin, took up the case for lack of anything more sensational, and the representative Party District Leader of Berlin, Goerlitzer, thinking the case might provide good propaganda material, decided to lead the demonstration himself. The arrest of the Director of the *Reichsbank* was then declared to be necessary because of politi-

cal considerations, and he was denied the protection of the law.[113]
The decisive factor here is that considerations operative in dealing with political cases are outside the domain in which they can
be 'properly handled' by the judiciary.

The attempt of the Prussian Supreme Administrative Court
(*Oberverwaltungsgericht*) to compromise by permitting practically unlimited discretionary powers to the political authorities
was not sufficient.[114] The National-Socialist state has insisted that
law be eliminated from the sphere of politics and that the definition of the boundary lines between the two rests in the hands of
the political authorities themselves. Minister Frick left nothing
further to be said on this subject when he declared: 'It is self-
evident that questions of political discretion should not be subject to review in the administrative courts.' [115] Not content with
this, Frick went even further by stating that it would not be
feasible for the administrative courts to review those matters
which—regardless of their 'political' significance from a *general*
viewpoint—were of *special* importance in furthering the interests
of the state.

More than 300 years ago a similar demand was made in England.
King James I, in his famous message to the Star Chamber (June
20, 1616),[115a] declared that in political questions the decision
rested with the Crown and not with the Courts.

'Encroach not upon the prerogative of the Crown. If there fall
out a question that concerns my prerogative or mystery of State,
deal not with it till you consult with the King or his Council or
both; for they are transcendent matters . . . As for the absolute
prerogative of the Crown, that is no subject for the tongue of a
lawyer, nor is it lawful to be disputed. It is atheism and blas-
phemy to dispute what God can do . . . so it is presumption and
high contempt in a subject to dispute what a King can do, or say
that a King cannot do this or that.' [116]

The straightforwardness of this message has scarcely been sur-
passed by any spokesman of the Third Reich.

The important result of the co-existence of authorities bound
by law and of others independent of law are these: when it is
politically desirable, the decisions of the courts are corrected by

the police authorities who confine persons acquitted by the judiciary in concentration camps for indefinite periods (the Niemöller case), and who set aside judgments rendered in civil courts, and reverse the decisions of the 'Court of Social Honor' by the activity of the Labor Front.The co-existence of legal and arbitrary actions, most impressively demonstrated by the confinement in concentration camps of persons who have been acquitted by the courts, is a crucial development of the recent German constitutional status. Significantly enough, the National-Socialist state does not acknowledge this fact willingly. The Dual State lives by veiling its true nature.

This is clearly shown by a decision of the *Reichsgericht* rendered on September 22, 1938, in regard to a minister of the Confessional Church who had offered the following prayer at the end of the sermon: 'Now we shall pray for those brothers and sisters who are in prison. I shall read their names. . . . Social worker L., Berlin, in protective custody since February 2, 1937, although the court had decided in her favor. . . .' [117] The *Reichsgericht* declared the minister guilty of committing a breach of the peace (affirming a decision of the lower court). The *Reichsgericht* stated that 'the minister's assertion about L. implied — by connecting the two sentences — the criticism that L. should have been freed and that the protective custody was unjustified' [118] and, according to the *Reichsgericht*, this endangered the public peace since the minister, 'in reading the list, might have led the congregation and others to the belief that the state was acting arbitrarily rather than in accordance with justice and law.' [119]

The fact that the *Reichsgericht*, highest authority of the Normative State, condemns as a disturbance of the peace the public announcement of an activity of the most important body of the Prerogative State speaks for itself. Although one key to the understanding of the National-Socialist state lies in its dual nature, none but a few high officials are permitted to allude to this fact.[120] One of them, Dr. Best, describes the activities of his agency in relationship to the activities of the court:

'If the administrative courts repeatedly grant peddler's licenses to Jews, to former members of the French Foreign Legion, or to other undesirables, the *Gestapo*, in executing its commission to protect the people and the state from the danger resident in such elements, will confiscate those licenses. If this entails a loss of prestige to someone, the *Gestapo* will not suffer the loss, since it always has the last word in such matters.'[121]

This statement is one of the most outspoken repudiations of the Rule of Law which we have found in National-Socialist literature. The difference between a *Rechtsstaat* (Rule of Law state) and the Third Reich may be summed up as follows: in the *Rechtsstaat* the courts control the executive branch of the government in the interest of legality. In the Third Reich the police power controls the courts in the interest of political expediency. [122]

The claim that the decisions of the regular courts can be and are rendered ineffective by the political authorities is difficult to prove by official evidence since those measures, lacking a foundation in law, cannot be justified by legal arguments and naturally are not published. All the more interesting for this reason is an article by Dr. Thieme, of the University of Breslau, in which he takes for granted the use of this procedure in cases before the Courts of Social Honor (*Soziale Ehrengerichte*) in the manner set forth in the revised Penal Code. Thieme argues that 'anyone acquitted in a case which is punishable in the light of wholesome popular sentiment should be handled through publicity or protective custody.' [123] This circumlocution may well be interpreted as an indication of the control the political authorities exercise over the courts.

If the political authorities go beyond the jurisdiction of the law their measures need not be justified by the attribution of illegality to the actions of those against whom they are invoked. In an article in the *Reichsverwaltungsblatt*, which discussed whether a citizen may be forced by the police to hoist a swastika banner on festive occasions, the author concluded that though it is not a legal duty to hoist a flag, it is evidence of the citizen's devotion to the Leader. Moreover failure to display the flag might be taken to indicate that the citizen in question lacked a National-Socialist background. The author suggests that the deficiency may be remedied in a concentration camp.[124]

This relationship between law and politics is a consequence of conflicting value-orientations. Awareness of this value-conflict has been expressed by the former National-Socialist Minister Franzen in his book *Gesetz und Richter*

'The criterion or the value-standpoint in accordance with which conflicts are adjudicated is in the case of the vast majority of legal norms a certain conception of justice. There are many norms, however, which contain no element of justice but which are based on simple political principles and are politically legitimated. Things to which we may be politically opposed are not necessarily bad. A political attitude is one which opposes its enemies and seeks to maintain its own existence. This is the prevailing criterion in the Third Reich.' [125]

With a typically National-Socialist cynicism Franzen emphasizes this point as an *arcanum imperii*. Since the broad masses of the population would not be able to appreciate this point of view it is necessary to deprecate the moral character of one's political enemy. According to Franzen, the political struggle must be so conducted that its followers will think of it as a moral and legal crusade.[126] The Prerogative State does not merely supplement and supersede the Normative State; it also uses it to disguise its political aims under the cloak of the Rule of Law.

In present day Germany, there is a double jurisdiction for all cases regarded as 'political.' The police execute administrative punishments in addition to or instead of the criminal punishments executed by the courts. This situation is illustrated by a decision of the Prussian Supreme Administrative Court (*Oberverwaltungsgericht*) regarding the refusal of a driver's license to an applicant who had spent six months in a concentration camp because of his attacks on the government.[127] Attacking the government is a crime within the jurisdiction of the courts.[128] The reason why this case did not come before the special court cannot be determined by an examination of the decision. Perhaps the facts were insufficient to provide grounds for an action. But in this case the applicant was deprived of any possibility of defense, subjected to heavier penalties and branded as an enemy of the state for the future without receiving 'due process of law.'

Not only does the Prerogative State replace the court but it also actively intervenes in pending proceedings.

A survey of legal developments in 1936 by an official of the Ministry of Justice in the course of a discussion of political crime and the conflict between the State and the Catholic Church has supplied us with a characteristic document on the relations between the courts and the political authorities of the Third Reich. In it we find the following statement:

'Among the more important political crimes are the ecclesiastical delinquencies, which can be classified into three groups: exchange manipulations, moral transgressions and malicious attacks on the state. Since August 1936, by order of the Leader, for political reasons none of these matters may be brought before the courts.' [129]

Thus the defendants may be kept in jail for political reasons indefinitely awaiting trial. The courts, whose legal duty is to speed up trials in cases where the defendants are under arrest, must postpone the trial by order of the Leader and thereby deviate from the law.

This self-revelation of the policy underlying the National-Socialist administration of justice is of particular significance for its disclosure of the wide range of actions which are designated as 'political.' Offenses against exchange regulations may be classified as 'political' in contemporary Germany, and malicious attacks against the government are, of course, political crimes. Why the homosexual practices of two monks should be considered a political offense, however, is more difficult to explain. It is clear that there is no intrinsic connection between such actions and those falling under the category, the 'political,' which is defined by the Prussian Supreme Court (*Kammergericht*) as 'that which involves the domestic and foreign security of the state.' [130] Neither the offense as such nor the person of a completely inconsequential monk has even the slightest connection with politics. In the Third Reich, sodomy becomes a political offense whenever the political treatment of such offenses is regarded as desirable to the political authorities. The conclusion one must come to is that politics is that which political authorities choose to define as political.

The classification of an action as political or non-political determines whether it will be dealt with according to law or according to the arbitrary preferences of the political authorities.

The legal system of present day Germany is characterized by the fact that there are no matters safe from the intervention of the political authorities who, without any legal guarantees, are free to exercise discretion for political ends.

In the first phase of the Hitler regime in 1935, the *Reichsgericht* had tried to prevent an 'arbitrary interpretation' of the Reichstag Fire Decree, but significantly enough, even then, when the *Reichsgericht* sought something absolutely immune from political intervention and therefore beyond the jurisdiction of the *Gestapo*, it could think of nothing but traffic regulations.[131] Meanwhile, however, the courts have systematically extended the sphere of the 'political.' Thus the Court of Appeals (*Oberlandesgericht*) of Kiel decided that the prohibition of a newspaper which 'defamed the medical profession and damaged its reputation' was a political question.[132] The reason given was that the newspaper obstructed 'the policy and aims of the state with respect to the protection of public health.'[133] The Third Reich does not confine its political concerns to questions of sanitation but extends them to the ownership of taxicabs as well. Whoever disagrees with the Third Reich regarding taxis runs the risk of being considered an 'enemy of the state in the wider sense.' For political reasons he may then be expelled from the executive committee of the local taxi owner's association of which he is a member. It was in such terms that the Supreme Court of Bavaria (*Oberlandesgericht* München) acknowledged the legality of a police order of the Ministry of the Interior.[134]

The Supreme Administrative Court of Prussia (*Oberverwaltungsgericht*) finally took the revolutionary step of revealing the political character of traffic regulation. The above-mentioned decision in the driver's license case, although admitting that political considerations had hitherto been irrelevant to the granting of drivers' licenses, justified its change of attitude by pointing out that the multi-party-state had since been succeeded by the one-party-state. The decisive point is, according to the court, that 'in the struggle for self-preservation which the German people are waging there are no longer any aspects of life which are non-political.'[135] In this way street traffic became a political question and an application for a driver's license may be rejected on the ground that the applicant spent six months in a concentration camp. For 'the community has a right to be protected from its enemies in every sphere of life.'[136] A decision of the Appellate Court of Stettin echoed this construction. It was held that an auto trip made by a Storm Trooper while in service must be considered a political act since 'all the activities of a Storm Trooper take place within the framework of the National-Socialist program and are therefore "political." '[137] No sphere of social or economic life is immune from the inroads of the Prerogative State.

A further illustration of this thesis is to be found in the litigation involving a request for the issuance of a birth certificate by a Jewish attorney who had emigrated after 1933.[138] One should first make clear that according to the German Law Regarding Vital Statistics (*Gesetz über die Beurkundung des Personenstands und der Eheschliessung*)[139] the registrar is required to issue birth certificates upon request. In this case the registrar submitted the application to the state police, who forbade its issuance. Accordingly the registrar refused to issue the certificate and upon the applicant's appeal to the Municipal Court, the court ordered that it be issued. The District Court reversed the decision and the reversal was affirmed by the *Reichsgericht*. The latter based its decision on the statement of the *Gestapo* that 'the issuance of a birth certificate to the applicant was out of the question. . . . The registrar is obliged to follow the instruction of the *Gestapo*. The court cannot review the grounds for the instruction. This is the necessary consequence of § 7 of the law of February 10, 1936. . . . But it was true even before this law was enacted. . . . since it exceeds the jurisdiction of the courts to examine whether certain executive orders are actually necessary for the preservation of public safety. It is unnecessary to state the reasons why the right of the individual to the issuance of a document prescribed in § 16 of the Law concerning Vital Statistics is being disregarded where the safety of the state is involved.'[140]

In a discussion of this decision an official in the Ministry of Justice, Dr. Massfeller, stated that further discussion was superfluous since any other decision 'would have been impossible.'[141] But for this very reason we think the decision worthy of discussion especially in three aspects: 1. The Supreme Court did not regard a *jus cogens* clause of the law as binding for the state police. It thereby recognized the theory that political authorities are not bound by legal norms. 2. The Supreme Court recognized the subordination of the courts to the political authorities although the law explicitly subordinates the registrar to the supervision of the courts. 3 . The Supreme Court acknowledged the right of interference of the state police out of considerations of 'public safety' even though the area of intervention was entirely non-political in the narrower sense of the word.

If it be admitted that a certificate of birth may threaten the 'security of the state' we have conclusive evidence that nothing is immune from police intervention and therefore we may say that any activity whatsoever may be dealt with as a political activity in the Third Reich. Since our whole thesis turns on this point it is perhaps permissible to add another decision which contributes to its corroboration.

In the above-mentioned decision of the highest Bavarian court (*Oberlandesgericht* München), the court, after having declared that the Reichstag Fire Decree was applicable to non-Communists, stated that the name of a member of the executive committee of the taxi drivers' association could be struck from the register of that society if the police authority ordered it. The court said:

'It is irrelevant to discuss whether S. is an enemy of the state in the broader sense of the word. Those regulations which derived from the second sentence of the Decree of February 28, 1933, confer authority on the police. The hitherto prevailing legal guarantees are now suspended in favour of the police. It makes no difference whether the association in question is an economic one—such as a commercial enterprise or a joint stock company. Any previous laws concerning associations are now superseded by the relevant sections of the Decree of February 28, 1933.' [142]

These words pronounced the death sentence on the Rule of Law.

The Rule of Law no longer exists. It has been supplanted by the Dual State, which is the joint product of the Prerogative State and of the Normative State.

4. THE PREROGATIVE STATE IN OPERATION

a. THE NEGATION OF FORMAL RATIONALITY

The Normative and the Prerogative States are competitive and not complementary parts of the German Reich. To illuminate their relationship one might draw a parallel between temporal and ecclesiastical law on the one hand and between normative and prerogative forms of domination on the other.

But in what sense can we say that the Prerogative State resembles the church? More than 50 years ago Dostoevski, in *The Brothers Karamazov*, said that the state tends to become like the church, a comment which becomes especially significant when we interpret it in the light of a statement by Rudolf Sohm,[143] the greatest German authority in ecclesiastical law, to the effect that the state and the church differed in their leading structures; the church concerned itself with material truth, the state was more interested in formal issues. The essence of the Prerogative State is its refusal to accept legal restraint, i.e., any 'formal' bonds. The Prerogative State claims that it represents material justice and that it can therefore dispense with formal justice.[144] Professor Forsthoff of the University of Königsberg calls the formalistically oriented Rule of Law State (*Rechtsstaat*) 'a state bare of honor and dignity.'[145] National-Socialism seeks to supplant the ethically neutral administration of law with a system of ethics which abolishes law. In 1930 Hermann Heller called National-Socialism 'Catholicism without Christianity.'[146]

National-Socialism makes no attempt to hide its contempt for the legal regulation of the administration and for the strict control over all activities of public officials. 'Formal justice' has no intrinsic value for National-Socialism, as we can see in a quotation from an official document, the Program of the Central Office of the National-Socialist Party for the Redrafting of the Penal Code: 'In the criminal law of the National-Socialist state there is no room for formal justice; we are concerned only with material or substantive justice.'[147] The first part of this quotation disregards formal justice in the German legal system. Whether formal justice has been replaced by a new type of material justice can be determined only by the examination of what National-Socialism calls 'material justice.' The second part of this treatise will amply demonstrate what kind of justice this new 'material justice' is. It will be shown that the Rule of Law has not given way to higher ideals of justice, but rather that it has been destroyed in accordance with National-Socialist doctrine for the purpose of strengthening the 'race.'

The practical significance of this point may be demonstrated by a decision of the Supreme Disciplinary Court (*Reichsdienststrafhof*). The question before the court was whether a public servant who refused to contribute to the Winter Relief Fund (*Winterhilfe*) was guilty of a misdemeanor in office. The accused, who for many decades had been a member of the nationalist movement, pointed out that he contributed a considerable share of his income to private charities and that his refusal to contribute to the Winter Relief Fund was without legal significance, since it always had been officially emphasized as entirely 'voluntary.' In a legal system adhering to principles of formal rationality it would be impossible to attach legal significance to the non-fulfillment of 'voluntary' obligations. The National-Socialist state ignores this 'merely' formal restriction. The Supreme Disciplinary Court dealt with the significance of the voluntary character of the contribution in the following argument:

'Even today the defendant's conception of liberty is of an extreme character. . . . For him liberty is the right to neglect all of his duties except where they are explicitly required by law. He has abstained from participation in community enterprises merely because he wanted to show that as a 'free' man he could not be coerced.'[148]

Because he believed that he was free, the state itself having emphasized the fact, he is now blamed for 'a despicable abuse of the

liberty which the Leader had granted in full confidence that the
German people would not abuse it.'[149] It was for this that he was
punished. The wrongdoing of the public servant did not consist in
his lack of charitable intentions. National-Socialism is not interested
in charity as such. It is primarily interested in enlisting and co-ordinating everyone in the official National-Socialist charity organization. The 'despicable abuse of liberty' consisted in having contributed to private charity. The 'value' which National-Socialism
attributes to activities in the welfare field is a function not of charitable interests but of the desire to add to the party's prestige.

Here again a parallel can be found with the period of personal
government in England between 1629 and 1640 dominated by the
regime of Archbishop Laud. Professor Tawney tells us that the
ecclesiastical courts, when confronted by cases similar to that
dealt with by the Supreme Disciplinary Court, imposed similar punishment. He explains that since the activity of the ecclesiastical
courts had not ceased with the Reformation these courts tried to
enforce the obligations of charity. They punished "the man who
refused to 'pay to the poor men's box,' or who was 'detected for
being an uncharitable person and for not giving to the poor and
impotent.' " [150] Laud's theocracy was guided by principles of
material justice and was therefore opposed to formal rationality.[151]

From this point of view, the great English revolutionary movement of the seventeenth century acquires a tremendous interest
for those seeking to understand our present situation. The political
movements of the twentieth century which have culminated in
National-Socialism and Fascism are a reaction against the heritage
of the English revolutionary movements of the seventeenth century. Despite this similarity, there is a marked difference between
the 'eleven years of personal government' in England and the National-Socialist dictatorship. Although the National-Socialist state
is by no means an agnostic state[152] it also lacks some of the central
features of the theocratic state. If a paradox were permitted it
might be said that the Third Reich is a theocracy without a god.
The structure of the Third Reich approximates that of a church,
although it is a church which is not devoted to a metaphysical idea.
The National-Socialist state seeks only its own glorification. But as

a quasi-ecclesiastical institution, it views those who transgress a-
gainst its rules not as criminals but as heretics.

b. THE PERSECUTION OF THE HERETICS

National-Socialist theorists who first asserted that the repressive
activities of the state were directed against political 'criminals' now
see the state's activity as a crusade against heresy. Thus Professor
Dahm of Kiel University has distinguished between 'crime' and
'treason.'[153] Acts constituting 'high treason,' according to Dahm,
cannot be precisely defined; therefore it is necessary to provide a
'general clause' which will allow sufficient discretionary power to
determine whether a breach of faith is treason.

Another National-Socialist theorist, Diener, criticizes the hitherto predominant definition of treasonable actions as those attempting to overthrow the constitutional order by violence. He regards
the 'technical illegality of treason against the constitution' as far
inferior to the National-Socialist concept of high treason for the
reason that 'the National-Socialist revolution has created a conception of the state for which every hostile attitude is treasonable.'[154]

A decision of the Special Court (*Sondergericht*) of Hamburg of
May 5, 1935, demonstrates practical consequences of this doctrine.
The question before the court was whether, in case of violence
during a treasonable enterprise, prosecution for a breach of the
peace should be added to the charge of treason. Contrary to the
ruling of the *Reichsgericht*, the Special Court ordered a penalty
for breach of the peace in addition to punishment for treason. It
offered no explanation for the fact that the Penal Code[155] explicitly
mentions violence in the high treason paragraph (§ 80) but held
that 'as applied to temporary Communism, preparations for treasonable actions include the organization and execution of large-
scale political murder. The Penal Code which was enacted in 1871
did not make violence a test of preparation for treason.'[156]

The Special Court of Hamburg seems to have forgotten that the

Penal Code of 1871 was prepared under the immediate influence of the Paris Commune. The political courts of Germany have applied the provision concerning treason in many cases for which the clause was not suitable. Frequently they have given maximum sentences for the preparation of treasonable actions although the acts themselves involved no violence whatever. When the facts of the case really demanded a verdict for treason, the use of violence having been definitely proved, the court interpreted the provisions for treason as not covering those facts and considered it necessary to supplement the charge with one dealing with a breach of peace committed by the accused.

Dr. Freissler, State Secretary of Justice, greeted Dahm's analysis as a theoretical achievement of revolutionary importance.[157] Its importance lies in the revelation that not only political authorities but courts also must handle political questions from a political instead of a legal point of view. As Professor Dahm says: 'We are faced with the general problem whether the substantive rules of law applicable to ordinary cases are also valid in the realm of politics. . . . Do not special standards obtain here just as they do in the procedural law of political trials?'[158] National-Socialism has no general 'standards.' A standard presupposes a scale of ethical values; but politics in Germany is entirely free from the controls imposed by ethical values. The treatment of political crimes in German 'courts' today is a fraud. The People's Tribunal and the other Special Courts are the creation of the Prerogative State. The term Special Court sums up the difference between the Rule of Law State (*Rechtsstaat*) and the Dual State: the Rule of Law refers political crimes to a *special* court despite the fact that they are questions of law; the Dual State refers political crimes to a special *court*, despite the fact that they are *political* questions.

That the political courts of Germany which function as agencies of the Prerogative State are courts in name only can be proved neither by the interpretation of the high treason statutes nor by pointing to the heavy sentences which they have imposed. Falsely reasoned decisions demonstrate nothing concerning the legal character of a judicial body. The situation is, however, quite different if we can prove that the 'courts,' unlike other judicial bodies, have failed to apply fundamental legal principles when political questions were brought before them.

One of the central principles of criminal law in all civilized states is the principle *ne bis in idem*, i.e. the prohibition of double jeopardy. The *Reichsgericht* adhered to this principle even as recently as September 8, 1938, and October 27, 1938.[159] This makes it all the more significant that the People's Court (*Volksgericht*) as well as the Prussian Supreme Court (*Kammergericht*) and the Bavarian Supreme Court (*Oberlandesgericht* München) have suspended this principle in decisions dealing with treason. The highest Bavarian court sentenced a defendant for distributing illegal propaganda, an action which in Germany is considered 'high treason.' The defendant had already served his sentence when the court, in a second trial, discovered that the facts of the case were of a more important character than had originally been realized. Although the court stated especially that 'general juridical theory and practice do not permit new proceedings against R., because of the identity of the act with the one for which he has already been punished, and that the fundamental principle *ne bis in idem* forbids the further punishment of the defendant,'[160] the court condemned the man once again. The court tried to belittle this principle by pointing out that it is based only on the law of procedure.

This may have been correct from the judicial point of view, but when the court denied the principle by condemning the man for a second time it set itself in opposition to universal juridical experience and observation. The significance of procedural questions is by no means inferior to those of substantive law. The prohibition of extraordinary courts, the institution of the jury, judicial review of the actions of state agencies are evidence of this. There is no proposition in the substantive law which can be compared in fundamental importance with the principle of *res judicata*. The distinction between a judgment of court and an administrative order is that the decision, once rendered, stands, while the order may be changed. The Bavarian Court showed little appreciation of the nature of judicial procedure when it declared that the application of the principle of *res judicata* should not interfere with the substantive law. Thus the court degraded its

status to that of an instrument of the Prerogative State by laying
down the following principle:

'In serious cases of high treason an adequate sentence has to be
imposed in all circumstances regardless of all legal principles! The
protection of state and people is more important than the adherence to formalistic rules of procedure which are senseless if
applied without exception.' [161]

Since other courts followed this decision [162] the opinion of the
Bavarian court is not an isolated phenomenon. The principle of
the inviolability of legal validity has yielded to political considerations and has been replaced by political reservations. Courts making their decisions only in the light of political considerations, i.e.,
courts which recognize their own decisions only with reservations,
cease to be judicial organs and their decisions are no longer real
decisions; they are measures (*Massnahmen*). This distinction was
formulated by Carl Schmitt very clearly about 1924:

'The judicial decision has to be just, it must be ruled by the idea
of law . . . the legal structure of the measure is characterized by
the principle of the *clausula rebus sic stantibus*.' [163] A decision
under reservation is controlled by the principle of *clausula rebus
sic stantibus*, the principal element of martial law.

Although German and Anglo-American martial law differ in
their presuppositions and legal content, the German political
courts may nonetheless be compared to those military courts
which, according to English law, are legal only in case of open
insurrection. An English court held in 1866 that 'the courts-martial,
as they are called, by which martial law . . . is administered, are
not, properly speaking, courts-martial or courts at all. They are
mere committees formed for the purpose of carrying into execution the discretionary power assumed by the Government.' [164]

Only when actual rebellion exists are they 'justified in doing,
with any forms and in any manner, whatever is necessary to suppress insurrection, and to restore peace and the authority of the
law.' [165]

In present-day Germany political courts are permanent institutions. Thus, what is permissible only in consequence of actual
conflict in the Anglo-Saxon countries is 'normal law' in Germany.

'The existence of this system,' said the above-mentioned English opinion, 'in cases of foreign service or actual warfare, appears to have led to attempts on the parts of various sovereigns to introduce the same system in times of peace on emergencies, and especially for the punishment of breaches of the peace. This was declared to be illegal by the Petition of Rights.' [166]

What has been considered a nightmare in English law for more than 300 years has now become the law of the land in Germany.

It is, however, impossible to present a completely satisfactory account of the political judicature of the Third Reich since decisions in political criminal cases are generally not published.[167] A general impression of German political justice can, however, be gained from a study of the political decisions of civil and administrative courts. Of course, it must be kept in mind that those decisions merely deal with the economic existence and not with the life and liberty of the persons involved.

A woman sympathetic to the Jehovah's Witnesses applied for a peddler's permit. The request was denied by the Bavarian Administrative Court (*Verwaltungsgerichtshof*) which supported its refusal by the following argument:

'Although no proof has been offered that Maria S. is a member of the forbidden association . . . it has been shown that she is a warm sympathizer. . . . She has also refused to promise that she would not work on behalf of the association in the future. . . . This mode of thought and the diffusion of such thinking is dangerous to the state . . . since it defames both state and church, alienates people and state and renders aid to pacifism, which is an ideology irreconcilable with the heroic attitude characteristic of our nation today.' [168]

The Supreme Administrative Court of Saxony (*Oberverwaltungsgericht*) refused to be outdone by this decision and denied a permit to a midwife because she was suspected of being a member of the Jehovah's Witnesses with the following argument:

'It is indeed true that until now Mrs. K. has not participated in any activities hostile to the people or the state. Nonetheless, her remarks leave no doubt that if a situation were to arise in which the orders of the state clashed with her interpretation of the Bible

and with the commandments of 'Jehovah,' she would not hesitate
to decide against the people and its leadership. . . . Although
persons of the type of Mrs. K. individually can scarcely be said
to constitute a danger to the state, their attitudes and opinions
encourage those who actually are enemies of the state and promote their destructive activities.' [169]

A similar tendency is revealed in a case involving the dismissal
of a postal clerk who was a member of the Jehovah's Witnesses
Association but who, following its prohibition, had not participated in its meetings. According to his religious conviction, the
Bible commanded that no mortal being should be greeted with
'Heil' since such a greeting was due only to God. Accordingly,
when he greeted anyone he raised his right hand and said only
'Heil.' His saying only 'Heil,' and not 'Heil Hitler' as was officially required, resulted in his dismissal as a postal clerk, a position which he otherwise would have held for life. In this struggle for his existence 'the accused was not allowed,' as the court
said, 'to appeal to religious scruples.' [170]

The Third Reich does not merely persecute those who spread
dangerous doctrines; it wages a perpetual warfare against all those
dictates of conscience not in harmony with its teachings. A decision of the *Reichsgericht* of February 17, 1938, is ample evidence
of this. In this case a sectarian family from Solingen was alleged
to have conducted family worship at home. The charge was dismissed by the District Court, which argued that family worship
did not infringe on the order prohibiting the sect. The *Reichsgericht* then reversed the decision and pronounced sentence on
the grounds that 'services of this type are prohibited and punishable even if held within the family circle among the former
members of the prohibited sect.' [171]

National-Socialism gives neither mercy nor justice to any German suspected of harboring ideas which are not in harmony with
its own principles. This was quite clearly expressed by Alfred
Rosenberg when he said that 'he who is not devoted to the interests of the people cannot claim their protection. He who is not
devoted to the community needs no police protection.' [172] Three
hundred years earlier Archbishop Laud enunciated the same idea

in other words: 'If any be so addicted to his private that he neglect the common state he is void of the sense of piety and wishes peace and happiness for himself in vain.' [173]

Having destroyed all voluntary associations and abridged the freedom of worship, National-Socialism next turned its attention to the destruction of the family. The saying of grace in a form required by the conscience of the members of a given family is prohibited by the state authorities. Interference with parents who are educating their children in a religion or philosophy not acceptable to National-Socialism is to be taken for granted. By a decision of the District Court (*Landgericht*) of Hamburg several members of the Jehovah's Witnesses Association were denied the custody of their children because 'their [the children's] spiritual welfare was endangered' by the fact that the parents wanted to bring them up in their own faith.[174]

Such dangers to minors are considered by the National-Socialist authorities more serious than moral dangers. Two decisions rendered simultaneously in Municipal Courts (*Amtsgericht*) provide a striking demonstration to the fact. Moreover they show that political and 'non-political' cases are not only differently handled in Germany but that the differentiation in treatment persists even when the facts in the case in question are practically identical. The Municipal Court (*Amtsgericht*) of Berlin-Lichterfelde held that 'exposing a child to Communist or atheistic influences is adequate reason for depriving the parent of the custody of the child.' [175] On the same day the Municipal Court of Hamburg declared that 'the fact that the mother of the child is a prostitute is not sufficient justification for the court to deny her the custody of her children who have been placed in unobjectionable foster homes.' [176]

The suspension of legal guarantees has affected the entire range of life in present-day Germany and has had disastrous consequences in the political sphere. No less disastrous have been the consequences of the outlawing of the parties in opposition to the regime. On April 15, 1935, the Municipal Court deprived certain persons of the custody of their children because they were Communists. On January 5, 1936, a similar decision was rendered but on the grounds that the parents in question were Jehovah's Witnesses. In 1937, the Municipal Court of Frankfurt a.M.–Höchst deprived a mother of the custody of her child because she wished to educate her in a Catholic convent.[177] In 1938 the Municipal Court of Wilsen placed several children in a foster home because their father had not enrolled them in the Hitler Youth movement. 'In this case the father kept his children out of the Hitler Youth and thereby abused his right of custody of his children.' [178]

According to the National-Socialist view, children who are educated according to tenets at variance with those of the Hitler Youth movement are 'neglected' by their parents.[179]

The National-Socialist state demands control over the minds of the growing generation. A Catholic priest who, during confession, warned a mother against sending her child away for the *Landjahr* (the 'year in the country') because her child might 'lose his faith there' was sentenced to six months in jail for malicious attacks against the government.[180]

National-Socialism at first justified its extreme measures by saying that the struggle against Communism made them necessary. Many persons at that time gave their approval to this outlawing of the Communist Party. But since then many more have come to understand the truth of Shakespeare's words (*Merchant of Venice*, Act 4, Scene 1):

BASSIANO: 'To do a great right, do a little wrong, And curb this cruel devil of his will.'

PORTIA: 'It must not be. There is no power in Venice Can alter a decree established. 'Twill be recorded for a precedent; And many an error by the same example Will rush into the state. It cannot be.'

CHAPTER II

THE LIMITS OF THE PREROGATIVE STATE

THE entire legal system has become an instrument of the political authorities. But insofar as the political authorities do not exercise their power, private and public life are regulated either by the traditionally prevailing or the newly enacted law. The birth certificate case page 44) is particularly enlightening. Hundreds of birth certificates are issued every day in Germany in accordance with the provisions of the law. Normal life is ruled by legal norms. But since martial law has become permanent in Germany, exceptions to the normal law are continually made. It must be presumed that all spheres of life are to be subjected to regulation by law. Whether the decision in an individual case is made in accordance with the law or with 'expediency' is entirely in the hands of those in whom the sovereign power is vested. Their sovereignty consists in the very fact that they determine the permanent emergency. 'The sovereign is he who has the legal power to command in an emergency' as Carl Schmitt has formulated in his book *Politische Theologie*.[181]

From this follows the principle that the presumption of jurisdiction rests with the Normative State. The jurisdiction over jurisdiction rests with the Prerogative State.

The limits of the Prerogative State are not imposed upon it; there is not a single issue in which the Prerogative State cannot claim jurisdiction. According to the practice of the courts, as we have already shown, the Decree of February 28, 1933 is valid for the entire field of the 'political.' In present-day Germany there is nothing which cannot be classified as 'political.'

The possibility, however, of treating everything as if it were 'political' does not imply that this method is always resorted to. Reuss, a National-Socialist authority on Administrative Law, distinguishes between 'actual' and 'potential' political relevance:

'The range of the "political" is variable. Even within the Third Reich and even within our own historical period, the sphere of the "political" widens and narrows at different moments, in different situations. The so-called "private sphere" is only relatively private; it is at the same time potentially political.' [182]

When Reuss speaks of the 'potentially' political character of private life he has in mind what we have called the jurisdiction over jurisdictions of the Prerogative State: i.e., where the Prerogative State requires the 'political' treatment of private and non-state matters, law is suspended. Where the Prerogative State does not require jurisdiction, the Normative State is allowed to function. The limits of the Prerogative State are not imposed from the outside; they are imposed by the Prerogative State itself.[183] These self-imposed restraints of the Prerogative State are of cardinal importance for the understanding of the Dual State. The self-limitation of the Prerogative State is as deeply rooted in the nature of National-Socialism as its existence.

Legally the Prerogative State has unlimited jurisdiction. Actually, however, its jurisdiction is limited. This is the most significant criterion of the constitution of present-day Germany.

In a decision of the Supreme Administrative Court (*Oberverwaltungsgericht*) of Saxony of November 25, 1938, these facts, so important to an understanding of the Third Reich, became especially apparent. The court had to determine whether it could deny a building permit without citing the grounds for the refusal. This raises the question whether building construction also falls within the scope of the Reichstag Fire Decree. The court said that it did because 'a building permit, such as is required under present building laws, may be denied on grounds deriving from the Decree of February 28, 1933. It must also be recognized that in such a case the reasons for the decision need not be adduced.' [184] The possibility of excluding decisions in building construction cases from the jurisdiction of the administrative courts by refusing to state the reasoning underlying the decision is limited to the sphere of the Prerogative State. The court vigorously opposed the extension of this principle of the Prerogative State into the sphere of the Normative State with the words: 'Nevertheless, the above-mentioned Decree of the *Reichspräsident* of February 28, 1933, involves an exceptional ruling, which leaves untouched the laws and procedural rules which are otherwise generally valid.' [185]

The same point of view was expressed with equal lucidity by the Prussian Supreme Administrative Court (*Oberverwaltungs-gericht*) in a decision of December 15, 1938, involving the Association Law. The Supreme Administrative Court repeated its earlier declaration that, in consequence of the Decree of February 28, 1933, all legislation concerning associations was under the jurisdiction of the police and declared that 'it still remained to be determined whether the administrative authorities in questions of associational law were deprived of the rule of the Civil Code [186] only in the sphere of the Decree of February 28, 1933, or whether they are generally deprived of the Civil Code. The court is of the opinion that insofar as the Decree of February 28, 1933, is not applied, the hitherto obtaining laws governing associations are still to be regarded as valid.' [187]

The existence of these self-imposed restraints indicates that the Third Reich cannot be interpreted as a 'totalitarian state' in an uncritical way. Dr. Herrfahrdt, Professor at the University of Marburg, considering whether or not the Third Reich should be called totalitarian, concluded: 'Either it is true of every state or it is particularly untrue of National-Socialism.' [188] What Herrfahrdt meant was that although the Third Reich reserves for itself the power of regulating every aspect of social life, it deliberately limits its use of this power. This, however, is nothing more than the repetition of an idea which had been energetically propagated by another opponent of the catchword 'Totalitarian State,' Secretary of Justice Freissler, who said that 'the National-Socialist state does not believe that the state is necessarily the best leader in all spheres of life. On the contrary, it prefers to leave large spheres of life to other organs of leadership.' [189]

The concept of the 'totalitarian state' is not unambiguous. The ambiguity in the term 'totalitarian state' may be explained by the

fact that there are two types of states with totalitarian tendencies. The common character of the totalitarian tendencies is the
subordination of all activities to the ends of the state. This may
be done on the one hand in the name of the masses. In the state
dominated by the masses, conservatives like Jacob Burckhardt and
contemporaries of the French Revolution like Hegel and John
Adams are likely to view with horror the swallowing up of other
values in the all-consuming interests of the society which is considered to be identical with the state. Burckhardt characterizes
democracy as a *Weltanschauung* in which the 'power of the state
over the individual cannot be too great.' [190] On the other hand a
state may be called totalitarian because of its absolute exercise of
power in order to strengthen the state in its external relationship.
This state may be a monarchy or an aristocracy; it is not necessarily a democratic state. Erich Kaufmann, in 1913, in his book
Die clausula rebus sic stantibus und das Völkerrecht [191] has expressed the idea of the *Machtstaat* as exponent of totalitarianism.

Thus the totalitarian state may be attacked by conservatives insofar as it is a state reflecting the purposes of the masses, while
it may be attacked by liberals because of its authoritarianism. The
Third Reich may be interpreted as a confluence of both of these
tendencies towards the totalitarian state. It is similar to France in
the revolutionary period insofar as it combines the Jacobinist
movement within the *Massenstaat* and the Napoleonic policy towards the outside world of the *Machtstaat*.

We have avoided using the term 'totalitarian state' because of
its complex connotations. Its use in Germany goes back to Carl
Schmitt's book *Der Hüter der Verfassung* [192] where the term totalitarian state was used for the first time in connection with Ernst
Jünger's concept of 'total mobilization.' [193] Carl Schmitt refused
to accept a definition of the 'totalitarian state' as one which controls every aspect of social and economic life. He distinguished
between two types of totalitarianism, the qualitative and the quantitative type. The significance of this distinction becomes clearer
if one takes into account the occasion on which it was formulated.
In November 1932 the *Rheinische-Westfälische Langnamen-
Verein* (Heavy Industry Employers' Association of the Ruhr Val-

ley) invited Schmitt to lecture on 'Majority or Authority.' In this lecture, Schmitt stated that a totalitarian state in the qualitative sense 'is a state which would refuse to tolerate movements hostile to the state. Fascism is a good illustration of this type.' [194]

A 'quantitatively totalitarian state,' however, represents a 'totality of weakness.' The Weimar Republic was, according to Schmitt, a quantitatively totalitarian state but not a qualitatively totalitarian state. 'The qualitatively totalitarian state concentrates in its hands all the major means of mass influence. But, alongside of this realm reserved for the rule of the state, there must in the qualitatively totalitarian state be room for a free individual business enterprise and for a public sphere which does not overlap the sphere of the state.' [195] In view of this speech it cannot be said that Schmitt's conversion to National-Socialism a few weeks later represented any significant inconsistency. Merely terminological issues separate Freissler's theory of the totalitarian state from Schmitt's theory of the qualitatively but not quantitatively totalitarian state.

In both its program and its actual fact, the so-called 'qualitatively totalitarian state' bases itself on private property.[196] In his first *Reichstag* speech on March 25, 1933, Adolf Hitler said:

'The government will on principle safeguard the interests of the German Nation not by the roundabout ways of a bureaucracy organized by the state but by encouraging private initiative and by recognizing private property.'

If the economic system of present-day Germany may be described as 'regulated capitalism based on private property' (as will be later demonstrated) it cannot be called a totalitarian state in the broader sense. To the extent that the Third Reich permits private enterprise to exist, National-Socialism limits the scope of the Prerogative State. Regulated capitalism is characterized by state activity in the economic field; but generally, state intervention in this sphere is not of the type associated with the Prerogative State. Werner Best, the legal counsel of the *Gestapo*, has perceived this situation more clearly than anyone who has written on the problem. In an article of the *Jahrbuch der Akademie für Deutsches Recht,* Best reiterated a theory already well known in Germany as a result of his earlier writings, namely, that the National-Socialist state recognizes a policy power free from all legal restraints. After describing the Prerogative State, Best turns to the Normative State:

'Our discussion of the National-Socialist state does not imply that any political activity may be undertaken without regard to rules and according to the arbitrary decision of any individual political authority. It is essential that many of the activities of the state should be carried out according to legal rules and that they should be calculable in advance, in order that the persons concerned may be able to orient themselves satisfactorily.' [197]

Once having laid bare the central fact of National-Socialist constitutional law, i.e. the co-existence of the Normative and Prerogative State, he approaches the decisive legal problem, the definition of the specific point at which the Prerogative State yields its jurisdiction to the Normative State. This self-restraint, the regulation of its future activities by legal rules, is according to Best 'appropriate where it satisfies the requirements of the constructive forces of the nation. In order that these forces maintain their ends, it is desirable that they should be able to predict the activities of the state.' [198] Best does not pursue this idea further. It is not by chance that the clearest analysis of the structure of the Third Reich available in National-Socialist juridical literature is the product of a man who, since he represents the Prerogative State (or rather its most powerful instrument i.e., the *Gestapo*) need not fear its criticism. Nor is it strange that Best should leave unanswered the pressing question as to exactly which 'constructive forces' of the nation require the protection of the Normative State.

The relevance of such an 'abstract' question would be denied by National-Socialism. If it were forced to take a general position on the question, National-Socialist theory would probably assert that racial forces are the 'constructive forces' of contemporary Germany. Accordingly, National-Socialism denies the protection of the Normative State to all non-Aryan subjects. Furthermore, whether or not any particular Aryan citizen is individually included in the 'constructive forces' of the nation is to be decided in each particular case.

A detailed analysis of the National-Socialist legal system will show that this viewpoint is inadequate for the solution of the problem under consideration. In the preceding pages, it was shown that any case, once it is declared to be 'politically' relevant, may be shifted from the jurisdiction of the Normative State to the Prerogative State. No person in contemporary Germany has any guarantee that his status as a 'constructive force' will not be denied by some agency of the party or of the state and that he will not lose the protection of the Normative State. A theoretical analysis of neo-German constitutional law, however, must not rest content with such a statement. Although National-Socialism would refuse to recognize such a question, it is still necessary to discover whether any criterion is available for distinguishing between 'destructive' and 'constructive' forces other than the racial ones and those which are adduced in individual cases.

This problem is a crucial one for any realistic analysis of the legal order. Because of its paramount importance, we shall attempt to state it as clearly as possible.

Thesis: The 'constructive forces' of the nation are, as a matter of principle, protected by the Normative State.

Question: 1. Is there a general distinction among the various groups of the Aryan German nation with respect to the extent to which they enjoy the protection of the Normative State?

2. Assuming that this question is answered affirmatively, is the extent to which the various groups enjoy the general protection of the Normative State indicative of the degree to which the respective groups are regarded as 'constructive elements' ?

3. This in its turn raises the question of the class structure of the Third Reich.

Here we need only point to the existence of the problem. (A more detailed discussion will be found at the end of the first part of this book—*vide infra* 'The Estates.') But perhaps at this stage of the discussion it may be noted that the leaders of private business are generally classified with the 'constructive forces' of the nation.

CHAPTER III

THE NORMATIVE STATE

---

1. The Dual State and Separation of Powers

a. PREROGATIVE STATE AND THE EXECUTIVE

ONE reservation always lurks in the background of the Normative State: considerations of political expediency. This political reservation is apparent throughout the entire German legal system. The character of this reservation was first made explicit in certain treatises on international law by Professor Carl Bilfinger of the University of Halle.

In 1929, Bilfinger wrote an article the fundamental importance of which is concealed by its non-committal title: 'Reflections on Political Law.' [199] In his discussion of certain questions of international law, Bilfinger asked how far political activity may be regulated by norms. Although he did not entirely reject the normative regulation of political activity, he emphasized the fact that general norms must be suspended whenever issues vital to the existence of the state are involved. The validity of all rules of international law is limited by the reservation that a state may repudiate anyone of them if and when its security is threatened. In the field of constitutional law, Bilfinger sees the same reservation contained in the provisions for emergency decrees and martial law.[200]

Proceeding from Bilfinger's ideas, Carl Schmitt, in his pamphlet *Nationalsozialismus und Völkerrecht* [201] pointed out that 'the "reservation" is to a great extent a more fundamental principle of international law than is a treaty.' A system of international law, according to Schmitt, may be useful and expedient for certain administrative institutions, but it should not be taken 'too seriously.' [202] The issues involved in questions bearing on the existence or non-existence of political entities transcend the limits of normative regulation.

The legal theory of the post-war German counter-revolutionists was decisively influenced by international events and the concept which permitted an unlimited sovereignty to ignore international law is the source of the theory that political activity is not subject to legal regulation. This was the presupposition for the theory of the Prerogative State.[203]

Even before the war of 1914-18 German jurisprudence had recognized certain legal limitations in the field of domestic politics. It had singled out one section of the functions of the state which it designated as 'government' (*Regierung*) in contradiction to the three functions defined in the classical theory of the separation of powers.[204] We quote from a leading textbook: 'Not everything is "administrative" that is neither legislative nor judicial. There is a fourth field in existence . . . excluded from administration are all those activities of the state which for the realization of its purpose lead it beyond those purposes.' [205] Eminent constitutional lawyers of Imperial Germany generally denied that the doctrine of the 'separation of powers' was of importance in Bismarckian Germany. However, the prevailing doctrine of constitutional law correctly pointed out that the constitutional structure of the limited monarchy could not be understood without reference to the theory of separation of powers.

But it must not be forgotten that during the course of the centuries the doctrine of the separation of powers has undergone considerable change especially in regard to the executive function.[206] Although Locke is generally looked upon as the father of the modern doctrine of the separation of powers he exerted no significant influence on the absolutist Germany of his time. It has frequently been pointed out that Locke not only recognized three separate powers, the 'legislative,' the 'executive,' and the 'federative' power, but that he also included the 'prerogative': 'Prerogative is nothing but the power of doing public good without a rule'. [207]

According to Locke, 'prerogative' is not a fourth power in the framework of the doctrine of the separation of powers but a deduction from a principle which was not integrated with the structure of the separation of powers.[208] Since the bearer of the 'prerogative' may, according to Locke, act not only independently of law but, if necessary, in opposition to it, and since there are no legal restraints imposed on him beyond the vague formula: *Salus rei publicae suprema lex*, a connection might be presumed to exist between the neo-German constitutional doctrine and Locke's theory. Such a hypothesis would, however, be incorrect.

Locke's doctrine of the prerogative was never accepted in England. When George III tried to invoke that doctrine in a politically inconsequential case he encountered the energetic and successful opposition of Parliament.[209] Nor was it influential in France or in the United States, in spite of the otherwise enormous influence Locke exercised on the political thought of these countries. Thomas Jefferson vigorously denied that the executive power was associated with the 'prerogative' as it had been during the colonial period.[210] By the identification of 'government' and the 'execution of the law' Jefferson is able to say that he 'proscribes under the name of prerogative the exercise of all powers undefined by the laws.' [211] Nor did Montesquieu adopt Locke's prerogative theory. Furthermore, he modified Locke's doctrine of the separation of powers decisively by declaring that the judiciary was an independent power, while Locke had placed it under the executive power. On the other hand, he maintained that the executive power included both the maintenance of public safety and the federative power as defined by Locke.

The doctrine of the separation of powers in Montesquieu's formulation exercised a deep influence on German constitutional development. There was, however, one point of difference: the German monarchs never admitted that government was nothing else but the execution of laws or that governmental functions were identical with administration. Ultimately influenced by Hegel, the German ruling groups always stressed the special importance of the governmental function as distinguished from the executive. This distinction between administrative and governmental function was very clearly expressed by Metternich in a letter written in April 1848:

'The major evil consisted in the failure of the government to govern and this was the result of the confusion of administration and government. Wherever this confusion exists an empire may appear to continue its existence without disturbance. Unused power, however, finds its way from the highest levels to the lowest and results in the overthrow of the existing order.' [212]

Pre-war German doctrine merely noted the existence of this specific function of government while stressing the function of administration in order to train efficient civil servants. In the post-war period, however, the constitutional theory, influenced by Rudolf Smend,[213] dealt with the state from the political viewpoint, a viewpoint which had previously been neglected. Smend went so far as to consider the legal order as a 'foreign body' (*Fremdkörper*) in the framework of the constitutional, i.e., the political system.[214]

The question arises whether the theory of the National-Socialist legal system is substantially different from the theory first put forth by Otto Mayer and later elaborated by Rudolf Smend. The question might also well be raised whether the 'fourth power' corresponds to what we have called the Prerogative State. If it does, no great change has occurred. Carl Schmitt wrote in 1927 that 'the legal state [*Rechtsstaat*], despite its legalism and normativism, is essentially a state and hence always contains, in addition to its legalistic and normative elements, certain special political elements.' [215] But is not this co-existence of administrative and governmental elements identical with the distinction between Normative and Prerogative State and is not our thesis that the dual form is peculiar to the National-Socialist state thus refuted? The answer to this question is 'no.' The crucial distinction between the 'fourth power' legal state and the Third Reich consists in the fact that in the Third Reich the 'political' does not represent a single segment of the state activities (rigorously delimited by legal restraints) but that potentially it comprises the entire political and private life. The 'political' sphere is not one sphere of the state separated from the others by law; it is an omnicompetent sphere independent of all legal regulation.[216] Since it claims unlimited jurisdiction for itself, it cannot be considered as one 'power' among several (as is the case according to the doctrine of the separation of powers). 'The separation and distinction of powers presupposes in principle the delimitability of all the activities of the state.' [217]

A potentially unlimited power, however, is the antithesis of a limitable one.

b. THE NORMATIVE STATE AND DISCRETIONARY POWER

The German theory of administrative law always considered discretionary power to be a characteristic of the executive power. It must be recognized that under National-Socialism all executive authorities, whether or not they are parts of the Prerogative State, have extended the scope of their discretion. Authorities belonging to the Normative State such as Foreign Exchange Control Offices (*Devisenstellen*), Reich Food Provision Estate (*Reichsnährstand*), Trustees of Labor (*Treuhänder der Arbeit*), and many other regulatory bodies operate under statutory provisions which are usually so vague that they are only general enabling clauses. These vague general principles authorize administrative bodies to intervene in the social and economic life of the nation, not only in matters which have always been subject to government regulation, but also in many new fields which prior to 1933 had not been subject to the state.

This raises the problem as to the existence of any fundamental difference between these activities and those of the authorities which we designated as organs of the Prerogative State. Might it not be argued that the Prerogative State is nothing but an extreme case of the administrative power in which the discretion of the administration is even greater than usual? If this were true, the qualitative distinctions between the Prerogative and the Normative State would disappear, since the difference would be a matter of degree only. A systematic treatment would then be impossible.

A decisive distinction between the administrative agencies of

the Normative State and the organs of the Prerogative State rests
on the differences between their respective sphere of jurisdiction
and is not a problem of varying degrees of discretionary power.
However extensive the discretion of an administrative agency —
such as the Foreign Exchange Control Office — its discretion can
be exercised only within the limits of its clearly defined jurisdiction. Were the Foreign Exchange Control Office to exceed its
jurisdiction, its acts could be declared null and void in a proceeding before the ordinary courts. The organs of the Prerogative
State, however, are not so limited in their jurisdiction. There are
no legally defined restraints which narrow their jurisdiction. Since
the jurisdiction of these authorities is unlimited, they cannot be
considered as regular administrative agencies. Administration may
be defined negatively as the state function which is neither
legislative nor judicial, while the organs of the Prerogative State
are characterized by their unlimited jurisdiction.

Although a clear distinction exists between administrative agencies and the organs of the Prerogative State it must be pointed out
that the activities of the ordinary administrative agencies have
been greatly influenced by the existence of the Prerogative State.
Since the jurisdiction of the organs of the Prerogative State is unlimited, a certain tendency exists among the agencies of the
Normative State to imitate this example and to enlarge the scope
of their own discretion. Furthermore, since the Prerogative State
has completely stifled all public opinion, resistance against such
an encroachment was decisively weakened. Such a development
was closely connected with the changes in the economic sphere.
In the period of competitive capitalism there were very far-
reaching limitations on the discretionary powers of administrative agencies. The continuously increasing activity of the state in
all fields of social and economic life has brought with it a corresponding enlargement of the area of discretion. Moreover, the
mere existence of governmental arbitrariness, as embodied in the
Prerogative State, has dulled the sense of justice to such a degree
that the existence of an agency with limited jurisdiction is considered as a legal institution even though the government exercises enormous discretionary power.[218]

The Normative State, however, is by no means identical with a state in which the 'Rule of Law' prevails, i.e., with the *Rechtsstaat* of the liberal period. The Normative State is a necessary complement to the Prerogative State and can be understood only in that light. Since the Prerogative and Normative States constitute an interdependent whole, consideration of the Normative State alone is not permissible.

The co-existence of the Normative and Prerogative States is indicative of the National-Socialist policy of promoting the power of efficiency of the state by means of increased arbitrariness. Justice Brandeis' statement, 'the doctrine of the separation of powers was adopted by the Convention of 1787 not to promote efficiency but to preclude the exercise of arbitrary power,' [219] has no meaning for the Dual State. The Prerogative State's jurisdiction over all other jurisdictions guarantees that the efficiency of the state shall have priority over the liberty of the individual. In National-Socialist Germany the 'gospel of efficiency' has been substituted for the worship of liberty.

2. THE GUARDIANS OF THE NORMATIVE STATE

a. NATIONAL-SOCIALISM AS THE GUARDIAN OF THE NORMATIVE STATE

Since the jurisdiction of the Prerogative State is not legally defined, there is no legal guarantee of the stability of the Normative State. The existence of the Normative State is not dependent on law. It depends on the complete permeation of the state by National-Socialist attitudes and ideas.

This view will appear paradoxical only to those who have not perceived that National-Socialism is a political phenomenon arising out of the recent stage of capitalistic development in Germany. Since, according to National-Socialism, the freedom of the entrepreneur within the economic sphere should in principle be unconfined, questions of economic policy are usually regarded as falling within the domain of the Normative State. This is not a function of law but of the preferences of National-Socialism. We quote a National-Socialist author: 'It would be a misinterpretation of the concept of substantive political issues if police authorities directed economic policy for political aims and for the use of the police power, and further, if they were to attempt to pass measures of economic policy as political issues. It would not be satisfactory to withdraw from the control which is implicit in judicial review such measures of the ordinary police authorities. The tasks of the *Gestapo* do not lie in the field of economic policy but rather in the investigation and suppression of activities which are dangerous to the state. In other words, all their duties fall in the sphere of state policy in its narrower sense.' [220]

In order to prevent a repetition of the experience of the sorcerer's apprentice (i.e., in order to master the spirits which he has invoked), Reuss, the author of the above quotation, appealed to the principles of the traditional administrative law as it functioned under the Rule of Law (*Rechtsstaat*), since he sensed 'the danger of *excès de pouvoir* in a particularly acute form.' [221] Legally speaking, however, there can be no abuse of discretionary power in contemporary Germany, no *excès de pouvoir*, of political authorities. The 'particularly' acute form in which the abuse of discretionary power takes place in National-Socialist Germany consists in informing the responsible official that he has infringed the basic principles of National-Socialism by disturbing economic life through the exercise of prerogative measures.

In spite of the existing legal possibilities for intervention by the Prerogative State where and whenever it desires, the legal foundations of the capitalistic economic order have been maintained. If one picks at random a volume of the decisions of a German civil court and examines it systematically, this conception will find complete corroboration. Freissler, Secretary of the Ministry of Justice, has clearly realized that economic law in a narrower sense (the National-Socialists call it 'community law') was left relatively untouched by the revolution of 1933. Even Freissler recognizes that the *mores* of the 'ethnic community' did not affect it. As late as 1937 Dr. Freissler said in his article *'Der*

Heimweg des Rechts in die völkische Sittenordnung' that although 'Penal Law has now oriented itself towards the *mores* of
the ethnic community, economic law has not in any legally effective way appreciated the biological position of the individual as a
cell in the German ethnic organism.' [222]

b. THE COURTS AS GUARDIANS OF THE NORMATIVE STATE

1. Internal and External Reservations

The courts are responsible for seeing that the principles of the
capitalist order are maintained—even though the Prerogative State
occasionally exercises its right to deal with individual cases in the
light of expediency and the special nature of the case at hand.
The decisions show that the courts have successfully maintained
the legal system necessary for the functioning of private capitalism. The legal institutions essential to private capitalism, such as
freedom of enterprise, sanctity of contracts, private property, the
right of the entrepreneur to control labor, regulation of unfair
competition, regulation of patent, trade-mark rights, etc., legal
protection for interest agreements, property and transfer for purposes of security, still exist in Germany. To this extent the courts
have striven to maintain the supremacy of the law. In order that
we may not complicate our analysis, we are not considering cases
touching on the Jewish problem. To generalize from the treatment of the Jews in the economic field would be misleading. At
the same time, it would be equally misleading to cite cases in
which the Normative State protected the rights of the Jews.
Whether a Normative State exists in Germany and whether it
extends protection to Jews are two separate problems. We shall
deal with the Jewish problem in § 3 of this chapter.

The parallel existence of the Normative and the Prerogative
States is well demonstrated by the legal regulations governing
in those areas where economic life and police functions overlap,
i.e. in the areas controlled by the Industrial Police (*Gewerbe-
polizei*). It is not necessary to discuss the question as to the power

of the political police to deal with individual cases as they please; we realize by now that they can. Of greater interest is an investigation of the cases in which there has been no intervention by the political police. Has the supremacy of rational law been abolished by the National-Socialist *coup d'état?* It would not be legitimate to speak of a Normative State if, in cases of conflict, the courts ignored the existing law in favor of general principles of National-Socialist origin. The Normative State would not exist if, even in cases where the political police do not intervene, the legal authority had to contend with this second reservation.

Of course, we realize that in addition to the already existing 'external' political reservations attempts have been made in Germany to establish 'internal' reservations which would not be subject to the will of the political authorities. So far, these efforts have been ineffective except where Jews are concerned.

Whether authorities are to adhere strictly to the law in cases which have not been defined as 'political' or whether all laws are to be applied with an 'internal' reservation has been treated by no less a person than Hermann Goering. In an important lecture entitled 'The Stability of the Legal System as the Foundation of the Ethnic Community,' Goering energetically rejected the latter possibility when he said:

'There may be circumstances in which the application of the ordinary law may lead to a profound injustice. The application of the law even in such cases is not a matter to be decided arbitrarily. The judges are bound by the law which is the promulgation of the Leader's will. An arbitrary deviation from the law would constitute a violation of the judge's loyalty to the Leader.' [223]

Thus even National-Socialism had been unable to avoid the dilemma of legal stability versus political expediency. In attempting to explain why Goering advocated the maintenance of formal rationality it would be unfortunate if we were to overlook the nature of his audience. The lecture of November 16, 1934, was given before a group of prosecuting attorneys and judges. Goering would probably have used a somewhat different tone had he been speaking to his appointees in the *Gestapo* — i. e., to the officials of the Prerogative State. Such lectures, however, are not published.

2. The Normative State as the Guardian of
Legal Institutions

a. *Entrepreneurial Liberty*. The dispute over the 'internal reservation' and therewith over the existence of the Normative State was bitterly fought in relation to the Economic Enterprise Law (*Gewerbeordnung*). This law is based on the principle of entrepreneurial freedom. Extreme National-Socialist circles tried to destroy this principle. They tried to brand entrepreneurial freedom as a holdover from the liberal epoch and, accordingly, antiquated and automatically rendered inoperative by National-Socialism. They asserted that restrictions on entrepreneurial liberty should be introduced not only when specially required by statute, but whenever desirable in the light of the general principles of National-Socialism.[224]

If we assume a case which stands outside the jurisdiction of the Prerogative State, it is still undecided whether the prevailing substantive law or vague principles allowing unrestricted discretion are to govern the actions of the inspectorial staff. But, in its decision of August 10, 1936, the Prussian Supreme Administrative Court (*Oberverwaltungsgericht*) declared itself in favor of the Normative State. The court referred to the fact that 'it has recently been claimed that in consequence of the revolution in legal conceptions associated with the triumph of National-Socialism, the fundamental principles of entrepreneurial freedom no longer obtain.'[225] As early as 1934 the Prussian Supreme Administrative Court had rejected this contention although other courts accepted it. Despite vigorous criticism, the Supreme Administrative Court held its ground; although, as the court said: 'It is true that National-Socialist law has added new legal regulations to those which were already in existence. As yet, entrepreneurial freedom has not been legally abolished. Further restraints and regulations may be imposed only through a new law.'[226] The court emphasized the dangers which would flow from the abolition of the trade regulation laws. One argument which the court offered was that: 'if the inspectorial staff are given the general power to regulate entrepreneurs, all the laws which are concerned with the

regulation of economic activity are out of date and practically
suspended.' [227] Thus the court emphatically refused to renounce
the basic principles of the traditional legal and economic order by
proclaiming the general principle:

'The suspension and modification of the law is not the task of
the judiciary, even when it considers the law to be in conflict
with the National-Socialist outlook. Legislation is the domain of
the Leader and the courts may not intervene in this sphere.' [228]

b. *Sanctity of Contracts.* A similar attitude was expressed by a
court in a case which was in many respects political and which involved the sanctity of contract. In the capitalistic society credits
can be given and goods can be transferred only if one has the
guarantee that contracts will be honored: *Pacta sunt servanda.*
National-Socialism has not abolished this principle though it by no
means treats it as a corollary of Natural Law. The difference between the western democracies and National-Socialist Germany
becomes particularly clear in their attitude towards the Natural
Law status of the sanctity of contracts as expressed in the sphere
of International Law. The foreign policy of Germany in the last
years has amply demonstrated the practical application of this system of ethics which regards contracts as terminable whenever it
appears desirable. The *clausula rebus sic stantibus* which had been
worked out by German international lawyers before the war plays
a central role in National-Socialist theory and practice in the field
of international law. As early as 1930 Carl Schmitt referred to the
principle *pacta sunt servanda* as a tendency of 'loan shark'
ethics.[229]

Is this attitude also dominant in the sphere of private legal relations? If it were possible to terminate any contract at will by
appealing to general National-Socialist principles, the Normative
State could not exist. This in turn would mean the destruction of
the capitalistic system. Some courts have at least definitely sounded a warning on this point. The Bavarian Administrative Court
(*Verwaltungsgerichtshof*) had to decide whether a specific
National-Socialist *clausula rebus sic stantibus* was valid in the internal legal order of the Third Reich. In 1882 a Bavarian munic-

ipality contracted with the Catholic congregation of the town to contribute to the living of the Catholic priest. When the National-Socialists came to power the municipality sought to terminate the contract, arguing that it was entered into under very different political circumstances and could not be considered binding after the National-Socialist revolution. The attempt of the municipality to evade its contractual responsibilities by appealing to general National-Socialist principles was blocked by the court, which held that 'the sanctity of contract is the foundation of the existing legal order. The sanctity of contract is an ethical value and an ethical imperative with which no legal order can dispense.' The court characterized the sanctity of contract as 'the basis of economic life and of the orderly existence of the ethnic community'[230] and declared that formal rationality had priority over National-Socialist ideas by proclaiming the following principles:

'A realistic attitude must be taken towards the objection basing itself on National-Socialist principles. This attitude must be grounded in the positive norms of the existing legal order which is the emanation of the ethical principles accepted as binding by the ethnic community. The court does not exclude all possibility of applying the *clausula rebus sic stantibus*...but reserves its right to do so for especially exceptional cases.'[231]

But this was also the attitude of the courts in pre-National-Socialist Germany. Where the capitalistic system in endangered the courts must function as guardians of the law. The Bavarian court emphasizes the fact that 'the judiciary has as its domain the care of the legal order. Political leadership is not within its domain.'[232]

c. *Private Property*. If the courts look at the traditional legal order as 'the emanation of the ethical principles accepted as binding by the ethnic community' they would be inconsistent if they refused their protection to property owners who are threatened with the intervention of non-political authorities hiding themselves under National-Socialist phraseology.

A case dealing with the farm-land law, a sphere in which National-Socialist ideology has allegedly made its most important gains, is instructive. This case centered around the question whether the owner of a herd of sheep had the right to let them graze on a piece of land belonging to another person. The owner of the sheep argued that the woods in which the sheep grazed had hitherto not been exploited for economic purposes, and that the refusal of the owner of the land to permit the sheep to graze there represented an interest in private gain which should be sacrificed for the benefit of the community (*Gemeinnutz geht vor Eigennutz*). The Prefect of the District (*Landrat*) had concurred in this argument and he had, by a special decree, decided in favor of the sheep-owner. The Prussian Supreme Court (*Kammergericht*) was impressed neither by the decree of the Prefect of the District nor by the National-Socialist argument that private gain should be sacrificed for the benefit of the community. The court clearly upheld the law of property as contained in the German Civil Code (*Bürgerliches Gesetzbuch*).[233] The court declared that limitations on property rights could be imposed only in legally specified exceptions and these must be made in the regular legal forms. [234]

The property system of Germany has not been transformed by the National-Socialist catchwords. Private property still enjoys the protection of the courts from official interference, except where political considerations are involved. The Rule of Law as it bears on the protection of property is especially relevant to the question of assessment of taxes. Rational calculation as part of the conduct of a business enterprise is impossible if tax assessments are unpredictable. The Third Reich therefore upholds the rule of the Normative State in regard to tax administration.

A decision of the Supreme Disciplinary Court (*Reichsdisciplinarhof*) discusses the question whether the Rule of Law still prevails with regard to fiscal problems. The case was one in which the mayor of a town had deviated from the letter of the law by assessing and collecting highway taxes. He defended himself with the argument that 'the urgency of the situation had necessitated immediate action' [235] and that National-Socialist principles emphasized the secondary significance of strict application of the law when there were undesirable conditions to be eliminated. The

court, however, did not follow this reasoning, and acting in accordance with the principles of the Normative State, declared that
'although National-Socialism seeks to overcome the inadequacies
of the former regime with speedy and energetic actions its extensive legislative activity demonstrates that statutory measures
and legal procedures are required for this end.' [236] The court emphasized that the fiscal administrators are as much bound by the
pre-National-Socialist laws as they are by the laws and orders of
the Leader. The mayor was informed that inasmuch as he was not
an agent of the Prerogative State he had to assure himself that 'in
the National-Socialist state the head of a community should avoid
arbitrary measures.' [237] In questions of road constructions and highway taxes the Third Reich permits the majesty of the law to
prevail.

d. *Competition.* The German courts have continued to uphold
the previously prevailing laws regulating unfair competition among
business enterprises. The Appellate Court (*Oberlandesgericht*) of
Cologne denied an injunction to an association of oil dealers who,
with permission of the Board of Trade and the Trustee of Labor,
had fixed gas prices. The injunction was to be applied against a
non-member selling at lower prices. The association pointed out
that the prices which they had fixed had been approved not only
by the Board of Trade but by the Trustee of Labor as well, i. e.,
by an authority erected by the National-Socialist state in order to
protect the interests of the community. In denying the motion for
the injunction, the court declared it 'irrelevant that the price fix-
ing of the applicant had the approval of the Trustee of Labor of
Düsseldorf and of the Board of Trade and Industry of Cologne
because these organizations are not legally empowered to fix
prices in a binding way on the motor fuel market. . . . The approval of the said organizations does not make the prices binding
on outsiders.' [238]

Three years later there occurred a case which indicated that the
capitalistic laws of the market, involving the right of the producer
to set any price upon his product, were still operative where they
did not come into opposition with the special regulations of the

government. A German statute in 1909 (*Gesetz betreffend unlauteren Wettbewerb*)[239] had provided that, although in general
competition in the market was not to be regulated, in special cases
of unfair trade practices legal actions could be taken by the competitors injured by these practices or by the association to which
the merchant or manufacturer belonged. On the basis of this statute the alarm-clock manufacturers' association in 1937 initiated
a suit against one of its members for selling inferior articles at an
exorbitant price. The plaintiff argued that the conduct of the
defendant was contrary to the doctrine of the *justum pretium*
which is inherent in National-Socialism. Unjust prices are im-
moral and are therefore at the very least contrary to the Law
against Unfair Competition.

The Appellate Court of Hamburg rejected this argument in
its decision of May 12, 1937. The court recognized that 'a transgression of the price regulations set by the National-Socialist government is unethical . . . but this did not apply to the case of the
merchandise sold by the defendant since the price of alarm-clocks
was not specially regulated by the state.'[240] The court based its
decision on the argument that the prices of merchandise not regulated by the state 'are even now determined by the conditions of
supply and demand, that is, the price is determined in the last
analysis in accordance with the interest of the consumer. So long
as the conduct of the business is in accord with the other requirements of fair trade practice there is no restriction on the prices it
sets for its products. Thus there may be cases of very high, or
even exorbitant prices in which there cannot be attributed unethical conduct on the basis of the exorbitance of the price alone.'[241]
It is fitting that this expression of commercial policy occurred in
Hamburg, with its definite commercial tradition.

e. *Labor Law.* The Normative State has also warded off threats
against the position of the entrepreneur in the firm. In a case before
the Supreme Labor Court (*Reichsarbeitsgericht*) a branch manager
complained of dismissal, without adequate notice. Sheltered by
the German Labor Front, she had attempted to rent for herself
the shop in which she was employed. The Labor Front had con-

ducted the renting negotiations while the employee remained in the background. The court was called upon to decide whether the Labor Front had overstepped its jurisdiction in interfering with the rights of the defendant in favor of the plaintiff. The court held that 'even if the Labor Front acted in its official capacity and within its jurisdiction, it was subject to the laws as was any other public corporation and might act only within the framework of the laws.' According to the court, 'a direct interference with the right of others in the case at hand in which the negotiations were carried on with the building owner behind the back of the defendant for the purpose of making a lease for the plaintiff is illegal.' [242] Even the German Labor Front must acknowledge the principle that the entrepreneur is 'master in his own house.' The complaint of the branch manager was dismissed.

A decision of the Court of Social Honor (*Sozialer Ehrengerichtshof*), an institution which is among the proudest accomplishments of National-Socialism, provides clear evidence that the Normative State is still operative. § 36 of the National Labor Code (*Gesetz zur Ordnung der nationalen Arbeit*)[243] prescribes penalties for certain specified offenses. Soon after this law went into force, the question arose whether the list of offenses in § 36 was an exhaustive enumeration or whether it was merely a list of examples which should occasionally be supplemented by practice and analogy. The Supreme Court of Social Honor ruled out analogy [244] as a method for applying law for all cases within its jurisdiction when it decided that '§36 of the Labor Code specifically enumerates the serious violations of the act which are punishable by the Court of Social Honor. It unambiguously indicates thereby that the inclusion of less important violations was not intended by the legislator.' [245] The foregoing again demonstrates that National-Socialism, although it passionately repudiates formal rationality in the application of the law as a vestige of a bygone era, adheres to the principle of formal rationality when the case concerns fundamental economic problems. The capitalistic system cannot exist without a minimum of formal rationality. It is no wonder then that Dr. Mansfeld referred to the decision of the Court of Social Honor as 'wise moderation.' [246]

f. *The Law of Non-Tangible Property*. The law of non-tangible property (copyright, patents, rights of publication, trade-marks, etc.) raises a crucial point in our theory of the Dual State, since it is here that the capitalistic system can least easily submit to interference with the existing system of private law.

The case which we shall cite is perhaps the most important civil case in Germany of recent years. It involved the suit of a phonograph record manufacturer against the German Broadcasting Company (*Reichs-Rundfunkgesellschaft*) in which the former sought to restrain the latter from playing his records without paying a fee. Two lower courts sustained the Broadcasting Company but the *Reichsgericht* on November 14, 1936, decided against it. The company had claimed that the courts had no jurisdiction in the case, since radio stations supplying vital political information were therefore an integral part of national policy. The court refused to accept this argument and, furthermore, denied that the radio station was entitled to use records without charge, because they were used in the interest of the national welfare. The court held that, even though the activities of the radio station were partly public, the obtaining of material for broadcasting purposes fell within private law since 'the broadcasting of a work without the consent of its author or owner, merely on the ground of the public position of the radio station, would amount practically to expropriation.'[247] This decision was all the more significant in view of the fact that during the course of the trial the press took an attitude conflicting with that of the court.

The same tendency was evident in a copyright litigation. The litigants disagreed over the question whether the German national anthem — the Horst Wessel Song — had been composed by Horst Wessel or whether it had been plagiarized. If someone in a public gathering had put forth the view that Horst Wessel had plagiarized the melody from an old song he would have suffered serious consequences. But when the same charge was made in court by representatives of a music publisher the court examined all the details of the case thoroughly, calling in experts, etc. This actually happened in a case decided by the *Reichsgericht* on December 2, 1936.[248]

3. The Normative State and the Party Program

a. *Public Interest precedes Self-Interest.* The general principles of the National-Socialist Party were formulated in the Party Platform of February 24, 1920. Followers of National-Socialism contend that the program of the party is the real constitution of the Third Reich. Its relationship to substantive law, therefore, is of interest, especially in case of conflict between the substantive law and the program. The National-Socialists who favor the acceptance of the platform argue that judges are empowered to review those pre-National-Socialist laws which have not been formally rescinded as incompatible with the 'constitution.' According to their opinion, the judge is forbidden to apply 'unconstitutional' laws or to make decisions which will lead to results opposed by the party program. Even opponents of National-Socialism reluctantly admit the tenability of this view, recognizing that Hitler has worked on the fulfilment of the program with uncompromising energy. As evidence of this contention, the National-Socialist solution of the Jewish question is cited. Whether the Jewish question really has been treated in conformity with the program will be discussed later.[249] But even if it had been so we should still not know the degree of completeness with which the platform as a whole has been realized.[250] For our examination of the achievements of the party, it is important to discover the extent to which the principle, 'general welfare precedes private welfare', has been honored.

The realization of this principle would have involved the repudiation of the Normative State and of formal rationality. This, however, did not occur. The courts, it is true, paid verbal deference to it while actually 'co-ordinating' it with the needs of the Normative State and the structure of private law; the *Reichsgericht* especially performed this task with deftness:

'Although the most recent tendencies of German law particularly emphasize the old saying 'general welfare comes before private welfare' and seek to realize it, it must be recognized that it is not entirely new since older laws had already recognized the principle. (Graf und Ziether, *Deutsche Rechtssprichwörter, II. Auflage* 1869, p. 487; *Preussisches Allgemeines Landrecht* § 73, 74)'[251]

This decision enabled the *Reichsgericht* to maintain the traditional principles of German private law in the economic sphere
and to provide them with new legitimation by concealing old arguments under new phrases. In the course of revaluation proceedings the *Reichsgericht* formulated the principle that 'economic considerations cannot induce a court to render a decision clearly in
conflict with the law.' The *Reichsgericht* emphasized in this decision that 'the old principle which guaranteed the stability of the
law. i. e., the preamble to the Code of Court Procedure[252] which
stated that the judge must obey the law, is still in force and that
Art. 336 of the Penal Code,[253] which punishes anyone who tam-
pers with the law with penitentiary sentences up to five years is
still valid.'[254]

To date the higher courts have not abandoned these principles,
although the lower courts sometimes tried to revolt. The District
Court of Breslau (*Landgericht*) for example attempted to abandon
the formal rationality of private law by holding that the transfer-
ence of property for purpose of security (*Sicherheitsübereignung*)
could not be reconciled with National-Socialist principles. It justified its decision by saying that 'the transaction made the debtor
the slave of the creditor and that this would be contrary to National-Socialist philosophy and should not be permitted by the
courts.' [255] The District Court, however, was admonished in the official journal of the Department of Justice (*Deutsche Justiz*) and
was advised that this type of judicial conduct was not admissible
in the field of private law. In commenting upon this decision of the
Breslau Court, Paetzold not only criticized it but warned against
its repetition[256] and said that 'the necessities originating from the
existing economic order cannot be ignored.'[257]

The attempt to replace the rational legal order of German capitalism as it was embodied in private law by the principles of the
party program was too abstract and much too general to serve as a
source of judicial decisions. In almost all borderline cases concerning economic problems it has been possible to construe the general
principles of the party program so as to satisfy both of the conflicting views. The discussion within the National-Socialist Party in
connection with a decision of the Joint Civil Senates of the Su-

preme Court (*Vereinigte Senate des Reichsgerichts*) on November 16, 1937, serves to illustrate this point. As a result of compulsory inoculation a child developed paralytic symptoms from
which he did not recover. Neither the physician nor any other
authorities were to blame. Claiming that inoculation had been
made compulsory in the interest of the general public, the child
demanded damages from the state for his injury. The complaint
was dismissed on the basis of positive law, the *Reichsgericht*, in its
comment on the decision, asserting that 'according to the National-
Socialist conception of the state, the duty of sacrifice should be too
strong to permit a claim for damages.'[258] This supplementary National-Socialist argument had met with violent criticism. Arguing
from the same theory of the ethnic community, the critics of the
Reichsgericht arrived at diametrically opposite results, contending
that their conclusion alone expressed the true National-Socialist
spirit. As long as National-Socialist arguments are only used to justify in political terms a decision based on legal principles this method is innocuous.

In a case before the District Court of Hamburg (*Landgericht*),
however, the problem arose whether the party program had been
substituted for positive law. A debtor who had failed to pay interests on a mortgage invoked as his defense Art. 11 of the party program. He argued that the charge against him was 'unconstitutional'
since the party program had promised the 'destruction of interest-
slavery' (*Brechung der Zinsknechtschaft*). The court did not take
this argument seriously and decided in favor of the plaintiff. The
court stated that it must 'be left to the Leader and the government
to decide when and to what extent they wish to realize this goal
(the abolition of interest) and to choose the means therefor.'[259]
As long as the courts decide that 'there is no danger under such
circumstances that a contract entered into according to law and the
claims deriving therefrom will be dealt with in a manner contrary
to "good faith" and "good morals," '[260] the German creditors need
not be disturbed. These anti-capitalistic sections of the party program are not being enforced.

The Third Reich has not transformed its economic organization
in accordance with the demands of the party program. The capi-

talist economy, founded upon self-interest, has no more been replaced by a predominance of public interests than 'class society'
has been supplanted by 'ethnic community.' The National-Socialists boast that by an intensification of racial consciousness they have
eradicated class hatred and arrogance. They pride themselves especially on having acquired social honor for the German worker
and on having freed him from his feelings of social inferiority. In
the course of a decision in a penal case, the Bavarian Supreme Court
(*Oberlandesgericht* München) had an opportunity to test whether
the National-Socialist revolution was more than a façade which
tried to disguise its emptiness with anti-Semitic propaganda. The
court was in a position to set a precedent for certain changes in the
class structure. It did nothing. According to a Bavarian police decree of November 18, 1887, unmarried laborers were to be punished if they possessed a certain type of knife. The possession of
such knives in general was not prohibited by the decree. The decree dealt only with special groups in the population: 'unmarried
laborers, beggars, vagrants, gypsies, and mentally deficient persons.' It hardly seems consistent with National-Socialist protesta-
tions regarding the 'National Community' that unmarried workers
should be classed with outcasts. Despite its ostensible acceptance of
the desirability of revising antiquated statutes in the spirit of National-Socialism, the Appellate Court of Munich refused to renounce its adherence to formal rationality in the application of the
law. For, as the court said, 'it cannot be claimed that the decree ar-
ranges members of the national community into a class system
which is contradictory to the National-Socialist philosophy or that
it accords them different amounts of social status.'[261] The fact that
it was not found legally necessary in a Bavarian decree to classify
unmarried workers with unmarried farmers, artisans, and students,
but with beggars, vagrants, gypsies and the mentally deficient, has
not caused National-Socialists to replace 'formal juristic' considerations with 'German principles.' We seek in vain in this decision
of the Appellate Court of Munich ideas like the following: 'Now
that German ideas are victorious, we cannot let their practical application be defeated by formal juristic considerations.'[262] They
are, however, found in a decision of the Probate Court of Berlin

in which the court withdrew an adopted Aryan child from its Jewish foster-parents. The most precious thing which these parents possessed, their adopted child, was taken away from them in a decision, typical of National-Socialist cynicism, which read: 'The principle, public welfare precedes self-interest, applies particularly to the Jewish members of the German state.'[263] This last decision certainly sacrificed the positive law in favor of the party program. It is no accident that the decision was one dealing with a Jew.[264]

b. *The Racial Idea.* Although the party program as a whole has not been substituted for the legal system which prevailed before 1933 we must raise the question to what extent one of the central points in the program, the racial idea, has been successful against the Normative State. To what extent have the authorities of the Normative State respected the claims of the racial idea? The racial problem in Germany includes the Jewish problem as its most important, though not sole, concern. In conformity with a previous procedure we shall suspend our consideration of the Jewish problem and deal only with the relationship between the non-Jewish aspects of the racial program and the Normative State.

During the first years of the National-Socialist regime, the courts generally tried to restrict the bearing of the racial idea to those areas where it was legislatively required. This is well illustrated by a decision of the *Reichsgericht* stating that 'the courts are not required to accord validity to National-Socialist views beyond the limits which legislative activity of the National-Socialist state itself has drawn.' The court underlined in this connection 'that National-Socialist legislation concerning racial problems has by no means attempted to enforce all the points of the National-Socialist program.'[265] This decision, however, has been obsolete for some time. It should not be overlooked that the 'Non-Aryan Laws' of 1933 were followed by the 'Anti-Jewish' legislation (Nürnberg Laws) of 1935.[266] Since 1935, persons classified as Jewish are subject not only to the Aryan Laws of 1933 but to the extremely rigorous 'exceptional' laws (*Ausnahmegesetze*) as well.

The racial laws are primarily directed towards family problems.

Family law is not of great relevance to the functioning of the existing economic system. Insofar, however, as the abolition of the Normative State in one section of the legal system may create a dangerous precedent, the regulation of family relations is of highest importance for the maintenance of the system. Actually after a long struggle the judicial authorities have refused to recognize a general racial reservation.

The question arose with respect to the problem of denial of paternity, which, according to the German Civil Code,[267] can only be accomplished within one year from the birth of the child.[268] This regulation is in conflict with National-Socialist ideas of blood relationship, which are of supreme importance in National-Socialist ideology. In order to prevent infringements of the National-Socialist ideology it would seem logical to abolish this section of the Civil Code. Although a number of appellate courts had ruled otherwise, the *Reichsgericht* rendered a decision on November 23, 1937, fundamentally in accord with the rules of the Normative State when it said that 'the judge is not entitled to make such great breaches in the substantive family law of the Civil Code as long as the limitations which it imposes on the question of the paternity of the child affect only the determination of the true blood relationship.'[269] The *Reichsgericht*, however, left an important loophole insofar as 'the question whether the court would have decided in another way if . . . racial differences were involved was not to be discussed.'[270] Thus the *Reichsgericht* which, in 1934, had proclaimed the general supremacy of the law over National-Socialist ideology still adheres to this principle but indicates the possibility of deviation where Jews are concerned. In a trial hearing on family law the Naumburg Appellate Court (*Oberlandesgericht*) on April 20, 1937 had decided that 'the law now — no less than before — is binding for every judge. He may, of course, interpret it within the framework of a racially oriented conception of law, but he cannot disregard it without very good reasons. Such judicial conduct is indispensable if the law is to possess stability and calculability. This feature must be regarded as essential to the state even when in individual cases they obstruct the dispensation of material justice. Even the interests of the ethnic community in the maintenance of

German racial purity cannot afford to ignore the pressing demand that the law be applied and legal stability be preserved.'[271] Massfeller, a high official in the Ministry of Justice, concedes the correctness of the Naumburg court in this particular case. But he doubts whether these principles should be universally applied.[272] They are inadmissible in the system of the National-Socialist law because they grant the Jews the protection of the law.

c. *The Legal Status of the Jews.* Inasmuch as the legal protection of the Normative State is reserved only for the 'constructive forces of the nation' (Best),[273] and inasmuch as the Jews are not considered a part of the German nation but rather are regarded as enemies, all questions in which Jews are involved fall within the jurisdiction of the Prerogative State. Although this was at first only a theoretical principle of National-Socialism, it has now become the regular practice of the Third Reich. The completion of the subjugation of the Jews to the Prerogative State was realized at the moment it was resolved to extirpate the Jews from economic life.

As long as the Jews were allowed to operate small and middle-sized shops and to carry on certain types of industrial production, a contradiction existed in the National-Socialist policy towards the Jews. Since the Jews at that time were more or less integrated into the capitalistic system of the Third Reich,[274] a strict application of the procedures of the Prerogative State would have disturbed the normal course of economic life. Therefore it was the task of the judiciary to guard the economy against disruption, even when that necessitated a certain protection of Jews. Some examples from the earlier phase of National-Socialism may illustrate this statement, although today they are only historically significant.

Since the rules of the practice of competitive capitalism are embodied in the Law governing Unfair Competition (*Reichsgesetz gegen den unlauteren Wettbewerb*)[275] one decision of the *Reichsgericht* which bears on this sphere of the law is especially relevant. With the intention of obtaining some of his competitor's clients, an insurance agent circulated a list of the directors of a competing company whose names appeared to be Jewish. The court was called upon to decide whether this method of competition was in accord with the Law governing Unfair Competition. The decision was in the negative. It asserted that 'to refer to the Jewish character of a firm is to adduce facts which are totally irrelevant to the commercial merits of an insurance company.... Nor can the defendant claim that the National-Socialist philosophy requires the protection of the rural population from Jewish influences.'[276]

From the very beginning, however, any effort to grant the Jews a minimum of legal security was bitterly opposed by the extremist wing of National-Socialism. For years an intensive battle was waged among the various state and party authorities. The process by which the extremist groups gained ascendancy is reflected in successive decisions of the courts. It was only against the strongest resistance that in 1935 the Prussian Supreme Administrative Court (*Oberverwaltungsgericht*) could still protect the entrepreneurial freedom of the Jews. The tremendous pressure which was brought to bear against the legal guarantees of the Jews is shown in the decision of the District Administrative Court of Cologne (*Bezirksverwaltungsgericht*), the court of first instance in this case: 'On the basis of centuries of experiences,' said this court, 'and on the basis of the National-Socialist theory which expresses the nation's ideas of honest and lawful trade, it must be said that Jewish merchants have a reputation for unreliability and must therefore be excluded from economic life. This is a general conviction of the nation and official bodies must respect it.' [277] At that time the superior court (the *Oberverwaltungsgericht*) paid no attention to the argument of the District Administrative Court of Cologne and required that Jews be dealt with according to the law in order to safeguard the principle of entrepreneurial freedom.[278]

Once Jews had been eliminated from the economic life, it was possible to deprive them of all legal protection without adversely affecting the economic system. Thus, the progress of anti-Semitism forced the Jews beyond the outer limits of the Normative State. A decision in the field of commercial law may serve to illustrate this. A half-Aryan and half-Jewish partnership owned a cigar and cigarette store for sailors whose ships were docked in the free port of Hamburg. Although the Jewish partner had fought in the Great War and was by far the more efficient of the two partners, the Aryan partner applied for an immediate dissolution of the partnership. He gave as a reason that the district leader of the National-Socialist Party had threatened to confiscate the store license because the 'economic activities of a non-Aryan firm caused unrest among the seamen.' [279] The application was successful. The behavior of the district leader conflicted directly with two orders issued by the Ministry of Economics. These 'orders did not influence the district leader,' as was demonstrated by his testimony. Even though the pressure brought by the district leader was in violation of the law, it had a legal bearing on the Jewish question. For according to the court 'the plaintiff cannot be expected to oppose the wish of the district leader. . . . If he were to do so he would be opposing the general sentiment of the people and also the National-Socialist Party which rules the state.' [280] This decision marked the defeat of Dr. Schacht's policy and the triumph of his opponents among the party authorities. Since 1937, the situation discussed in the foregoing decision has frequently recurred. The party authorities, as agents of the Prerogative State, have used their power to exclude the Jews from all economic activities.

A parallel case came before the *Reichsgericht*. A partnership between a Jew and an Aryan was being dissolved. When the Jew requested that he be provided with monthly reports according to the law, the Aryan partner refused, declaring that 'the district leadership of the party has forbidden the defendant or his employees to prepare and send an account to the plaintiff. It has indeed prohibited all direct communication between the defendant and the plaintiff.' [281] The defendant argued that 'under such conditions his failure to obey an explicit prohibition of the district leadership cannot constitute any ground for issuing judgment against him.' [282] In a state wherein the dominant party uses such methods, it does not really matter whether a Jewish complaint is occasionally successful. Only in the most unusual circumstances will a Jew bring a charge in court against an Aryan. A municipal government alleged before the Supreme Labor Court (*Reichsar-beitsgericht*) that a complaint should be dismissed for the sole reason that the plaintiff was Jewish, and justified this attitude by saying that 'among the regulations designed to solve the Jewish problem is included the order withdrawing from the jurisdiction of the courts claims of state employees dismissed because of their non-Aryan origin.' [283]

The courts capitulated to the political authorities. It has become pointless for Jews to appeal to them for the protection of their rights. In 1937 the Supreme Labor Court (*Reichsarbeits-gericht*) justified the denial of all legal protection to the Jews by saying that 'the racial principles expounded by the National-Socialist Party have been accepted by the broad mass of the population, even by those who do not belong to the party.' [284] If the higher court is supine before the terror of the street, it is not surprising that the lower courts fail to resist the anti-Semitic measures of the Prerogative State.

The Labor Court of Saalfeld (*Arbeitsgericht*) was required to deal with the case of a dismissal of a Jewish employee of a textile factory. The employer defended himself by saying that 'the Leadership of the National-Socialist Party would have withdrawn its patronage if after June 30, 1937 Jews were still employed in the firm.' [285] The dismissal was justified, the court holding that 'the employer could not be expected to run such a risk which, aside from financial hardship, would generally be understood as a withdrawal of confidence by the Party Leadership. The employer was further justified by the fact that the retention of a single Jewish employee would exclude him from the *Berufswett-kampf* of the German Labor Front.' [286] By means of such procedures, the Labor Front has succeeded in achieving the dismissal of nearly every Jew still employed in an Aryan firm. We know of no German court which has dared oppose the prerogative exercised by the German Labor Front.

Until 1938 the war of annihilation against the German Jews aimed at narrowing, and finally denying, their access to sources of livelihood. In 1938 a new stage was begun. National-Socialism, having cut off all opportunities for Jews to earn money, began to make it almost impossible for them to get food or lodging, or to engage in the most elementary life processes.

The legal manifestation of this new development was most unambiguously formulated in connection with the problem of living accommodations. Geman law protects the tenant from eviction unless he is in arrears with his rent or otherwise guilty of violation of a lease.[287] At least as early as the beginning of 1938 the problem whether Jewish tenants should enjoy this protection was raised. Without it the Jews would be unable to rent living quarters in many sections of Germany, since Aryan landlords either would not wish or would not dare to accept Jewish tenants. The tenancy law did not differentiate between Jews and Aryans and no attempt to change this law had been made by the National-Socialists. The courts therefore had to choose between doing their duty and applying the law for the protection of the defenseless victim or sacrificing justice to the demands of National-Socialism. A number of municipal courts dared to uphold the law for Jews and Aryans alike and for this were insultingly attacked by the National-Socialist press.[288] As a result, the courts then attempted to show by a 'National-Socialist interpretation of the law' that it did not apply to Jews. The municipal court of Charlottenburg denied Jews the right to inhabit apartments built from public funds on the grounds that the Jews had been excluded from membership in the German ethnic community (*Volksgemeinschaft*).[289] This decision prevented Jews from exercising a legal claim to utilize institutions erected for the public welfare. Still more extreme was the decision of the Municipal Court of Berlin-Schöneberg of September 16, 1938, which refused to apply the law to Jews on the basis of the law itself. This court explicitly denied that it was transcending the law when it declared that inasmuch as Jews were not members of the ethnic community (*Volksgemeinschaft*), they could not be considered members of 'residential communities' (*Hausgemeinschaften*) which constituted an essential part of the 'ethnic community.' Actually, the part of Berlin falling within the jurisdiction of this court was a tenement district and the judge was familiar with the fact that families could live in those tenements for years without even greeting each other; moreover he knew that a 'residential community' did not exist in the area in question. To prove that 'residential community' existed the judge pointed out that the necessity of air raid protection made it potentially significant.[290]

The step from these artificial legal constructions to an outright denial of the application of the civil law in general was not difficult and was finally made by the Appellate Court of Berlin (*Landgericht*), which held that 'the question before the court is not a problem of the law of landlord and tenant, but a question involving a fundamental outlook on life.' [291]

This was the decisive step. National-Socialist actions are placed above the laws. In the struggle between political aims and legal order, the former was victorious, as the following quotation proves:

'The view that every single act against Jews must be ordered by the government individually is not correct. If this were the case, it would not be permissible to interpret the law to the disadvantage of the Jew and the Jew would enjoy the protection of the law. It is obvious that this makes no sense.' [292]

This judge had rather a strange conception of what 'makes sense' in judicial matters. While this decision was being rendered, the party and the government were busily engaged in the preparation of the burning of synagogues as part of the pogrom of November 10, 1938. An outbreak of extreme fury exercised by the agencies of the National-Socialist Party coincided with the declaration of allegiance by the Berlin Court to the principle of barbarism, both representing different kinds of inhumanity:

'Man can be opposed to himself in a twofold manner: either as a savage, when his feelings rule over his principles; or as a barbarian, when his principles destroy his feelings.' (Friedrich Schiller, *4. Brief über die aesthetische Erziehung des Menschen*).[293]

The absolute withdrawal of legal guarantees from one group in the population has serious consequences for the functioning of the Normative State. This is clear to any observer who is capable of perceiving the deeper significance of these developments. Kohlrausch, Professor in Criminal Law at the University of Berlin, criticizes a decision of the *Reichsgericht* on 'racial disgrace'

(*Rassenschande*) thus: 'A judicial decision not derived from a legal principle neither convinces nor educates. It does not increase respect for the law but arouses doubts as to its correctness. . . . Another danger is that arbitrary decisions influence other courts which before never would have dared to apply the principle *Sic voleo, sic jubeo; stat pro ratione voluntas* with sanction of the highest court.' [294]

In the early years of the Hitler regime, a theoretical treatise on the legal status of the Jews would have had to investigate whether the Jews were being more or less justly treated. Such a question would not be relevant today. It must be remembered that in dictatorial countries the dichotomy of justice and injustice has been supplanted by one of legality and lawlessness. Finally, the *Reichsgericht* itself has refused to recognize Jews living in Germany as 'persons' in the legal sense. In a decision of June 27, 1936 the highest German court condemned German Jews to 'civil death.' In February 1933 a contract was signed between a motion-picture stage manager and a film company. The contractual reasons for the termination of the relationship were: 'sickness, death or similar causes rendering the stage manager's work impossible.' [295] A short time after the signing of the contract, when the anti-Semitic wave started on the grand scale, the company denounced the contract and refused to pay the salary agreed upon. The court had to determine whether the Jewish origin of a motion-picture stage manager was equivalent to 'sickness and death' as a reason for the dissolution of the contract. The *Reichsgericht* declared that an analogy did exist and dismissed the complaint of the stage manager. It argued that 'the former (liberal) theory of the legal status of the "person" made no distinction between races. . . . The National-Socialist philosophy, however, requires that German law recognize only persons of German origin or those who by law are declared equal to them and that only Aryans should enjoy all legal rights and privileges. It is merely a renewal of old principles to distinguish between groups having all legal rights and those who have only a limited number of rights. The complete deprivation of all rights is described a "civil" death: the case before this court permits an analogy. Since the contract in this case could be dissolved only if "sickness, death, etc." prevented the plaintiff from fulfilling his obligations the analogy to "civil death" is regarded as unqualifiedly applicable because the racial characteristics of the plaintiff were equated with sickness and death.' [296]

'Unqualifiedly applicable' (*'unbedenklich anwendbar'*) — only an understanding of the nuances of the German usage can reveal the enormity of this decision. When the highest court of Germany does not hesitate to condemn more than 600,000 persons to 'civil death' and then justifies itself with a few technical terms, little remains to be said.

In 1920 the National-Socialist program demanded that the Jews be dealt with according to laws regulating the behavior of foreigners. Since 1938, the Jews are no longer protected by a law for aliens. They are outlawed, *hors la loi*. The party program does not account for the 'legal status' of the Jews in Germany. Only the nature of the Prerogative State can account for it. Not the party program but martial law is the constitution of the Third Reich. Permanent martial law has notoriously allowed a curtailment of the legal rights of whole sections of the population — it has deprived one minority of the most elementary rights. This 'unqualified application' of permanent martial law in the future is likely to affect even the majority adversely. The extirpation of all but the most primitive ethical values from the law must ultimately injure all those connected with it.

Goethe's words:

> 'Sollt Ihr strafen, sollt Ihr schonen,
> Müsst Ihr Menschen menschlich sehen.'

have found no echo in National-Socialist Germany.

C. THE ESTATES AS ORGANS OF THE NORMATIVE STATE

1. *Economic Self-Government*

In Jewish affairs the courts surrendered to the pressure of the Prerogative State. Fearing political pressure on the courts in other spheres, business circles have supported all efforts to prevent political authorities from intervening in the administration of their internal economic affairs and to establish autonomous administration wherever possible. This is clear in the law concerning cartels. An order of the Minister of Economics of November 12, 1936, transferred a great deal of responsibility for the supervision of the activities of the cartels from governmental authorities to bodies of the economic self-administration. The Minister wrote:

'It is my intention to obtain the co-operation of private economic organizations in the execution of the supervisory activities of the cartels which my ministry has hitherto exercised alone. The administrative bodies of the private economic organizations should be responsible for seeing that the cartels are in harmony with the economic policy of the government in every respect.'[297]

The most important attempt of private business, however, to free itself from the intervention of the police authorities is to be found in the estate system (*Ständewesen*). In order to realize the theory that the jurisdiction of the political authorities must be limited, and to preserve the essence of National-Socialist economic policy, the organization of economic life into a 'system of estates' has been undertaken. This name, however, is not very revealing; the 'estate system' of the Third Reich resembles the old estate system about as much as National-Socialism resembles Socialism. The symbol 'estates' merely serves as a protective ideological coloring adopted by business-men to protect themselves from the interference of the Prerogative State.

Their protection is simply this — that matters within the jurisdiction of the estates are *de facto* outside the police power. That the creation of the estates is an indication of the National-Socialist repudiation of the 'totalitarian state' in the quantitative sense is shown by a contribution to the official *Handwörterbuch der Rechtswissenschaft*, which reads: 'In an epoch in which the state was regarded as the exclusive bearer of public power, the estates, as far as they could be said to exist, could be regarded as bearers of delegated power only. National-Socialism, which views the state only as a means, not as an end, as form, not as content, deprived the state of its omnipotence.'[298] One axiom of the National-

Socialist theory of law is that the police power has been replaced by the estates in those matters solely of interest to the estates. Since this allegation may seem astonishing and contrary to the usual concept of totalitarianism, we quote several well-known writers on police law.

Knauth:

'There are two diametrically opposed theories: one gives fundamentally unlimited jurisdiction to the police power . . . and the other views its scope as smaller than heretofore. For this reason the creation of independent organizations, which has taken place in many spheres, is evidence of the tendency to restrict the power of the police in the sphere in question. The true reason for this development is that the considerations in the light of which these matters are to be settled usually lie outside the jurisdiction of the police.' [299]

Schmidt:

'The police must keep in the background in matters connected with systems of a different nature. The police are not concerned with the estate system, their jurisdiction is limited to issues involving the regulation of the whole community.' [300]

Hoehn:

'The limits of the police power are set by the tasks which the existing concrete orders impose on the police.' [301]

Hamel:

'The exclusion of certain organizations from the jurisdiction of the police has gained new importance. The police are not totalitarian . . . the natural structure of these groups is neither the responsibility nor the concern of the police.' [302]

Koehler:

'Although in some ways the police power has been increased, it has been indirectly diminished to the extent that the new estate organizations operate as self-supervising bodies. . . . The

state does not subject the vested rights of ethnic comrades to unjustified or arbitrary restrictions.' [303]

The final opinion we shall quote is one of the most extreme.
Professor Koettgen requires on the one hand the death penalty
for all violations of the ethnic code and on the other argues:
'The function of the police in an ethnic community comprising
numerous groups is merely supplementary. They are required
to become active only where particular norms have shown themselves to be inadequate. Where concrete orders inside the state
are operative the police have no function.' [304]

In summarizing this point we may say that the police, who
are the embodiment of the state, are qualitatively but not quantitatively 'totalitarian' (cf. p. 60).

The statement that the estates protect the business world against
interference from the Prerogative State does not present the
complete picture. In order to attain their goals, business-men in
contemporary Germany require not only that the Prerogative
State abstain from intervening in their enterprises but also that
the state help them in a positive way. One of the most important
writers of National-Socialist legal theory, Reinhard Hoehn, claims
that the police authorities must execute the decisions of the
estates without any review. The police authorities are no longer
organs of the state exclusively (as in the period of competitive
capitalism) but are now also the organs of the business-men's
estates. Hoehn formulates this:

'The new conception of administration leads to a transformation of police law. In the hitherto prevailing system the police
were an organ of the state administration — now the functions of
the new estate organizations overlap with those of the police and
a change in the previous position of the police is necessitated.
Police action is no longer initiated by the police administration
alone; but it is also responsive to the estate organization which it
is supposed to serve. It is for this reason that the old liberal conception of the status of the police must be given up.' [305]

Thus the estates, which are the most inclusive associations of
business-men, give the purest expression of the Normative State.

They are a part of the Normative State, and in principle, their activities are treated as non-political. Though the police authorities have the *power* to intervene in these activities (since their jurisdiction is unlimited), they do not regularly do so. Membership in the guilds is (within the jurisdictions of the guilds) a *de facto* guarantee against the Prerogative State. To the extent that the estates abstain from actions which the police call 'political,' they enjoy security from the Prerogative State.

The principles governing the relations between the estates and the political authorities were formulated by the *Reichsgericht* on April 28, 1936, in a decision dealing with freedom of the press in National-Socialist Germany. The defendant was charged with a malevolent attack on the government because of his statement that there was no freedom of the press in Germany. The Supreme Court distinguished between unlimited and regulated freedom of the press and admitted that National-Socialism had eliminated unlimited freedom of the press. The new Press Law was formulated in the legislation regarding the Press Chambers and the journalistic profession.[306] Within the limitations specified by these statutes, the 'orderly' press 'enjoys a freedom of a special type' — 'regulated freedom of the press.' The supervision of this 'regulated freedom' is the responsibility of the self-governing bodies of the press. Those bodies, however, do not possess an unrestricted monopoly over the supervision of the press. Although pre-censorship does not exist, the *Reichsgericht* has recognized that 'any conceivable violation can be dealt with (aside from the measures of the self-governing bodies) by the state on the basis of the Decree of February 28, 1933.'[307] This decision is interesting because of its attitude towards the competition between political and estate authorities. No profession borders so closely on the 'political' as journalism. A collision between the estates and political officials is scarcely avoidable. In spite of this, the Third Reich preferred to form a press estate so that it could at least deal with economic aspects of the press within the framework of the Normative State. The estate should be adequate to take care of the everyday economic questions of the press, while as a last resort the Decree of February 28, 1933, can always be applied. This example typifies the relationship between estates and police power.

2. *The German Labor Front*

There are certain groups not included in the estate system of National-Socialist Germany, the most important one being the industrial working class. The claim that the German Labor Front (*Deutsche Arbeitsfront*) is the estate of the working class is not very convincing. Even National-Socialists admit that the German Labor Front is not an estate 'but rather the inclusive organization of producers who accept the viewpoint that all economic and social activities belong to an integrated national process.' [308] The same opinion is to be found in an article by Dr. Mansfeld, the head of the Section for Labor Law of the Reich Ministry of Labor, who makes the Labor Front responsible for the soul and spirit of all working Germans. 'Better things,' he says, 'can be achieved here than in the destructive struggle over industrial working conditions.' [309] The destructive struggle for better wages and hours is not just an activity outside the jurisdiction of the Labor Front. It is entirely prohibited to German workers. The National-Socialist leadership principle allots the determination of wages and working conditions to the entrepreneur, within the limits set by the state.

The Third Reich has created estates to regulate the economic affairs of all non-proletarian groups. These estates must be left untouched by the political authorities as long as questions of economic policy are at issue. The justification of this attitude may be found in a recent article of Professor Koettgen who emphasizes that 'the economic duties of artisans or journalists can be passed on only by persons intimately acquainted with the problems of the group interests in question. The practical consequence is that problems of professional or vocational honor can be decided only by members of the particular profession or vocation, and that the police thereby are deprived of the right to interfere in questions of professional duty. . . .' Thus, according to Koettgen, 'vocational law does not nullify police law and a complete occupational self-government will exclude police interference with special exceptions.' [310]

But what about the workers? The workers have no special code of duty, nor is their honor protected by persons in their own vocations. They are subject to unrestricted police interference. An attempt to arrive at an independent decision regarding economic problems on the part of the working classes is branded as 'class-struggle' — a political matter to be dealt with by the Prerogative State. Whether a person in Germany is entitled to come to independent conclusions concerning economic policy and has the right to be protected by the Normative State depends on whether he is a member of an estate. Those who are not members of an estate are not protected against the Prerogative State. Whereas the estates are largely exempt from the control of the Prerogative State, the German Labor Front is considered a political body and subject to the Prerogative State.

The estates and the Labor Front represent the two extremes of the National-Socialist state.[311] If we acknowledge the fact that the workers have been deprived of any right to participate in the determination of economic policy and are considered as enemies of the state if they attempt to influence it, while all other vocational groups are allowed considerable autonomy in the resolution of their own problems, the class character of the National-Socialist state should be evident.

The chief legal adviser of the *Gestapo*, Dr. Best, is of the opinion (p. 62) that the state's restriction of its own power is entirely appropriate if the restrictions apply only to 'the constructive forces of the German people.' Especially significant is Best's statement that it is essential to the effectiveness of 'these constructive forces of the nation that the activity of the state shall be predictable.' With but one exception, the whole German nation is 'constructive.' This exception, which is outside the estate system, is the working class.

An apparently unimportant amendment to the Law concerning Social Insurance (Art. 3 § 8, which amends § 615 of the Insurance Law) gives an unambiguous clue to the class structure of the Third Reich. It reads: 'A pension may be suspended if the recipient has committed acts hostile to the state after January 30, 1933. Whether such activities actually took place shall be submitted to the decision of the Minister of the Interior and the Minister of Labor.' [312] This provision did not pretend to be a protection against violence and it retroactively deprived helpless cripples and invalids of their pensions (their only source of income). It is no accident that the Third Reich chose the Law concerning Social Insurance as the first instance in which the activities of the unrestrained Prerogative State were enacted in statute form.

PART II

THE LEGAL THEORY OF THE DUAL STATE

Justitia remota quid aliud est regnum quam grande latrocinium ?

AUGUSTINUS

CHAPTER I

THE REPUDIATION OF RATIONAL NATURAL LAW
BY NATIONAL-SOCIALISM

THE complete abolition of the inviolability of law is the chief characteristic of the Prerogative State. This repudiation carries with it the elimination of the fundamental principle of the inviolability of law from the entire legal order. If inviolability within the sphere of the Normative State exists only under certain conditions, then it does not hold true as a principle, and conditional inviolability is necessarily the opposite of inviolability. This repudiation of the principle of the inviolability of law (its actual as well as its potential abrogation) raises the general question of the significance of law.

Shortly before the National-Socialists' accession to power in 1933, Gustav Radbruch[313] discussed the principle of the inviolability of law as defined by Otto Mayer, a well-known German authority on administrative law. According to Radbruch, the principle grew out of Natural Law and was later incorporated into the system of positive law. The principle is that, once the sovereign has promulgated a law, he may not violate it at his discretion. Thus the principle that legislative power is vested in the sovereign because he is sovereign is restricted by Natural Law.[314]

Since the doctrine of the inviolability of law is part of the heritage of rational Natural Law, its explicit rejection in the legal system of the Third Reich raises the question of the whole attitude of National-Socialism towards Natural Law. Regarding this question an important source is available. In his speech to the Reichstag on the occasion of the fourth anniversary of his advent to power,

on January 30, 1937, Adolf Hitler made several important com-
ments upon the relationship between law and National-Socialism.
He declared:

'Man is incapable of perceiving the meaning and purpose inherent in the existence of the races which have been created by
Providence. The meaning and purpose of human institutions can,
however, be measured by their utility for the preservation of
ethnic groups. . . . Only the recognition of this axiom can prevent man from adopting rigid doctrines where there can be no
doctrines and to falsify means into imperatives where the end
ought to be regarded as the sole imperative. In the course of time
our attitude towards law has been led astray, partly through the
incorporation of foreign ideas and partly due to our own inadequate understanding. Two opposite extremes characterize this
state of affairs:

1. the assumption that law as such has any intrinsic value,
2. the assumption that the main function of the law is the
   protection of the individual.

'Besides these potentialities, claims of the higher interests of the
community as a whole were acknowledged only in the form of
concessions granted to the *Raison d'état*.

'The National-Socialist revolution, on the other hand, provided
law, jurisprudence and the administration of law with an unambiguous basis. Their task is the maintenance and protection of
the people against anti-social groups which desire to evade or
who otherwise fail to fulfil all obligations required by the community.' [315]

In this speech Hitler officially promulgated only what National-
Socialist theories had always acknowledged. The same line of
thought was succinctly expressed by Professor Gerber in declaring that National-Socialist political thought is 'existential and biological, its data being the primal unique life process.' [316] Unlike
liberal political thoughts, it does not consist in 'rational abstract
constructions which possess universal validity' [317] and which are
on that account worthy only of contempt. Gerber states explicitly
that the traditional notions concerning the nature of justice have
lost their validity. 'National-Socialism insists that justice is not a

system of abstract and autonomous values such as the various types of Natural Law systems. This perception helps us appreciate the historical fact that each state has its own concept of justice.' [318] Consequently, justice cannot be viewed independently of a particular existing state. *Tot res publicae, tot justitiae!* After showing how the cosmopolitan idea of a divinely appointed universal justice has been supplanted by the doctrine of a Danish monarchical and of a Portuguese republican justice, Professor Gerber presents his conception of the real nature of justice as 'nothing more than the certainty of the people that it represents a primal social individuality.' [319]

With this conclusion, Gerber is in agreement with Alfred Rosenberg, who, in a somewhat more popularized formulation, had already presented the same ideas in 1934.[320] Rosenberg stated that the distinction between 'good' and 'evil' is obsolete — an idea which he had expressed in his much reproduced quotation of an Indian proverb: 'Right and wrong do not walk about saying: "Here we are." Right is what Aryan people think is right.' [321]

It was not by accident that the first act after the National-Socialist *coup d'état* (i.e., after the Decree of February 28, 1933) resulted in the abolition of the rule of *Nulla poena sine lege*, heretofore a major principle of German positive law. The *Lex van der Lubbe* provided retroactive capital punishment for a crime, subject at the time of its commission only to imprisonment. By the promulgation of this act, National-Socialism demonstrated unmistakably that it deemed itself bound neither in theory nor in practice by this old principle of Natural Law, which, until the *coup d'état*, had formed an unquestioned component of the German conception of justice. The *Lex van der Lubbe* made perfectly apparent the transvaluation of values. The National-Socialist legal theory perceives this clearly and even emphasizes it. The *Lex van der Lubbe* 'struck the intellectual revolt of the nineteenth century at its very heart. It attacked a system which had dared to substitute a hypostatized order of values, norms and rules for the creative vigor and power of living peoples and which therewith wholly destroyed the immediacy of ethical and political life.' [322]

It is interesting to note that in 1928 Rudolf Smend had envisaged the emancipation of the modern state from any 'non-
political legitimation as the very inception of the modern *Rechtsstaat.*' [323] But the reduction of the legal state to a precisely articu-
lated legal machine meant the beginning of its end. Smend had
denounced the legitimation of the state in the name of any kind
of 'transcendental order' as intolerable. The significant silence
which he maintains today may justify the conjecture that the
legitimation of the state by biological facts (which, to be sure,
are non-transcendent) is no less intolerable. In the preface of his
Mythus des 20. Jahrhunderts,[324] Rosenberg stressed the fact that
his book expressed the attitude of a generation which had lost its
faith in the traditional absolute and universal values. Since this
spokesman of disillusionment and cynicism has become the supreme director of the 'philosophical' education of a party which,
in turn, rules a people of eighty millions, the conclusion is perhaps justified that the skepticism of the preceding generation had
become the faith of the generation now coming to maturity. Carl
Schmitt's statement that we are today experiencing the bankruptcy of *idées générales* [325] therefore seems less important than
the following declaration of a member of the young National-
Socialist generation. In the review *Jugend und Recht*, Leuner
states with striking frankness that 'there is no right residing in the
stars; there is no equal right which is innate in the individual;
there is therefore no universal transethnic Natural Law. There
is only one norm which is equally valid for all individuals, namely
that they live in accordance with the imperatives of their race.' [326]

In connection with the National-Socialist assertion that law has
no intrinsic value of its own it is apropos to cite Hitler's famous
assertion that in the Third Reich law and morality are identical.
However, it should not be overlooked that this dogma [327] may
have a double meaning. On the one hand, Hitler's remark may
imply that contemporary German law can claim validity only
insofar as it corresponds to the maxims of morality. On the other,
it may imply that, in the National-Socialist state, moral norms
can claim validity only insofar as they are in harmony with a
legal system which is based on its own values. Actually the iden-

tification of law and morality in the Third Reich has resulted in the assimilation of morality to National-Socialist law. This opinion has been expressed unambiguously in the National-Socialist literature. Dernedde, for example, writes: 'The present promulgation of the indissoluble identity of law and morality signifies the integration of both of these categories into the ethnic community. It is the opposite of an acknowledgment of a transethnic universal Natural Law which limits the power of the legislator.' [328]

It is evident that such a sweeping simplification of the deepest problems of political theory contributes greatly to huge propagandistic successes among the masses of the people. Ideas which Machiavelli presented to a small circle of initiates are disseminated by Adolf Hitler by means of all the modern techniques of communication even to the adolescent members of the Hitler Youth organizations. Figgis' comment on Machiavelli applies equally to Hitler: 'He did not start from any ideals of government or desire to find them, he did not meditate on the philosophy of law. Social justice has to him no meaning apart from the one great end of the salvation of his country. He had the limited horizon and the unlimited influence which always come of narrowing the problem.' [329] But the reverse side of this outwardly successful enterprise is the destruction of the ethical tradition of Western civilization. Hermann Heller said that 'once conscience becomes a problem of cattle breeding, moral problems lose their inescapability.' [330]

The actual repudiation of Natural Law is less surprising than the form in which it is renounced. The doctrine of Natural Law, after all, has been discredited for more than a century. It has been refuted time and again by political science, and yet it has not lost its vitality. For more than a hundred years, we have been intellectually denying every type of Natural Law while our conscience has simultaneously been demanding its acknowledgment. At a time when, thanks to Bergbohn's unfortunate influence, positivism flourished in Germany, American legal philosophy was fully aware of this discrepancy. Morris Cohen, in a lecture delivered in 1914, said: 'To defend a doctrine of natural rights today requires either insensibility of the world's progress or else considerable courage in the face of it.' [331] The quarter of a century which has since elapsed has not accomplished the removal of these intellectual obstacles, yet the demands for the recognition of Natural Law principles have increased. Carl Becker, pleading for the cause of Natural Law against intellectual doubts, states that although we have lost the formula, something of the old faith remained. . . . 'We hold to it, if not from assured conviction, then from necessity, seeing no alternative except cynicism or despair.' [332] This ambivalent attitude towards Natural Law reflects the twofold origin of our culture; in the words of Werner Jaeger: 'No theoretical attempts to bridge the gulf between them can change the historical fact that our morality goes back to the Christian religion and our politics to the Greco-Roman conception of the state.' [333]

Whereas Italian Fascism deliberately identifies itself with the idea of the *Imperium Romanum* and the Roman theory of the state, National-Socialism explicitly announces its antipathy towards Roman Law. Sophisticated analyses of the legal evolution in the new Germany have, however, already revealed just what is involved in the substitution of 'German Common Law' for Roman Law. Referring to Hoehn's studies, which claim to demonstrate that Otto von Gierke, the prophet of the German Law of Associations (*Genossenschaftsrecht*), is no longer significant,[334] Manigk explains that 'the philosophical kernel of German Law (particularly the concept of the *Genossenschaft*) is in contradiction with our state as it exists today. . . . The idea of authoritarian leadership was realized in Roman antiquity. The separation of powers was unknown and the Senate called the Princeps "our Leader".' [335]

When we discuss the classical conception of the state, we do not refer to the *politeia*, the political Utopia. We have in mind rather the *polis*, the historical reality, as it existed in the Greek city-states. Late Grecian antiquity did of course produce Stoicism, a political theory which stood in direct contradiction to the ideal of the *polis*. A. J. Carlyle writes that 'there is no change in political theory so startling in its completeness as the change from the theory of Aristotle to the later philosophical view repre-

sented by Cicero and Seneca.' [336] Carlyle sees the same cleavage
in the various notions concerning the equality or inequality of
man. He sets the doctrine of primitive equality alongside the
ancient view of inequality. The specifically 'modern' political
theory is of Stoic origin and has been influential both in Christianity and in the Enlightenment. In this doctrine 'there is only
one possible definition for all mankind, reason is common to all ...
there is no race which under the guidance of nature cannot attain to virtue.' [337] For Germany, however, this doctrine had ceased
to be 'modern.' National-Socialism postulates its opposite—namely,
the racially conditioned and humanly unchangeable inequality of
man. Therewith the decisive step from Aristotle to Cicero comes to
nought and the long tradition of Christianity and Humanism, of
occidental science and philosophy passes into discard.

Moreover, owing to its repudiation of Natural Law, National-
Socialism is opposed to the medieval doctrine of the power of the
absolute prince. The foremost characteristic of the dictator is not
the fact that he makes law in accordance with his will. The theory
of modern dictatorship can only be apprehended by considering
again a distinction current in the Middle Ages which was forgotten in the era of democracy and the Rule of Law. McIlwain[338]
points out that in present times distinctions which were made
during the Middle Ages are ignored. The medieval king was considered to be absolute and practically irresponsible, but his power
was not an arbitrary one. The old maxim, 'What the king has
willed has the force of the law,' was—according to McIlwain—only
valid if this will was expressed in a way prescribed by law and
tradition and was restricted to certain purposes. There existed
definite limitations for the will of the medieval prince which were
usually expressed by the formula: 'The king is bound by the Law
of God and the Law of Nature.' This distinction sheds new light
on the approach pursued in the first section of this book. By the
'Enabling Law' [339] Hitler became Germany's absolute ruler after
he had previously (by the Decree of February 28, 1933) acquired
the power of a despot. McIlwain, who obviously alludes to the
present German situation, regrets that at present both concepts are
regarded as being practically identical.[340] Furthermore, he points

out that antiquity conceived of law as a matter of politics, where-as 'modern' thought attaches politics to the category of law. From this point of view, also National-Socialism cannot claim to be 'modern.'

With this repudiation of every trace of rational Natural Law, Germany has turned her back on the community of nations which consciously adheres to the traditions of occidental civilization. National-Socialism certainly cannot be said to be — as Friedrich Engels once said of Marxian Socialism — the heir of Classical German Philosophy. It is rather its complete negation.

CHAPTER II

THE NATIONAL-SOCIALIST CAMPAIGN AGAINST
NATURAL LAW

1. THE CHRISTIAN SYSTEM OF NATURAL LAW

THE flat rejection of the rationalistic traditions of Natural Law resulted in a conflict between National-Socialism and the proponents of Natural Law traditions. Only a study of the two opposing groups will enable us to fathom the historical significance of the National-Socialist attitude towards Natural Law.

The evolution of Natural Law in Western Europe cannot be comprehended without reference to the role of the religious elements. It is no longer possible, in view of Ernst Troeltsch's[341] solidly ground conclusions, to disregard the religion component in the development of Natural Law. Troeltsch did not hesitate to regard the Christian theory of Natural Law in its final development as the *Kulturdogma* of the church. He asserted that for the church this dogma held the same importance as, for example, the dogma of the Holy Trinity. Though the various churches and sects assumed different attitudes against Natural Law, none has ever completely repudiated it. The Christian tradition is, in this respect, closely connected with Zeno, the founder of Stoicism. Zeno, who witnessed as a contemporary the absorption of the small Greek city-states into the empire of Alexander the Great, came to glorify the 'Empire of Reason' which is independent of political frontiers.[342] After the establishment of the Roman Empire, this concept attracted new admirers such as Cicero, Seneca and Marcus Aurelius, and was given its most significant expression in the legal system of the *Corpus Juris*. As the heir of the *Imperium Romanum*, the Roman Catholic Church took over its Natural Law doctrines although they were subjected to extensive modifications in order to adapt them to the needs of the Church.

The adaption of the abstract principles of a universal and rational Natural Law to the requirements of a church intimately involved in temporal concerns was effected by the medieval doctrine of 'relative' Natural Law. According to this theory man was unable, after the Fall, to acquire anew the pure Natural Law of his previous state. Therefore he has had to be content with 'relative' Natural Law although he is still accorded the privilege of striving to approximate a state of 'absolute' Natural Law as nearly as possible. Troeltsch has shown[343] how this theory, in the course of centuries, was time and again opposed by those who never doubted the possibility of the realization of an absolute Natural Law. This opposition, coming from those who believed in the existence of a community regulated by the principles of an absolute Natural Law, was crystallized in the sects which, despite merciless persecutions, steadfastly adhered to the belief in absolute Natural Law.

While these sects denied the relativistic character of the Catholic theory of Natural Law, Lutheranism asserted its relativity. Holding that the legal regulation of interhuman relationships is a worldly affair bearing the strains of sinfulness, Lutheranism preached unconditional obedience to every secular regime. This 'extremist conservative glorification of autocracy' (Troeltsch) by Lutheranism was the consequence of an attitude which attributed only slight importance to worldly affairs. To Lutheranism, true Christianity resides in the inner soul of man ('*Innere Herzens-Christlichkeit*'). It is independent of the political and legal order of the temporal world as long as freedom of religious conscience is not violated. The Christian must submit humbly to a harsh and unjust regime which he is to regard as a punishment imposed by the Lord. But any restriction of the freedom of conscience constitutes an attack on the fundamental principles of Christian Natural Law.

The National-Socialist doctrine, with its intense enmity to

Natural Law, could only be established in a country where absolute Natural Law theories, as represented by Christian sectarianism, though always present to a small degree, were never consolidated into a real tradition. Christian sectarianism in Germany seldom transcended the stage of inchoate local movements after the total suppression of Thomas Münzer's Anabaptist movement, in which Luther's unequivocal attitude was not the least important factor. Hence, it is all the more remarkable that the sectarian movement of the Jehovah's Witnesses experienced such an astonishing growth during the last seven years. These sectarians, whose absolute pacifism requires them to eschew all compromise and whose exclusive worship of Jehovah involves the negation of every kind of secular authority, must be considered as the embodiment of behavior exclusively in accordance with norms derived from absolute Natural Law. No illegal group in Germany is more uncompromisingly opposed to National-Socialism than this obstinate sect. Its rapid growth must be interpreted as a reaction to the contemptuous negation of all Natural Law principles by the Third Reich. Only this fundamental antagonism explains the profound National-Socialist hatred for Jehovah's Witnesses, who have become true martyrs in the religious wars of contemporary Germany. The lack of any tradition of absolute Natural Law principles presumably furnishes one of the deeper reasons for the incomplete understanding of present-day Germany in the Anglo-Saxon countries. Influenced by a variety of sectarian movements, the whole public life of the Anglo-Saxon countries has been penetrated by the principles of Natural Law.

It was predictable that the purely political National-Socialist doctrine (which at bottom is devoid of any rational principles) would clash with the relative Natural Law institutionalized in the Roman Catholic Church. More surprising, however, was the conflict with the Confessional Church, especially in view of the fact that the Lutheran Church had not only failed to offer any resistance to the National-Socialist regime but had actually assisted it during the first phases of the Third Reich. The Lutheran Church in Germany is now divided into two groups in respect to their attitude towards National-Socialism: the 'German Christians' have capitulated to the requirements of the National-Socialist regime, the Confessional Church, soon after Hitler came into power, came into opposition with Nazi doctrines. Yet, compared with the absolute resistance of Jehovah's Witnesses, the attitude of the Confessional Church seems somewhat ambiguous. Its resistance is limited to the defense of the Christian freedom of religious belief and offers no opposition to the dissolution of the *Rechtsstaat* and the establishment of tyranny. It refrained from doing so even when it was still possible. The Confessional Church is a Lutheran Church, and because of this it could not have acted differently.

Luther proclaimed: 'If you are oppressed and wronged accept it; it is the essence of the worldly regime. If you want to live in this world you must expect this. The wish to undergo a different fate from that of Christ is not realizable. If you want to live among the wolves, you have to howl with them. We serve in a house where the devil is master and the world is mistress and many wicked desires are the servants. All of them are foes and adversaries of the Gospel. If your money is stolen and your honor destroyed — such are the ways in this house.' [344]

The conflict between National-Socialism on the one hand, and the Catholic and Lutheran Churches on the other may be explained in part by the fact that the doctrine of the Third Reich (until 1938 predominantly a Protestant country) was formulated largely by apostate Catholics. The existentialist philosopher Heidegger, the jurist Carl Schmitt, the propagandist Goebbels, and many other leading National-Socialist intellectuals have tried to disintegrate the solid structure of Catholicism which had shaped their spiritual development. As apostates from a theory of the state based predominantly upon Natural Law, they adopted the Prussian idea of the state with the passionate enthusiasm of converts. Since this Prussian idea of the state had been elaborated largely by Lutheran thinkers these converts, as former Catholics, were unable to appreciate the specifically Lutheran check on the power of the state: namely, freedom of conscience. Luther had declared: 'The worldly regime has laws which are supreme over body and property and every thing earthly, yet over the soul the Lord will not recognize any ruler but himself. Hence, whenever worldly power dares to make laws affecting the soul the Lord interferes.' [345]

In its conflict with the Confessional Church, National-Socialism points to Hitler's declarations that he did not conceive himself as a religious reformer. Yet his repeated assurances that National-Socialism is only a temporal movement, leaving the regulation of man's relations with the Lord to the churches, could not allay existing suspicions. As long as National-Socialism claims the power to decide authoritatively what is temporal and what is spiritual, and as long as the Third Reich seeks to 'govern the souls of men,' it will be unable to establish peaceful relations with the Confessional Church. For the latter would have to renounce its most fundamental principles in order to assent to the political control of the conscience.

For Confessional Lutheranism freedom of conscience is an absolute value; to compromise it is equivalent to a renunciation of principle.

In order to understand the tensions between church and state in the Third Reich one should not emphasize superficial characteristics or attach undue importance to the new cult of Wotan, in which a few secondary-school teachers take particular interest. Devotion to the latter cult would never have provided National-Socialism with the impetus necessary to initiate and conduct the church struggle. The strife arose when National-Socialism was confronted with remnants of a faith in absolute Natural Law asserting its independence in the face of the will of the state. National-Socialism has always been willing, and is still willing, to acknowledge the claims of Christianity except where they are incongruous with Art. 24 of the National-Socialist Party Program, which requires that the Christian religion subordinate itself to the vital necessities of the German people. Thus in the sphere of religion we meet the same reservation as in the sphere of law, the potential superiority of political considerations which impels National-Socialism to fight the representatives of all ideologies influenced by Natural Law doctrines. In 'Christianity with reservations' Christianity is of less importance than the reservations. Although for propagandist reasons National-Socialism does not disclose its religious policy as unambiguously as its legal policy there is no basic difference. National-Socialism refuses to regard either religious or ethical values (as embodied in legal systems) as absolute. The value of a religion is not judged according to its inner truth but according to its political expediency. Ludendorff's hatred of Christianity rested on the assumption that in the next war Christianity would be unable to implement the maximum exploitation of all the psychic resources of the soldier. During the Party Congress of Nürnberg in 1937, Adolf Hitler hinted that 'since we ascribe eternal existence to it, the *Volk* is the embodiment of the ultimate value. . . . Religions are only of value if they help to preserve the living substance of mankind.' [346] It is only a question of time until cynicism of a National-Socialist *Reichskommissar* of Religion will apply this subjectively sincere formula to religion, i. e. that its value is determined by its relevance to the vital necessities of the German people.

Machiavelli may be regarded as the spiritual father of this politically oriented critique of Christianity. In his *Discorsi* we find ideas which recur very frequently in the anti-Christian racial pamphlets of National-Socialism. Of course Machiavelli is not quoted, and the Machiavellian references to classic antiquity are replaced by glorifications of German tribes. According to Machiavelli 'the Pagan religion deified only men who had achieved great glory, such as commanders of armies and chiefs of republics, whilst ours glorifies more the humble and contemplative men than the men of action. Our religion, moreover, places the supreme happiness in humility, lowliness, and a contempt for worldly objects, whilst the other, on the contrary, places the supreme good in grandeur of soul, strength of body, and all such other qualities as render men formidable; and if our religion claims of us fortitude of soul, it is more to enable us to suffer than to achieve great deeds. These principles seem to me to have made men feeble.' [347]

Historians, in their evaluations of Machiavelli, have always concluded that a religion oriented towards the requirements of the tribal state is equivalent to paganism. The tendency to deny the absolute character of all but political values and to recognize them only insofar as they serve political ends is Neo-Machiavellian paganism, which represents one of the most essential elements in the National-Socialist outlook. Machiavelli praises the Roman king Numa Pompilius because he invented gods particularly appropriate for the city of Rome: '. . . if the question were discussed whether Rome was more indebted to Romulus or to Numa, I believe that the highest merit would be conceded to Numa; for where religion exists it is easy to introduce armies and discipline, but where there are armies and no religion it is difficult to introduce the latter.' [348] This admiration for early antiquity is expressive of a yearning for a *polis* in which there was no conflict between universalistic ethics and particularistic *raison d'état*.

In rejecting belief in the validity of all universal ideas of justice, National-Socialism substitutes a nationally restricted idea of utility for the humanistic values of Natural Law. Considering the close relationship between Christianity and Natural Law, the conclusion seems justified that the Third Reich is tending from the universal God to the local Deity, from Monotheism to Xenotheism. [349]

However, the rejection of all universal values by the National-Socialist Prerogative State is a two-edged sword. Whereas the Prerogative State has a particular power arising from its rejection of all universal values, this is partly compensated for by the new enemies it makes. These allies for its adversaries come from groups on which the foes of National-Socialism had never counted as possible sources of assistance. Gürke, a National-Socialist international lawyer, hits the nail on the head when he states that the various enemies of National-Socialism (Democrats, Socialists, Catholics) despite their differing outlooks, have in common 'doctrines aiming at the inclusion and liberation of the whole of mankind.' [350] In Germany today all the proponents of the various types of rational Natural Law are being consolidated into a single *bloc* as a reaction against the complete negation of all absolute values by an opportunistic Leviathan.

The two main groups in the Natural Law *bloc* base their Natural Law views respectively on religious and on secular presuppositions. The following section will examine the special characteristics of the secular Natural Law group.

2. Secular Natural Law

While it is true that the Christian religion is both historically and doctrinally bound to Natural Law, rationalistic Natural Law is not necessarily dependent on the Christian notions with which it has often been associated.

The schoolmen of the later Middle Ages had already examined the question whether law is rational because it is the will of God or whether God willed it because it is rational.[351] The schoolmen finally chose the latter alternative and by doing so prepared the way for the doctrine of the existence of rational law independent of God. With the proposition of Hugo Grotius that an eternal absolute law dictated by reason would exist even if there were no God, the classical age of secular Natural Law was initiated. In Pufendorff's writing, the theory of rational law, far from constituting a revolutionary ideology, provided a justification for absolutist monarchy, while in Rousseau it legitimized a radical form of democracy. Secular Natural Law influenced Frederic the Great's legislation and found its most enthusiastic interpreters in the philosophers of German idealism, Immanuel Kant and the young Fichte. Kant calls Law the apple of God's eye, and the state the guarantor of the law. Despite the attacks of National-Socialist theorists who claim that it is un-German, Natural Law, as it is known today, is largely the creation of German thinkers.[352] To what extent do residues of the classical type of Natural Law still persist in Germany? How are they related to contemporary National-Socialist doctrines which express their hostility towards universally oriented Natural Law in the crude form of anti-Liberalism?

During the eighteenth century, Natural Law legitimized the existing distribution of powers.[353] When, however, in the course of the French Revolution, it became apparent that it could also legitimize revolutionary demands, Natural Law incurred the hatred of all those who were interested in the preservation of the *status quo*. The reaction against Natural Law (which had thus been compromised by the radicalism of the French Revolution) is best represented by Burke and Hegel.[354]

In opposing the revolutionary form of rational Natural Law, Burke appealed to the tradition of centuries of evolution. When he confronted the judgment of reason with the pre-judgments of history, Natural Law with Historical Law, when he stated that prescription is the most sacred of all legal titles, Burke was laying the ground for the romantic concept of history and for the Historical School of Law and ultimately for the theory of the Restoration.[355] It is superfluous to point out that Burke's ideas, particularly in the form given them by Savigny, exerted a tremendous influence on the evolution of the nineteenth century legal thought. He particularly influenced the movement which demanded the repudiation of rational Natural Law. For our present purposes we need only state that National-Socialism has denied its connection with Burke and Savigny, despite their common rejection of rational Natural Law. Burke's appeal to irrational forces of historical development is indeed applicable only where tradition is unbroken but not where all traditions have disintegrated. The National-Socialists are not the protectors of an inherited tradition. They represent a generation which has lost its guiding tradition. The 'good old law' is no more sacred to them than new law derived from rational principles. The notion that a right must be respected because it has been respected for a long time and is supported by an old tradition is as alien to National-Socialism (which is guided strictly by considerations of political opportunism) as the belief in rational Natural Law. National-Socialism would have respected Burke for his assault on the French Revolution. But they would have regarded as treasonable his sympathy with the revolt of the North-American colonists, whose vested rights had been denied. However much the rational and the traditional theories of sovereignty may differ, they agree in their acknowledgment of law as the decisive element in social and political life. In this respect they are sharply opposed to National-Socialism, which declares that law has no intrinsic value. Thus there exists an unbridgeable abyss between traditionalistic respect for irrational law and irrationalistic contempt for traditional law.

It is true that the National-Socialist legal theory tries to explain its rejection of the Historical School of Law on other grounds.

Larenz asserts that National-Socialism and the Historical School of Law share the same conviction that all law derives from the customs of the 'ethnic groups' (*Volk und Volkstum*). But he continues by asserting that their conceptions of the 'ethnic spirit' (*Volksgeist*) are poles apart. 'Our criticism of the Historical School of Law', he says, 'must in the first place be directed against the identification of the spirit of the ethnic group [*Volksgeist*] with the totality of the group's beliefs.'[356] National-Socialism rejects the romantic view that the law can be 'discovered' if the judge immerses himself into the soul of the nation and follows traditional legal usages. The Historical School of Law is reproached for its hostility towards enacted laws. It is not for the judge to determine the legal belief of the nation. That is the task of the Leader, of the 'great man.' The Historical School of Law regarded the legal feeling of the ethnic group as the genuine source of law. Larenz, however, places on the 'great man' the responsibility for deciding whether the group beliefs are to be followed. He alone can decide whether group beliefs are 'genuine' and are therefore to be acknowledged, or whether they 'merely represent public opinion' and are therefore to be disregarded. If the Leader can decide whether or not he will endorse the convictions of the group concerning 'good' and 'evil,' then the doctrine of the 'spirit of the ethnic group' has been subtly supplanted by an ideology which permits the Leader to decide in accordance with his own convictions regardless of the legal status of his decisions.

Hegel changed his attitude towards Natural Law during the course of the French Revolution and the ensuing decades. Hegel's book on the constitution of Germany,[357] written in 1803, seems of special importance for the purpose of the present study. Burke had been impressed by the social dangers to his class arising in consequence of the French Revolution. Hegel, however, considered these dangers as reacting upon the political weakness of the Holy Roman Empire. In view of this danger, Hegel postulated the supremacy of 'politics' over all law, whether written or based on traditional customs. Hegel's idea that the essence of the state is politically determined by its antagonism towards other states was entirely alien to the rational theory of Natural Law. What appeared essential to the viewpoint of Natural Law, namely, the co-operation of the citizen for the promotion of peaceful objects, is not recognized by Hegel as belonging to the sphere of the 'state.' Hegel goes even so far as to attack contemporary state theorists, because they have identified the 'state' with civic society.[358]

Hegel's thesis opposes Kant's idea of securing permanent peace through the erection of a League of Nations. Hegel explains that even a League of Nations is bound to have enemies because inter-state antagonism is an essential characteristic of any state.

Since the state is an individual Hegel believes that it can only be conceived of as an enemy to other states. Hegel emphasizes that, by definition, a state must create enemies.[359]

Notwithstanding his acceptance of the doctrine of political interests, Hegel does not discard the concept of Natural Law. Through the argument that 'the absolute moral totality is nothing but a nation'[360] he uses Natural Law to justify the existing state whose *raison d'état* cannot otherwise be justified. Thus Hegel legitimized the appeal to the *raison d'état* just as one would 'give legitimacy to a bastard.'[361] (In the age in which Natural Law was dominant, the *raison d'état*, though playing an important role in practice, was generally despised by political thinkers.)

National-Socialist philosophers are by no means unanimous in their attitude towards Hegel. *Reichsminister* Dr. Hans Frank speaks of him as perhaps Germany's greatest political philosopher.[362] Alfred Rosenberg, on the other hand, denounces Hegel's theory of the state as an 'empty construction.'[363] But even writers who are to be taken seriously, such as Koellreutter, state that National-Socialism and Hegel's theory of the state are 'philosophical antitheses.'[364] He maintains that Adolf Hitler has nothing to do with Hegel's deification of the state, for he (Hitler) builds his philosophy upon the *Volk* (nation) and not upon the state. In contrast with these, Huber and Larenz claim Hegel for National-Socialism. Larenz,[365] a Hegelian himself, points out that in his earlier writings Hegel saw the embodiment of morality less in the state than in the community and in the *Volk*. This discussion of Hegel, however, as it is carried on in National-Socialist literature, dwells exclusively on superficial textual problems. Loewenstein[366] has already pointed out that Hegel employed the terms *Volk* and *Staat* indiscriminately and that in two references to the same Greek passage, he once used the word *Volk* and at another time the word *Staat*. Behind these philological skirmishes, however, deeper differences of opinion are to be discovered. Insofar as National-Socialism rejects rational Natural Law and accepts a conception of the 'political' derived from the notion of the 'enemy,' there are indeed close connections between itself and Hegelianism. To the extent, however, that National-Socialism gives a specific content to its concepts of politics (as in its racial theory and its theory of 'blood and soil'), not even the remotest relationship exists.

Dealing with the Jewish question, Hegel asks for civil rights for the Jews. He condemns a policy by which the Jews would be deprived of full rights both in state and society. This attitude of Hegel's is the more interesting since he characterizes the Jews as a nation. He justifies his attitude towards the Jews by the idea that the Jews are men and therefore have a right to be treated as men.[367]

Hegel swept away the remnants of rational Natural Law which the Historical School had not destroyed. His work and that of Savigny undermined the great German tradition of secularized Natural Law and the attempts of some Kantians to restore it were of no avail. Nevertheless, the scientific refutation of secularized Natural Law did not lead to its disappearance. As early as 1910, Ernst Troeltsch raised the question of how much the socialist-labor movement had been influenced by ideas derived from Natural Law. At this time, however, he did not attribute much importance to this influence, asserting that 'contemporary Marxian Socialism does not base its theories on the absolute Natural Law theory of freedom and love as found in Christian doctrine . . . it rests rather on a conception of the natural laws of economic development.' [368] Only three years later, however, Troeltsch strikingly enough modified his opinion and characterized Social-Democracy as the heir of 'radical Natural Law'[369] declaring that Social-Democracy was now the bearer of the traditions of the sects.[370]

This discussion of the interrelationships between Socialism and Natural Law[371] raises the question as to what extent the remnants of proletarian Socialism can co-operate with groups believing in rationalist Natural Law in a common front against National-Socialism. The advocates of proletarian socialism have today the problem of determining what expression they can give to their spontaneous reaction against the arbitrariness of National-Socialism and its hostility towards Natural Law, without running the risk of becoming utopian. The reawakening proletarian Socialist movement must, during its present period of illegality, decide on this crucial question. It is an actual fact being discussed by many illegal groups within Germany today.

It is a well-known fact that Marx and Engels fought for more than four decades against the attempt to base the claims of Socialism on rational Natural Law. Their opposition to every variety of 'Natural Law Socialism' recurs constantly in their writings. They derided such attempts as absolutely utopian. Engels wrote: 'Proudhon . . . demands from present-day society that it shall transform itself not according to the laws of its own economic development, but according to the prescriptions of justice. . . . Where we prove, Proudhon . . . preaches and laments.'[372] In his *Critique of the Gotha Programme*, Marx emphatically dismisses justification for Socialism on the basis of Natural Law rather than on that of social science. He says: 'The German Worker's Party . . . shows that its socialistic ideas are not even skin-deep, in that, instead of treating existing society (and that holds good for any future one) as the basis of the existing state (or the future state in the case of future society) it treats the state rather as an independent entity that possesses its own intellectual, moral and free basis.'[373] In his *Anti-Duehring*, Engels, like his conservative adversaries, emphasized the destructive consequences which a rationalistic Natural Law attitude had produced during the French Revolution. Engels, of course, was referring not to the revolution as such but to its degeneration into the Napoleonic dictatorship. The progress from 'Utopia to Science' consists in substituting historical sociological laws for the rationalistic constructions of Natural Law.

Marx would not have been a true disciple of Hegel had he not assimilated Hegel's sharp and unclouded eye for political realities. Hegel proved with relentless clarity that there is no legal solution of political conflicts, but only the test of power. Marx was perfectly in accord with the Hegelian tradition, justifying the class struggle for the shortening of the working day in the words spoken by the laborer in *Capital*:

'I demand . . . a working day of normal length, and I demand it without any appeal to your heart, for in money matters sentiment is out of place. You may be a model citizen, perhaps a member of the Society for the Prevention of Cruelty to Animals, and in the odour of sanctity to boot; but the thing that you represent face to face with me has no heart in its breast.' And Marx sums up the argument: 'There is here, therefore, an antinomy, right against right, both equally bearing the seal of the law of exchanges. Between equal rights force decides.'[374]

Thus Marx dissolves the concept of justice *in toto* and substitutes for it 'relative justices' which are appropriate to the existing economic situations. He says:

'The juristic forms, in which these economic transactions appear as activities of the will of the parties concerned, as expressions of their common will and as contracts which may be enforced by law against some individual party, cannot determine their content, since they are only forms. They merely express this content. This content is just, whenever it corresponds, and is adequate to, the mode of production. It is unjust, whenever it contradicts that mode. Slavery on the basis of capitalistic production is unjust, likewise fraud in the quality of commodities.'[375]

It is quite understandable that the liberal Benedetto Croce should have referred to Marx as Machiavellian. And yet this characterization is misleading since it takes into consideration only one aspect of Marx.[376] Even the most influential thinker of the nineteenth century could not transcend the contradiction inherent in our epoch between conscience, guided by a belief in Natural Law, and intellect, demanding its rejection. The famous slogan, 'the proletariat has no ideals to realize' is supplemented by another, 'the proletariat should set in motion the process of liberation.' Karl Marx states that Utopianism consists in thinking that, under the present circumstances, good intentions will suffice to establish a regime of justice. However, according to Marx, this state of har-

mony will, with historical certainty, be achieved as soon as the con-
flict-creating capitalistic society has been displaced as a consequence of the class struggle. The class struggle itself, to be sure, is
governed by the laws of political reality, but the classless society
which is its outcome is the fulfilment of the imperatives of Natural
Law. In one of the last chapters of the third volume of *Capital*,
Marx wrote:

'Freedom in this field (i.e., the field of production) cannot consist of anything else but of the fact that socialized men, the associated producers, regulate their interchange with nature rationally, bring it under their common control instead of being ruled
by it as by some blind power; that they accomplish their task with
the least expenditure of energy and under conditions most adequate
to their human nature and most worthy of it. But it always remains
a realm of necessity. Beyond it begins that development of human
power, which is its own end, the true realm of freedom, which,
however, can flourish only upon that realm of necessity as its basis.'[377]

The historic function of the class struggle, therefore, is the creation of an economic basis for the order of Reason, as Marx expressed in one of his earliest writings: 'Only under Communism does
the nobility of man become perceptible. Already today this can be
seen in a meeting of French workers in which the establishment of
the true society is the concern of all and where brotherhood is
truth and not an empty phrase.'[378]

Thus Marxian theory is characterized both by the rejection of
all utopian applications of Natural Law for the duration of the class
struggle, and by the vision of an order governed by Natural Law
following the termination of class conflict. If this interpretation of
Marxism is correct, there can be no objection to the affiliation of
the German Marxists with the United Front, which is composed of
groups whose ethical demands are based on Natural Law. The
Marxists, however, insist that their opposition to National-Socialism is owing primarily not to its suspension of the inviolability of
law for a limited period, but rather to the refusal of National-Socialism ever to subordinate its state to a legal ideology derived
from absolute values.

The clarification of the relationship between Marxian Socialism
and Natural Law is of decisive significance because, to a certain degree, the failure of Syndicalism and Reformism to consider the
problem paved the way for Fascism. It is of the most vital significance that the intellectual origins of George Sorel were Marxist.
Sorel[379] shared Marx's hatred of *'l'arbitraire,'* i.e., the utopian attempt to derive political decisions from rational calculations. Sorel
stripped the class struggle of its visionary goal and approved it as
a movement for its own sake. He transformed it into a myth because, to him, the movement was everything and the goal was
nothing. Thus Sorel became the prophet of politics without ultimate goal — the advocate of action for the sake of action. In the
course of his life he applauded the various militant movements not
because he believed in their aims but because he loved their mili-
tancy. Vaugeois, who was a member of *l'Action Française* and who
had been close to Sorel, once exclaimed: 'Toute force est bonne
autant qu'elle est belle et triomphe.'[380] This aspect of Sorelian
philosophy is expressed in the writing of Ernst Jünger, the most
gifted nationalist author of post-war Germany, who formulated
this attitude: 'Not what we fight for, but how we fight, is essential.'[381]

Whoever believes that political action is nothing more than ac-
quiescence in the laws of social development will share the fate of
Sorel. Like Sorel, he will pass from Syndicalism to *l'Action Française;* like Mussolini, a disciple of Sorel, he will shift from Socialism to Fascism; like Carl Schmitt, an admirer of Sorel, he will de-
sert political Catholicism for National-Socialism, as soon as he is
convinced that integral nationalism is the order of the day. In the
respects in which Machiavelli and Hegel can be regarded as the
spiritual ancestors of National-Socialism, Sorel should also be so regarded. Even though Sorel's influence was indirect, through the
medium of Italian Fascism, and its direct influence was exerted
only upon a small group of intellectuals, the following *credo* indicates his influence:

'One of the most important experiences which led me as a jurist
to National-Socialism was the conversation with a world-famous
American jurist. In 1932 he summarized his diagnosis of the con-

temporary world in one sentence: "We are witnessing today the bankruptcy of *idées génerales.*" ' (Carl Schmitt)[382]

The fact that the most brilliant political theorist of post-war Germany adheres to a political movement, not because of its ideas, but because of its lack of ideas, is a symptom of the degree of development of that political estheticism that worships violence for its own sake. It should be noted, however, that the bankruptcy of the *idées génerales* does not constitute the experience of a whole generation, but only that of an uprooted social group of that generation. This group transforms its necessity into a virtue, its lack of general principles into a principle, and its spiritual poverty into a political theory.[383] Whether one is a Fascist or an anti-Fascist may depend on one's attitude towards the validity of *idées génerales.* Only a believer in the existence of such principles will be ready to struggle, at the possible cost of his life, against National-Socialism as a political system and as a philosophical nihilism. It is the personal sacrifice exacted of every antagonist of National-Socialism in Germany which keeps the remnants of the Marxist opposition aware of the relevance of Natural Law: no-one has ever been willing to risk his life because of his belief in the 'laws of social development.' As Leon Trotsky has remarked, 'Awareness of the relativity of values does not give one the courage to practice violence and shed blood.'

On the other hand, the present political impotence of Marxism in Germany prevents it from repeating the fatal mistake to which it has been especially subject, i.e., propounding Natural Law imperatives as programs for practical political activity. The tragedy of the Marxian political movements in Germany lies in part in the fact that they became, in spite of many warnings of their founders, the victims of their belief in Natural Law even under the rule of capitalism. Alfred Meusel[384] has convincingly shown that Social-Democracy gradually replaced the Marxian analysis of imperialism with an analysis motivated by a utopian pacifism. He says that Kautsky had correctly analyzed the dominant trends in the age of imperialism and had predicted their consequences. However, his morally admirable devotion to peace impelled him to find a way out of the vicious circle of world war and world revolution. Hence he endowed political democracy with a golden glamor and inclined toward the belief that it is possible to replace imperialism by free trade and disarmament, not, it is true, without a struggle, but still without the painful expense of war and revolution. The theoretical issue of 1912 became the fateful decision of 1919. Trusting in democracy and the League of Nations, German Social-Democracy found itself in the current of Wilsonian thoughts, which were based on principles of absolute Natural Law. Hence Social-Democracy developed from a Marxist to a utopian party whose program was formulated by reference to Natural Law. Social-Democracy, which originally had torn the ideological veil from the economic system of capitalistic society, in turn witnessed its ideology being unveiled as utopian by National-Socialism. The premature attempt to realize an order based on utopian Natural Law was fatal to Social-Democracy. The National-Socialist Party matured during its battle against the democratic and pacifist utopianism of post-war Social-Democracy. The attempt of National-Socialism to extirpate all traces of Natural Law represents the other extreme and awakens the conscience of all those who think that life is purposeless unless one strives to achieve a state in which principles of justice prevail.

CHAPTER III

NATIONAL-SOCIALISM AND COMMUNAL
NATURAL LAW

I. SOCIETAL AND COMMUNAL NATURAL LAW

THE NATIONAL-SOCIALIST rejection of rational Natural Law has aroused all social groups for whom rational Natural Law is still of positive importance, but this is only one phase of the relationship between National-Socialism and Natural Law.

The conception of Natural Law lacks precision as far as the term 'law' is concerned; but it is no less ambiguous in regard to the phenomena which can be classed as 'natural.' Professor Carl Becker has pointed out this difficulty in his analysis of the intellectual and historical development preceding the Declaration of Independence. His exposition makes especially clear the relationship between the classical Natural Law of the Age of Enlightenment and the development of Newtonian physics. After having explained that the higher law (which is identified with Natural Law) has taken on different forms in different times, Becker deals especially with the law of God as revealed in nature. Becker distinguishes with regard to the concept of Natural Law between two kinds of nature. According to Becker, 'nature' may be conceived either as 'subject to rational control' or as a 'blind force subjecting men and things to its compulsion.' [385] Since Natural Law at any period is related to the current system of natural science, it was to be expected that there would be changes in the conception of Natural Law with the replacement of classical physics as the predominant natural science by evolutionary biology.

Insofar as National-Socialism is based upon a race concept it has already accepted the dominance of biology.[386] Its race theory rejects the rational optimism associated with classical physics which viewed the discovery of universally valid natural rules as the highest aim of scientific work. What we may call its 'biologistic' political thought and action is based upon the recognition and promotion of 'vital' forces. These vital, irrational forces are the basis of race and their political form is the racial community. Thus, in addition to rational and societal Natural Law, we may add to the long list of historical variants an irrational and communal Natural Law, founded in biology.

The distinction between societal and communal Natural Law was stressed by the publicists as early as the 17th century. This distinction is indicated in the terms *societas* and *socialitas*. Gierke discusses several long-forgotten legal theorists who must be viewed as exponents of a kind of communal Natural Law.[387] These men would hardly deserve attention were it not that Leibniz was among those who, as Gierke says, 'derive law from the community and sees in every community an organic component of the realm of spirits in *universum*.' [388] Leibniz' theory of communal Natural Law is contained in his unfinished *Vom Naturrecht*. A few passages from this should be quoted because of the importance of distinguishing societal Natural Law originating in Reason from communal Natural Law originating in instinct. Leibniz wrote: 'A natural community exists if Nature wishes it to exist. Signs which permit the conclusion that Nature wishes something are given whenever Nature endows us with impulses and with capacities to satisfy them; for nature creates nothing without a purpose.' [389] Leibniz never went very far in differentiating the forms of the natural community from the connubial community, the family, the household community and finally from the civil community. It is all the more remarkable that Gurvitch,[390] a French jurist, has recently concerned himself with this almost forgotten theory of communal Natural Law.[391]

In the following pages a number of features of the ideal types of the two main forms of Natural Law will be presented. However, the numerous concrete subtleties of Natural Law will be left undiscussed. The aim of this procedure is not the description of particular facts but the formulation of ideal types.

Societal Natural Law assumes the isolated individual living in a constant struggle with all other isolated individuals except when the war of one against all is replaced by an order created through a deliberate act of Reason.

Communal Natural Law teaches that there exists among individuals harmonious order based on natural impulses. It originates in and takes its form from the spontaneous impulse of the members of the community (*Wesenswillen*).

Societal Natural Law views Law as the primary source of human co-operation.

Communal Natural Law views Law merely as a manifestation of the community, the cohesion of which is a function of other than legal forces. Law, at best, has a reinforcing function.

Societal Natural Law is supreme. As a manifestation of omnipotent Reason it is unlimited. Societal Natural Law represents the triumph of the mind over the body; it despises biological impulses because it exists only through their suppression. Actually, its legitimation rests on the suppression of these impulses.

Communal Natural Law is the bearer of delegated power. Its content is determined by the earthly forces which gave it birth. From these, it derives its dominion, which is limited both temporally and spatially. Communal Natural Law rejects Reason if Reason questions the legitimacy of those biological instincts upon whose sanction Communal Natural Law is based.

Societal Natural Law is universal. Limitations on the scope of law would create an era of anarchy. The prevention of anarchy is the very essence of Societal Natural Law. Societal Natural Law is valid for the whole world (*jus gentium*). *Jus gentium* as Natural Law is in contrast with *jus civile* as positive law.

The validity of *Communal Natural Law* is limited in space and time and to the persons under it. The communal consciousness to which it owes its existence emerges only in the course of differentiation from other communities. Since Communal Natural Law applies only to a particular societal group, it is particular law which is Natural Law, whereas international law is by definition positive law.

Societal Natural Law is equalitarian. It presupposes the existence of equal, rational individuals who have by common agreement willed the creation of law.

Communal Natural Law is non-equalitarian in analogy with the family which is the elementary form of all communities and which is organized on the basis of unequal relationships among its members.

Before terminating this series of contrasts, the respective relations between 'state' and 'ethnic group' under societal and communal Natural Law should be pointed out.

To the *Societal Natural Law* the nation appears as a plurality of citizens who form a unified group by virtue of their common citizenship. The people (*Volk*) is a juridical concept derived from the state which is legal in nature.

To *Communal Natural Law* the state is merely the superficial form of the essential unity of all *Volksgenossen* (ethnic comrades). The ethnic community is a biological entity which exists even when it is not organized into a state. The state is an organic phenomenon derived from the biological ethnic community.

This fundamental difference in modes of thinking is well examplified by two passages from Justice Holmes and Adolf Hitler respectively. In *Missouri* v. *Holland*, Justice Holmes said of the Fathers of the American Constitution that 'it was enough for them to realize or to hope that they had created an organism, it has taken a century and has cost their successors much sweat and blood to prove that they created a nation.' [392]

On the other hand, Adolf Hitler argued that the state, far from being an end itself, is only a means. According to Hitler there must be created and maintained a community of members equal both physically and spiritually. It is the purpose of the state to serve this community, and states which do not do so are unjustified in their existence. Since this passage of Hitler's *Mein Kampf* which has been summarized above is frequently quoted as the kernel of National-Socialist political philosophy, we are reproducing the German text: '*Der Staat ist ein Mittel zum Zweck. Sein Zweck liegt in der Erhaltung und Förderung einer Gemein-*

schaft physisch und seelisch gleichartiger Lebewesen. . . . Staaten,
die nicht diesem Zweck dienen, sind Fehlerscheinungen, ja sogar
Missgeburten. Die Tatsache ihres Bestehens ändert sowenig daran,
als etwa der Erfolg einer Filibustergemeinschaft die Räuberei zu
rechtfertigen vermag.' [393]

The rational Natural Law concept prevailed at the time of the
emergence of the United States, while irrational Natural Law
thinking was in the background of the creation of the Third
Reich. The present-day German interpretation of Communal
Natural Law is perhaps best expressed by Theodor Buddeberg,
who states that 'the legal system of a state can exist in the long
run only if it is based on the close ethnic kinship of its citizens. . . .
Only ethnic kinship provides them with the common view of
what is law (Natural Law) and with the common belief without
which law cannot exist (Divine Law).' [394] According to this conception, Divine Law manifests itself in the subconscious ethnic
impulses. It becomes secularized into Natural Law as soon as it
passes the threshold of consciousness. As a further illustration
of this attitude we quote Pfenning: 'Only men of the same race
and of the same hereditary biological qualities can co-operate in
a collective understanding. . . . The members of a *Gemeinschaft,*
because of their racial identity, will react in the same way to any
crisis which will threaten the whole ethnic community.' [395]

As long as we consider only the rejection of rational Natural
Law by National-Socialism, it remains possible to find its intellectual roots in occidental civilization. The biological mysticism
frequently encountered in National-Socialist literature was, however, imported with those White-Russian *émigrés* whose influence
on National-Socialism cannot be overemphasized. It is not surprising that Alfred Rosenberg, the author of the *Mythus des 20. Jahrhunderts,* the preacher of the crusade against Bolshevism, the pope
of National-Socialism, is a White-Russian *émigré.*[396]

It was about this particular type of thought that Max Weber
said: 'The central idea of the oriental mystic conception of the
Church is the firm conviction that Christian brotherly love, if
pure and strong enough, must lead to unity in all things, including matters of belief. Thus if human beings love one another mys-

tically in the Johannean sense — they will all think in the same
way, and motivated by the irrationality of this feeling will act
with a divinely willed solidarity . . . this is the kernel of the Slavic
conception of *Gemeinschaft* inside and outside of the Church.' [397]

The practical significance of the theoretically intriguing difference between the concepts of societal and communal Natural Law
is to be found in National-Socialist theories of international law
as they have been revealed by the foreign policy of the Third
Reich.

There is an interesting inconsistency in Dietze's study *Naturrecht der Gegenwart.*[398] After attacking the application of societal
Natural Law to domestic politics, he accepts without reserve all
those principles drawn from Natural Law which in the field of
foreign politics legitimized the remilitarization of Germany: the
principles of the equality of rights, self-determination and the
freedom to choose instruments of defense, etc.

If, however, we study the more recent German literature, especially publications after March 7, 1936 (when the Rhineland was
remilitarized), we discover a remarkable change.[399] Gürke, Professor of International Law at the University of Munich, formulated with especial clarity the new National-Socialist theory of
international law as derived from the concept of 'International
Law Community': 'International law presupposes the racial and
cultural affinity of states in addition to their continuous relationship.' [400] The practical consequences of this theory are likewise
indicated by Gürke. He points out, for example, that as long as
Bolshevist Russia is ruled by Jews and inspired by Marxism, it
remains a racial and cultural alien to the concrete 'community'
of nations, and therefore stands, according to the National-Socialist
doctrine, outside the pale of international law. It is no less important that in National-Socialist thinking, the ethnic community (*Volk*) extends beyond the boundaries of the state. The fact
that there were ethnic comrades (*Volksgenossen*) living under the
sovereignty of foreign states had definite implications for National-
Socialism. Societal Natural Law served as the basis of international law as the Third Reich was rearming. In the second phase
of its development, the National-Socialist regime regarded com-

munal Natural Law as a more adequate basis for international law.

The German-Russian pact on the eve of the second world war indicated the sacrifice of these ideological distinctions and the adoption of a course of pure opportunism. Thus National-Socialism adopted in international relations the same ideology of transgression of law as was used to justify opportunism in the conduct of domestic affairs.

In analyzing the differences between societal and communal Natural Law the author has been guided by the categories of Ferdinand Toennies, the great German sociologist. Toennies,[401] in discussing Hobbes' theory, elaborated the main propositions of societal Natural Law which he then contrasted with the hypo-thesis of communal Natural Law. Toennies was influenced by Maine's thesis concerning the evolution of law *from Status to Contract.* [402] He regarded the communal Natural Law as a mere hypothesis and believed that in Western civilization the age of the 'community' (*Gemeinschaft*) was undergoing a progressive disintegration.

Wolgast and Dietze, who incessantly claim to be disciples of Toennies, treated communal Natural Law as a political reality, whereas Toennies had envisaged it only as a hypothesis. How-ever, in their attempt to monopolize Toennies for National-Socialism, Wolgast and Dietze wilfully distorted his theories. The German Youth Movement had distorted Toennies' sociologi-cal concept of *Gemeinschaft* into a panacea for all the sufferings of society.[403] It was from the Youth Movement that National-Socialism took over the fetish of the *Gemeinschaft* which Hans Freyer in 1930 called the 'vital lie of our age.' [404] Thus Ernst Troeltsch's prophecy that the end of the idealization of groups would be 'to brutalize romance and to romanticize cynicism' [405] has proven true.

2. Communal Natural Law and Concrete Theory of Order

In National-Socialist doctrine, the theory of community is the criterion of what is purely German and therefore National-

Socialist.[406] This attitude is evident in an article by Professor Heckel of the University of Munich,[407] in which he seeks to discredit Stahl, the founder of the Prussian Conservative Party, because he was a Jew. He completes the argument by pointing out that Stahl at heart was a liberal Marxist. As evidence, Heckel offers the fact that Stahl did not view the state as a *Gemeinschaft* and that his attitude was therefore un-German.[408]

A pure Aryan German attitude does not necessarily lead to the adoption of the theory of the *Gemeinschaft*. The claim that there is a connection between German race and thinking in terms of *Gemeinschaft* is as false as the claim that Jewishness and normative thinking are related. The characterization of any system of thought as Jewish constitutes, in the eyes of National-Socialism, its most vigorous condemnation. Accordingly, the foremost requirement of 'German' thinking is an uncompromising opposition to 'Jewish' intellectuality, which is condemned because its main concepts are said to be abstract and universal. This rather negative characterization of National-Socialist communal theory serves as a justification of what we have called the Prerogative State. The proposition that there should be norms of general validity in order to protect the individual's liberty from infringement by the political sovereign, the dictum that the individual can only be punished in accordance with law, the doctrine of equality before law — all these ideas are labelled and condemned as 'Jewish' normativism. The coldly impersonal and abstract norm which is rationally arrived at and rigidly fixed does not guarantee the welfare of the community and hence is prejudicial to the triumph of 'justice.' Only the completely unrestricted power of action based on 'the circumstances of the case' guarantees the supremacy of the legal system, the aim of which is the protection of the central value of life, i. e., the protection of the community.

The idea that the community constitutes the sole source of law has a corollary, the doctrine that there can be no law outside the community. Dernedde expresses this dogma by insisting that 'beyond the vital needs of the ethnic group there are no legal values. These needs should not be opposed by restraints deriving from the law.' [409] According to National-Socialist doctrine, in the relations with those who are outside the community, only political imperatives are valid. Those who stand outside the community are actual or potential enemies. Relations within the community are marked by the prevalence of peace, order and justice. Relations with those outside the community are marked by power, war and destruction. From the viewpoint of National-Socialism the establishment of a legal norm governing extra-community as well as intra-community relations would hamper the successful prosecution of politics. The doctrine of communal Natural Law, therefore, is not in conflict with the arbitrary regime of the Prerogative State. Rather it presupposes its existence, for only the community and nothing but the community is of value. Gerber writes: 'The political system of National-Socialism rests upon the *Gemeinschaft* as the supreme value, i.e., on the essential nature of the German ethnic group; National-Socialism is the expression of the German people's conception of justice.' [410]

In addition to expressing the German conception of justice, the National-Socialist theory of communal Natural Law also has another function. This function is the legitimation of the existing economic and social order. Professor Herrfahrdt of the University of Marburg has shown how the legitimation of the present social order on the basis of the ideology of community is brought about. He says that it is 'precisely in matters of the rule of law and legal security that German judicial activity has proceeded along lines which correspond to the communal theory of National-Socialism. As far as residues of liberalism still exist, they constitute permanent values which are also accepted by National-Socialism. Among these is the free existence of the maximum number of independent individuals in the field of business.' [411]

Since the community has been elevated to semi-divine status, it is necessary only to characterize an institution as communal in order to glorify and legitimize it. But why should the concept of community be restricted to the nation as a whole? Is not the family the prototype of the community? And if the family is a community, is not the household also one? And if this is true, then is not the workshop a community and the factory as well?

Thus the doctrine of community revolutionizes the legal relationship among members of the ethnic group.

The doctrine of community is the pivot of the whole National-Socialist system. The doctrine of the *Gemeinschaft* acknowledges the dualism of two legal systems: of the Normative State and of the Prerogative State.

The relationship between communal Natural Law and the Normative State still remains to be demonstrated. This relationship emerges most clearly in Carl Schmitt's *Über die drei Arten des rechtswissenschaftlichen Denkens*, which is the most influential juridical study of recent years. In this essay Schmitt distinguishes three kinds of legal thinking:

1. Normativism, characterized as thinking in terms of laws and abstract norms,

2. Decisionism, as thinking in terms of decision without regard to any legal basis.

He places in juxtaposition to both the 'concrete theory of order' (*konkretes Ordnungsdenken*) which he describes as thinking with reference to the concrete communities existing within the ethnic group. Schmitt states: 'To the concrete theory of order, order, even juridically, does not consist primarily of individual rules or the total system of rules. Rules are rather components of order and means for maintaining it.' [412]

This is not an especially new idea in the sociology of law in Germany. It is simply a re-formulation of the proposition asserted by Eugen Ehrlich that the law actually being enforced in a given situation is not to be found in statutes but in the legal customs practiced by the members of the legal unit in question. The statement, however, that the 'concrete theory of order' (*konkretes Ordnungsdenken*) is neither original nor even characteristic of National-Socialist thought does not exhaust the significance of Schmitt's theory, which, as Maunz [413] rightly maintains, represents a new stage in the development of National-Socialist legal philosophy. It is not the 'concrete theory of order' as such but its association with the concept of 'community' (*Gemeinschaft*) which gives it significance. Ehrlich went no further than to state that social order is spontaneously produced by members of the society more frequently than academic jurisprudence imagines. When Schmitt remarks that 'the introduction of the concept of community revived the concrete theory of order'[414] he attributes to the bearers of the concrete order the same mystic quality that characterizes the National-Socialist concept of the community.

Schmitt's opposition to legal normativism is in complete consistency with his attitude during the Republican period. Schmitt also stole from Hegel the tendency to use the 'concreteness' as a weapon against 'abstraction.' According to Hegel the principles of reason must be conceived as concrete in order that true freedom may come to rule. Hegel characterizes the school of thought which clings to abstraction as liberalism and emphasizes that the concrete is always victorious against the abstract and that the abstract always becomes bankrupt against the concrete.[415] However, Schmitt, who had discovered the sovereignty of the state under martial law, who had frequently reiterated Hobbes' doctrine that authority and not truth is the creator of law, and who in 1932 had coined the phrase that 'the best thing in the world is a command,'[416] turned away from decisionism after dictatorship had been achieved and martial law made permanent under the authoritarian state. This naturally caused some distress to his admirers. [417]

A critical analysis of Schmitt's theories reveals that, according to the theory of concrete order, the concrete communities are not the primary sources of law. If they were, then every concrete group, so long as it constitutes an orderly whole, would have to be regarded as equivalent to a concrete community order. But if this were the case Schmitt's theory would logically imply a liberal theory of group autonomy. But this conclusion does not follow because Schmitt's 'concrete theory of order' really contains a decisionist element connected with the conception of the 'community.' Only those groups are to be regarded as the bearers of the 'concrete order' to which the character of the 'community' is granted by National-Socialism.

The clarification of this problem is not merely of theoretical import. It is a practical problem of considerable political importance as well. Völtzer, the Labor Trustee for the District of Northwestern Germany,[418] wrote an article which, considered together with Kühn's article on the organization of industry, acquires considerable significance. After examining the relationship between the National-Socialist conception of the state and the newly founded estate-system, Kühn concludes that the new organization of industry has grown organically out of National-Socialism. He says that in the sphere of the estates 'self-administration was firmly established when the National-Socialist state was organized. National-Socialism adopted self-administration in complete consistency with its own principles.'[419] Kühn also points out the intellectual bond between the National-Socialist theory of the state and the 'estate-system.' 'The co-ordination of occupations as it is embodied in the estates today contributes greatly to the formation of the community.'[420]

But if the co-ordination of occupations is a particularly adequate basis for a community which is the embodiment of concrete order, why, then, are all occupational groups deemed fit to form such communities with the single exception of the proletariat? According to the National-Socialist viewpoint, the labor unions before 1933 were infected by Marxism and infested with Jews. But on May 2, 1933, the National-Socialists took the labor unions in hand and exterminated every trace of Marxism and Jewry. Why were the purified labor unions not preserved? Why were the entrepreneurs, the craftsmen, the peasants, professional people, the artists deemed fit to form communities, but not the workers? Why must the worker be satisfied with the German Labor Front of all Productive Germans (*Front aller schaffenden Deutschen*), while the other groups form autonomous estates which are accorded the status of communities above and beyond their affiliation with the German Labor Front? Völtzer answers this question directly. After describing the seizures of the union headquarters by the Storm Troopers, he continues: 'In practise the result was the existence of two independent bodies of employers and employees, each internally co-ordinated. Today it can be admitted that these organizations did their best to wage a spiritual class struggle under the aegis of National-Socialism.'[421]

The experiences of this labor trustee are a valuable source of information. They reveal that the German labor unions' adherence to the ideas of the class struggle is not due to their 'infection by Marxism or their corruption by Jewry.' Since the same labor unions, under National-Socialist auspices, were about to engage in the same kind of class struggle as before, it must be inferred that organized labor tends to carry on the class struggle even if its chiefs are ideologically opposed. Therefore, from the National-Socialist viewpoint, labor unions cannot be regarded as 'communities.'

There is no norm or abstract principle by which it can be decided whether or not a given group is a community. The problem of the concrete theory of order transcends the limits of the system of the concrete 'communities.' This problem demands solution by decisionism and, since there is no norm, this decision—to employ Schmitt's terminology — must be derived from a 'void.' In reality, however, this 'void' is not a 'void' at all. It is the value system associated with the class structure of present-day society. This decision is a political decision par excellence. Therefore it falls within the scope of the Prerogative State.

Viewed in this light, the essence of Schmitt's theory may be summarized as follows: the National-Socialist legal system is embodied in concrete communities. The question as to which groups constitute concrete communities is decided politically, i.e., the decision is not made in accordance with pre-existent norms, but in accordance with the 'demands of the situation.' The theoretical shortcomings of the concrete theory of order have been obvious even to National-Socialists. Havestädt,[422] in an article in the *Verwaltungs-Archiv*, cautions his readers against the attitude which opposes the concrete theory of order to the theory of law. He says that such an abandonment of normativistic thinking would only result in a kind of pluralism. Havestädt also very clearly penetrates to the decisionistic element on which the concrete theory of order is based when he says that 'any occupational community which forgets its task ceases to form a "community" and therewith renounces the claim to be an order.'[423] The 'reality' of an order thus consists not in the fact of its existence but in fulfilling a purpose which is imposed on it externally. The concrete theory of order evaporates completely once it is reduced to its normativistic and decisionistic elements.

It is not by accident that Schmitt has neglected the analysis of decisionistic elements in his recent writings. National-Socialist literature is replete with treatises on the 'community' as the prototype of the National-Socialist theory of law. There are also a considerable number of studies dealing with problems of political law. There is, however, not a single systematic treatment of the relationship of political law to what is called the law of the 'community.' Professor Huber of Kiel is the only one who even touches on the problem. He raises the question as to whether legal principles have as much validity in politics as they have in the other spheres of life. He writes: 'If the follower in the political order enjoyed no legal status comparable to the legal status of the member of the community, we would be confronted by a tremendous unbridgeable disjunction within the legal order. The dualism between the political law of the political order and the unpolitical law of the other spheres of life would be worse than the old dichotomy between public and private law.' [424]

It is worthy of emphasis, however, that Huber arbitrarily confines his discussion of various types of principles in the political and non-political sphere to the problem of the status of 'followers.' First of all it should be pointed out that on June 30, 1934 Röhm and his associates were not accorded the benefit of the legal guarantees appropriate to their legal status as Adolf Hitler's political followers. Further, a serious academic treatise should have pointed out that the desired subjection of the followers of a political party to legal norms would constitute an extraordinary exception to the contrary principle that political questions stand outside the law.

In the course of this study, Professor Huber has shown himself to be one of the most extreme proponents of the substitution of the Rule of Law for a state whose political order is unconfined by binding legal norms. Scarcely a single writer has contributed more than Huber to the introduction into the German legal order of that 'extraordinarily important distinction' and thus to the

construction of a 'dualism which is worse than the old distinction
between private and public law.' Now that it is no longer the
political foes, but the political friends and followers of the leader,
who are endangered, he shrinks from the conclusion which he
and his like-minded colleagues have advocated for years — namely
the elimination of law from the realm of politics! If Huber had
not avoided the question which he himself raised he would have
had to face the phenomenon of the Dual State with its distinction
between the Prerogative and the Normative State, two alternatives
between which there can be no reconciliation.

Hans Peter Ipsen believes it possible to evade the problems of
the Dual State by shifting them from the realm of substantive law
to that of jurisdictions. Ipsen's treatment of the question of *Politik
und Justiz*[425] narrows the cardinal problem of recent German constitutional law to mere formalism. The legal criterion of what
Ipsen calls 'acts of sovereignty' is not to be found in their *Justiz-
losigkeit*, i.e. their independence from judicial control, but in their
exemption from the rule of material law. Hence, Ipsen describes
not the phenomena themselves but their symptoms. He says:
'Independence from judicial control begins where the qualified
bearer of sovereignty — of the state or of the party — decides,
in concreto. The normatively determined limit of the judiciary
against acts of sovereignty as fixed by legal norms, i.e., the jurisdiction of the judiciary — is valid only in general, and is suspended whenever a concrete qualification provides otherwise.' [426]
Although Ipsen believes that all acts of state, whether independent of or subject to judicial control, are consequences of one and
the same legal system,[427] he is unable to disregard the question
whether or not such acts are justifiable from the viewpoint of
justice. In the preface to his book, Ipsen makes the idea of justice
even more relative than other National-Socialist jurists. He states
that there is not only a 'German justice' in contrast to other 'national justices' but that in addition there is a special justice for
National-Socialists which is valid only for the party followers
of Adolf Hitler. The main conclusions of his treatise, he says,
'can be accepted only by those who are convinced by their sense
of justice that the given order is just and who are certain that

the resolution of litigations independently of the judiciary and its norms is just. . . . In the National-Socialist state all who approve of it can be sure that their expectations will be fulfilled.' [428] But what about those who do not 'approve of it'? Does Ipsen imply that the ethnic outsiders, the foreigners or the Germans whose attitude towards the regime is neutral or hostile, cannot expect justice? It is probably not moral scruples which prevent Ipsen from declaring overtly: 'Justice is only for us, others are to be judged as we see fit.' The inhibitions are intellectual. If Ipsen would acknowledge that the National-Socialist state not only treats friend and foe differently within the same system, but that in reality there are two contradictory systems of domination in contemporary Germany, his whole thesis would be untenable and would serve only to mask the real problem. Thus Ipsen has no choice but to evade the embarrassing question. This is all the more significant since Ipsen reveals exceptional knowledge and intellectual skill and his book is one of the very best that has appeared in National-Socialist Germany. Ipsen actually ends his preface by writing: 'He who does not approve of the National-Socialist state cannot contribute to the scientific analysis of German law.' [429] That the essential point is not the contribution to German legal theory but equality in the German legal order has become clear to everyone who has had the opportunity of clashing with the Prerogative State. Ipsen's evasion of this problem is ample evidence that even the most specialized monograph cannot be written in a scholarly manner so long as there is no freedom of scientific research. Furthermore, Ipsen's contention that only a National-Socialist can contribute to the analysis of National-Socialist law must be rejected as groundless. If it were to be accepted, a complete repudiation of all Conflict of Laws would follow in as much as Conflict of Laws is based on the fact that a judge from one legal system is accorded competence to interpret the norms of a different legal system.

This whole problem has been thoroughly treated by Max Weber in his *Der Sinn der Wertfreiheit der soziologischen und ökonomischen Wissenschaften*. Regarding a hypothetical case of an anarchist as a legal scholar, despite his rejection of the norms

which he is analyzing, Weber said: 'That Archimedian point beyond the self-evident conventions and presuppositions (i.e., his
rejection of law) can give him the capacity to perceive problems
in the accepted legal theory which escape those to whom they
are self-evident. Radical doubt is the source of knowledge.' [430]
These remarks constitute the methodological justification of the
present book.

In the National-Socialist state, the primary function of science
is not the scientific analysis of legal and social phenomena. Hans
Frank, German Minister of Justice, unequivocally stated the task
of science:

'The substance as well as the objectives of scientific work must
be National-Socialism. Empty abstraction and the satisfaction in
highly theoretical results for their own sake must not be the content of intellectual studies. Their objective must rather be the
furtherance of our people. Neither the book itself . . . nor the
satisfaction "that my work has led to the perfection of a new
approach" should be the goal. Only the conviction that the
scientific work undertaken serves the promotion of National-
Socialism is acceptable as justification for science.' [431]

This quotation illustrates the fact that in present-day Germany
the 'political' is supreme not only in law and religion but also in
science. Frank, the author of the much quoted phrase: 'Law is all
that is useful to the German people,' clearly expresses in the
above passage the idea that National-Socialist Germany recognizes as truth only that which promotes the current aims of the
ruling party. Such a theory of 'conditional truth' would mean
the end of science. [432]

PART III

THE LEGAL REALITY OF THE DUAL STATE

Les institutions périssent par leur victoires.

RENAN

CHAPTER I

THE LEGAL HISTORY OF THE DUAL STATE

1. THE DUAL STATE AND THE DUALISTIC STATE

IN present-day Germany, many people find the arbitrary rule of the Third Reich unbearable. These same people acknowledge, however, that the idea of 'community,' as there understood, is something truly great. Those who take up this ambivalent attitude towards National-Socialism suffer from the two principal misconceptions:

1. The present German ideology of *Gemeinschaft* ('community') is nothing but a mask hiding the still existing capitalistic structure of society.

2. This ideological mask (the 'community') equally hides the existence of the Prerogative State operating by arbitrary measures.

The replacement of the *Rechtsstaat* (Legal State) by the Dual State is but a symptom. The root of the evil lies at the exact point where the uncritical opponents of National-Socialism discover grounds for admiration, namely in the community ideology and in the militant capitalism which this very notion of the *Gemeinschaft* is supposed to hide. It is indeed for the maintenance of capitalism in Germany that the authoritarian Dual State is necessary.

Any critical examination which attempts to reveal the social structure of the National-Socialist state must discover whether or not the essential criteria of the Dual State have appeared in any earlier historical period. In contrast to similar 'dualistic' forms in previous epochs the organization of the National-Socialist Dual

State is monistic. In the early 'dualistic state,' two independent powers (prince and peers, king and people) had to collaborate in order to produce a legal act of state; the Dual State, on the other hand, is characterized by the unity of its leadership. 'One Leader, one People, one Reich!' Despite its organizational unity, vast variety and contrast in the contents of the degrees and statutes issued by the state may well exist.

In the dualistic state every single act of legislation or fiscal policy expressing the will of the state is the result of a particular agreement. The constitutional history of the dualistic state is the history of perpetual compromises. The Dual State, however, is primarily characterized by the prevalence of one general and all-inclusive compromise. A Dual State may be said to exist whenever there is organizational unification of leadership, regardless of whether there is any internal differentiation in the substantive law. Viewed sociologically, the Dual State is characterized by the fact that the ruling class assents to the absolute integration of state power on the following conditions:

1. that those actions which are relevant to its economic situation be regulated in accordance with laws which they consider satisfactory,

2. that the subordinate classes, after having been deprived of the protection of the law, be economically disarmed.

Ferdinand Toennies and Werner Sombart saw the principal characteristic of the modern state in its dual nature ('Zwieschlächtigkeit').[433] This is true not only of the dualistic but also of the monistic, absolutist state in which the two-sideness is disguised by organizational and juridical forms.

Only in England, a country which has never known the phenomenon of the Dual State, do these distinctions lose all significance. Hintze, one of the leading historians of modern German government, says that there is only one state in which one could say that the Rule of Law has existed: England. The militaristic, absolutistic and bureaucratic governments on the continent faced different problems. Here the question was not how to secure the supremacy of law but how the two antagonistic legal systems, the old common law and the new administrative law, could be balanced and harmonized. Hintze considers this antagonism between these fundamentally different systems a decisive factor in the history of German law. 'I am inclined to assert,' he remarks, 'that at bottom it remained in Germany the essential problem of the state.' [434]

We lack space for a discussion of the basic reasons for the divergence between England and the Continent. Some importance must be attributed to the effect of the armed forces (the German army and the English navy) on the domestic politics of the respective countries. According to Hintze, 'the army is an organization which penetrates and shapes the structure of the state. The navy is only a mailed fist which extends into the outside world. It cannot be employed against the "internal enemies." ' [435] This observation may serve as a starting point in our attempt to discover the reasons why England never has been a Dual State. Her insular condition and the overwhelming importance of her navy for defensive purposes have prevented the intermingling of the spheres of law and power. Michael Freund says that 'English political theory in the sixteenth and seventeenth centuries was able to elaborate a distinction between the spheres of law and power which was intended to apply not merely structurally but spatially as well. . . . Absolute on the high seas and in the colonies, the seat of the Empire was ruled by common law and the laws of the estates.' [436] When, in the course of the struggle over the ship-money writs, the threat of a Dual State really became acute in England, the central legal issues were formulated in a way which is still relevant to our analysis of contemporary Germany.

In the case *Rex* v. *Richard Chambers*, one of the judges, in characterizing the threatening change, said that 'there was a Rule of Law and a Rule of Government, and that many things which might not be done by the Rule of Law might be done by the Rule of Government.' [437] In England, however, the danger was recognized and overcome in time in a great struggle for the preservation of law. Three hundred years ago the principal participants of this struggle were aware of the fact that the partial elimination of law would necessarily bring about the destruction of all values. D'Ewes, in his autobiography, had remarked that 'if this could be done lawfully, then by the same right . . . no man was, in conclusion, worth anything.' [438] This English aversion to the Dual State was brought to America by those emigrants who were driven out of England by Archbishop Laud.

When, some centuries later, during the Civil War, a Dual State seemed imminent, the Supreme Court halted the development. In *ex parte* Milligan, Justice Davis upheld the Rule of Law:

'No doctrine, involving more pernicious consequences, was ever invented by the wit of man than that any of its provisions can be suspended during any of the great emergencies of government. Such a doctrine leads directly to anarchy or despotism, but the theory of necessity . . . is false. . . . Martial Law cannot arise from a threatened invasion. The necessity must be actual and present. . . . Martial Law can never exist where the courts are open, and in the proper and unobstructed exercise of their jurisdiction.' [439]

When this opinion is compared with the permanent state of martial law in Germany today, one sees the correctness of Morstein-Marx's [440] statement that the German and American constitutional situations represent opposite extremes. The more astonishing is that Reinhard Hoehn, who expounds National-Socialist political theory at the University of Berlin, has asserted that between the National-Socialist antipathy to legal norms and the Anglo-Saxon adherence to the Rule of Law 'there is not a real but only a verbal conflict.' [441] According to Dicey's classical definition 'the Rule of Law may be used as a formula for expressing the fact that with us the law of the constitution, the rules which in foreign countries naturally form part of a constitutional code, are not the source but the consequence of the rights of individuals, as defined and enforced by the Courts.' [442] According to National-Socialism, rights of the individual in the sphere of public law are, at best, reflexes of the statutes of public law, whereas under the Rule of Law public law is nothing but a bundle of individual rights.[443] Hoehn's statements only further corroborate the contention that one cannot take seriously the study of political science and jurisprudence in National-Socialist Germany as intellectual disciplines. Since February 1933 an unbridgeable gap between German and Anglo-Saxon thinking has become apparent.

At present the legal situation of the seventeenth century has been reincarnated. The tendency defeated in England in the seventeenth century gradually attained success in Germany. During that period a fateful decision took place. After having broken the political backbone of the estates, the monarchy supplemented the traditional law of the estates by a system of absolute power directed towards political goals.

A historical sketch of the changes in Brandenburg and Prussia after the establishment of absolutism by Friedrich Wilhelm, the Great Elector (1640-88), may show the 'dual nature' of the state with reference to the Dual State. This sketch will be confined to the territories dominated by the Hohenzollerns. Southern, western and northwestern Germany (the free peasant country), developed somewhat differently.

2. THE HISTORY OF THE DUAL STATE IN PRUSSIA AND GERMANY

a. THE ESTABLISHMENT OF THE ABSOLUTE MONARCHY

With the destruction of the feudal power of the nobility by the absolute monarch during the seventeenth and eighteenth centuries, the 'dual nature' of the state did not by any means come to an end. At first the renunciation of political power by the estates could only be obtained in return for other social privileges. For example, the Diet of Berlin, in its resolution of August 5, 1653, expressly stated that 'the institution of serfdom will be preserved wherever it has been introduced or is customary.' [444] In addition, the Diet's decree precluded the possibility that the authority of the Electorate Treasury would interfere with the judicial jurisdiction of the courts of the nobility. In these courts the legal burden of proof was fixed in a manner which clearly reflects the realities of power: in all cases in which the *Junkers* laid claim to services the peasant had to provide the evidence that these services were *not* due. After the Law of 1681 concerning Farm-Hands had approved of migration from one village or estate to another, the new socio-political compromise was given full effect in another Law concerning Farm-Hands (*Gesindeordnung*) which was decreed in 1722 and confirmed in 1769. Henceforth, local customs were sanctioned even to the extent of permitting the sale of serfs.[445]

Only in exchange for such important concessions would the landed nobility renounce its political power and allow the institution of the *miles perpetuus* to be established.[446] The result was an absolute but not totalitarian monarchy, since the well-nigh complete surrender of the peasants to the landed nobility placed restrictions on the power of the state in its relations to the economic position of the serfs. Thus the power of the Prussian state ended with the *Landrat*.[447]

But more significant than the concessions which were obtained by the *Junkers* was the fact that, apart from traditional law which was applied by the courts, there grew up an administrative order guided by the monarchical *raison d'état*. This new administrative practice was organizationally and functionally independent of the traditional substantive law and of the jurisdiction of the courts. This innovation was based on the principle that 'in political questions there is no right of appeal.' The absolute state was strong enough to suspend or abolish both the jurisdiction of the estates and the rule of the status oriented laws in any matter important to it. However, it was neither able nor willing to eliminate the rule of this substantive status law from those spheres which did not seem vital to its aims.[448] Thus the estates were able not only to preserve the integrity of the traditional law in all matters which were of importance to their economic privileges. They even succeeded in laying the foundations for a system of autonomy in economic matters. Not only did the *Ständisches Kreditwerk* (Agricultural Financing Institute for Mortgaging the Manors of the *Junkers*) remain intact (it was not terminated until 1820): in 1719 there was added a *Marsch-und Molestienkasse* providing (significantly enough) for the 'liturgical' defraying of military expenses by the individual members of the estates. Of even greater significance were the provincial loan societies (*Landschaften*) supervised by the nobility. The structure of these bodies is adequately portrayed in § 28 of the *Reglements* of the *Ritter-*

schaftliches Pfandbriefinstitut für die Kur-und Neumark. These units were exclusively ruled by the nobility and royal officials were explicitly excluded from participation.[449]

If one examines the legal position of the estates in the German principalities at the turn of the eighteenth century, one sees a reduction of their traditional privileges to a merely intermediate position. The power of the princes had been extended above them and the power of the feudal lords beneath them. The protection of the court was fully accorded only to the privileged landed nobility.[450] On the basis of the absolute power of the estates over the serfs, a state was erected which eliminated the dualism of powers which had previously existed. But its 'dual nature' persisted in a different form, in the sense that a legally regulated order functioned alongside of a politically regulated order. Max Weber characterized this situation when he spoke of the co-existence of both the indestructible power of traditions and the arbitrary power of the cabinet (as a substitute for the supremacy of rational rules.)[451]

b. ENLIGHTENED DESPOTISM

During the second half of the eighteenth century the realm of law was extended into spheres which it had hitherto left untouched. The absolute monarch, Frederic the Great (1740-86), by way of introducing certain protective rules on behalf of the peasantry, placed certain legal restrictions on the power of the landed nobility. Guided by the Enlightenment, the strengthened monarchical absolutism tended to impose the doctrines of Natural Law on those spheres which had been regarded as the proper domain of the *raison d'état*, and which were, therefore, outside the legal order. Otto Hintze views these activities of the enlightened despotism as the beginning of the *Rechtsstaat* (Rule of Law State), the characteristic system of the nineteenth century.[452] Enlightened despotism, represented in its purest form by Joseph II of Austria (1765-90) and, to a lesser degree, by Frederic the Great of Prussia, involved an attempt to eliminate completely the two-sideness of the state. Its aim was the absolute supremacy of the monarchy as the exclusive bearer of political authority and, concurrently, its subjection to Natural Law. The program of the absolute monarchy required not only the centralization of authority but a universally valid legal system as well.

Of course there was a considerable discrepancy between the program and its realization. Professor Hugo Preuss said: 'the *Preussisches Allgemeines Landrecht* [Prussian Code of Public and Private Law 1792] sounded as if the premises had been written by the philosopher of Sanssouci, while the practically more important conclusions had been written by the King of Prussia.' [453]

The Enlightenment did not alleviate the unnatural tyranny of the estates over the serfs or the despotic *raison d'état*. Frederic the Great thus described the tension between the ideology of Natural Law and the reality of the positive legal order: 'There are provinces in most of the states of Europe in which the peasants fixed to the soil are the serfs of their masters. This is the most miserable of all conditions and the most revolting to mankind. Such abuses are justly detested and it may be thought that it is only necessary to desire to abolish this barbarous custom in order for it to disappear. But this is not true. This custom rests on old contracts between the owners of the soil and the colonists. In attempting to abolish this abominable institution, the whole rural economy would be disrupted. It would be necessary to indemnify the nobility in part for the losses which their revenues would suffer.' [454] In the face of this deep-rooted skepticism as to 'what the economic system could bear,' it is incomprehensible why all attempts at reducing compulsory service from six to two or three days a week should have failed,[455] and why the Neumark Farm Labor Law remained in effect despite the existence of the *Allgemeinen Landrecht* guaranteeing civil freedom to the peasantry.[456]

The same failure can be observed in the state. The instructions for the General Directory which the Natural Law theorist Coceji (Secretary of Justice under Frederic the Great) wrote in 1747 contain the rule, 'all complaints and lawsuits must be handled by the ordinary courts even when they involve the state or the treasury.' But a new regulation of June 6, 1749, contradicts this. It upheld the above-mentioned general principle, but it specified numerous exceptions to the applicability of the law and it is of particular significance that all matters which concern the *status oeconomicus et politicus* fall under the jurisdiction of the political agencies, i.e., the Chambers and Boards (even if they are only slightly connected with the *status politicus*).[457] Thus, in spite of Natural Law, the absolute monarchy of Frederic the Great was ruled by the principle that all political questions are beyond the competence of the judiciary. The sphere of the *status politicus* remained isolated from the rule of positive law.

The two decades between the death of Frederic the Great and the temporary downfall of his state in the Napoleonic era are marked by the developments toward the *Rechtsstaat*. The Prussian *Allgemeine Landrecht* contains the famous definition of police functions. Under the influence of Natural Law, the tasks of the police are defined as protection from danger and maintenance of order. It is true that the *Allgemeine Landrecht* also contains a provision to the effect that the royal prerogative is not subject to legal control. Even this provision represents definite progress over the previous rules because the concept of royal prerogative is undoubtedly much narrower than the vague concept of *status politicus*. The decree of 1797 for the province of New East Prussia provided for far-reaching judicial control of administrative acts. A decree of the Cabinet in 1803 provided that the courts and not administrative boards should have jurisdiction in all cases of private and public law.[458]

After the catastrophe of 1806 this development towards the *Rechtsstaat*, instead of continuing and being perfected by the reforms of Stein and Hardenberg, actually suffered a serious reverse.

C. THE ABSOLUTE BUREAUCRACY

The French Revolution and its consequences brought to an end the association of rational Natural Law and utilitarian *raison d'état* which had developed in the course of the eighteenth century. With the abolition of serfdom, the precarious basis on which enlightened despotism rested disintegrated. Simultaneously, as a result of the French Revolution, the politically dominant circles discarded Natural Law because its potential dangers had become only too apparent. The partial restitution of bureaucratic for patrimonial methods of administration, which had become necessary after the liberation of the peasantry, was not confined to the rural areas. It permeated the whole state and transformed the despotism of the enlightened monarchy into the absolute domination of the state bureaucracy. It was this absolute bureaucracy which Hegel had in mind when he wrote about the state in his *Philosophy of Right*.

Georg Friedrich Knapp's pioneer investigations into the social consequences of the liberation of the peasantry render it unnecessary for us to dwell upon this particular point. The abolition of serfdom can only be understood in the light of the Regulatory Decree of September 14, 1811 and the Declaration of May 29, 1816.[459]

At the same time, the legal protection which the absolute monarchy had introduced for the prevention of the eviction or 'putting down' of peasants (*Bauernlegen*) failed. Consequently the economically weaker strata of the peasantry became agricultural day-laborers. Otto Hintze [460] calculated that of the 145,000 serfs in the old Prussian provinces (excluding Silesia) only about 45,000 became independent farmers after the abolition of serfdom. The rest were 'put down' by the *Junkers* and became part of the agricultural proletariat.[461]

The abolition of hereditary serfdom was accompanied by a strengthening of the tendencies towards a police state. The modification of the police-idea which had been effected under the influence of Natural Law during the age of enlightened despotism can be fully appraised only with reference to the social structure of the period. The overwhelming majority of the population had not even been touched by the new Natural Law oriented legislation since they were under the patrimonial jurisdiction of the *Junkers* and not of the agencies of the state. For the upper classes, enlightened despotism meant a lessening of the pressure of the police administration since the formerly autonomous estates were now socially and economically assimilated into the absolute monarchy. The more the large estates in eastern Germany were transformed into agricultural capitalistic enterprises the better they were adapted to the rigorously organized Prussian state.[462]

This economic development had highly significant political repercussions. The younger sons of the Prussian *Junkers* were forced to gain their livelihood as officers in the Prussian army. Mercantilist policy was supported by the large landed estate system, and is itself the effect of the operation of the capitalistic system on the manor.[463]

The abolition of hereditary serfdom by the decree of October 9, 1807 presented new problems to the Prussian administration. The administrative domain of the Prussian state, which hitherto had not extended over the *Landrat*, now included the lowest strata of the population. The simultaneous introduction of freedom of movement, the termination of the compulsory guild system and other restrictions on industry liberated the urban population from the bonds which before had facilitated the state's control over the industrial and commercial population. Even before the decree of October 9, 1807 (which stipulated that after St. Martin's Day 1810 there should be only free persons in Prussia) had come into force, the police law had undergone a decisive change. By § 3 of the decree of December 26, 1808, the police legislation of the *Allgemeine Landrecht*, which had borne the imprint of Natural Law, was repealed. 'The negative as well as positive care for the welfare of our faithful subjects' was turned over to the police administration of the provincial governments. The elaboration of the police law begun by the enlightened despotism was cut short by the liberation of the peasantry and replaced by a grant of unrestrained police powers to the absolutist bureaucracy. Insofar as the exercise of the police power remained with the *Junkers*, the newly introduced police law compensated them for the power over the serfs which they had lost.

The new police law greatly diminished judicial control over police activities. Friese, the spiritual father of the decree of December 26, 1808, clearly recognized this change. If the police exercised not only negative and protective functions — as the *Allgemeine Landrecht* allowed — but also 'positive' ones (involving unlimited jurisdiction), and if it were admitted that 'a certain degree of legislative power was inherent in police administration,' then the police were also entitled 'to intervene in lawful activities and to decree actions for which they had no specific legal jurisdiction.' [464] Correspondingly, § 38 of the decree reduced control over the police to a minimum. This meant that, in practice, the police (to the extent that the *Allgemeine Landrecht* did not otherwise specify explicitly) were able to erect an independent system of authority alongside the legal order of the state.

Thus, the events of 1653 were repeated under more complex conditions in the years 1808-1816. Just as in 1653, following the Thirty Years' War, a basis for the absolutism of the territorial princes was created after the politically dispossessed estates had been compensated by an extension of their social power, so the defeat in the Napoleonic wars provided the ground for a new compromise. 'The absolute monarch was able to strengthen himself vis-à-vis the nobility in return for a reinforcement of hereditary serfdom. The absolute bureaucracy sought to strengthen itself vis-à-vis the nobility by turning over to it peasantry in a modernized way: by the abolition of serfdom.' [465]

Does German history provide a corroboration of the hypothesis that military defeat promotes political absolutism? The military reorganization which followed the Treaty of Westphalia brought with it the *miles perpetuus*, while the Peace of Tilsit (1807) was followed by the introduction of universal military service. Both of these reforms which deeply affected the structure of the state were closely connected at least with the strengthening if not with the establishment of the absolute state. This process could be consummated only by a compromise with the dominant classes. The power position of the upper classes in Germany seems to have arisen partially from the consolidation of the power of the state in the absolutistic period, for this could only be realized with the collaboration of the dominant classes and at the cost of the lower classes.

However that may be, the political structure of the Prussian state in the period of post-Napoleonic reaction differs essentially from the monarchical absolutism of the period of enlightened despotism, despite the retention of a monistic form of state organization. The liberation of the peasantry meant that the landed nobility exchanged social privileges for economic power. The losses and gains of this change made it possible for the *Junkers*, adapting themselves to the pattern of economic development, to transform their patrimonial estates into capitalistic enterprises oriented towards export. This new type of enterprise was easily integrated into bourgeois legal order, which was being modernized by concurrent reforms of the legal regulation of industry and commerce. The interests of the dominant landed aristocracy were, to a large extent, in harmony with the economic aims of the commercial and industrial bourgeoisie, which had been freed from the shackles of mercantilism. For 'as long as industrial backwardness forces large-scale agriculturalists to export, the landed proprietor will be well disposed towards industry and trade.' [466] The free trade tendencies of German tariff policy were the expression of this attitude, which made possible the strengthening of the bourgeoisie, whose political weakening was the chief goal of the absolutistic bureaucracy. However, the subsequent development of industry reinforced the influence of the bourgeoisie and threatened the political power of the landed *Junkers*.

The domestic policy of the governing aristocratic bureaucracy [467] had as its mainspring the persecution of popular agitators and forerunners of national unity by the police. In other words, its domestic policy was essentially oriented towards defending itself against the revolutionary democratic movements (in this period identical with the national movements) which were surging over Europe subsequent to the formation of an industrial proletariat. At the same time the governing aristocratic bureaucracy, in its role as executive organ of the agrarian-capitalist *Junker* aristocracy, was moving towards a liberal free-trade policy and a rational system of private law. During the Restoration the dual nature of the monarchy manifested itself in the conflict between the judiciary and the administration.

The Restoration saw a revival of the study of law. Its most distinguished theorist, Savigny, denied the possibility of changing the historically developed law by means of legislation. Characteristically, his definition of law referred only to private law.

The same Savigny, as Minister of Justice, asserted that the state could declare its police organs independent of judicial control. This rejection of the Natural Law doctrine of the Enlightenment implied (in the sphere of private law) that law as it had historically developed, was inviolable, whereas in the sphere of state administration the rejection of Natural Law tended to be associated with the scrapping of whatever had been public law in favor of the legally unrestricted power of the police. Illustrative of this trend are the repeated attempts to obstruct the judicial control of punishments imposed by the police. Conditions reverted to what they had been in 1749. The rescript of April 17, 1812 assigned jurisdiction over the lesser criminal cases concerning domestic servants exclusively to the police, and specifically excluded the right of appeal. It is interesting to note that punishments of lower class persons by the police included corporal punishments and that in the rural areas the *Junker* nobility in most cases remained in possession of the patrimonial police authority. Thus, along with the law administered by the courts, there existed another body of law created and applied exclusively by the police. In the succeeding years, the police-state increasingly blocked the legal control of police measures, even in those cases in which the unrestricted power of the police could have been limited by legalistic interpretation of the decree of December 26, 1808.

The end of this evolution was foreshadowed by the first signs of the revolution of 1848. § 6 of the 'Law concerning Admissibility of Legal Appeal from Orders of the Police' of May 11, 1842 provided that a review of police cases by the courts is admissible only if the police order has been declared by a higher administrative body to be in conflict with law. The year 1847 witnessed the introduction of the *Konflikt* (see p. 29) which National-Socialist Germany has adopted from the Restoration — the darkest period of reaction in modern Prussian history.

If one takes into account that the police had also 'positive tasks,' that the control of the police by administrative courts did not exist and judicial control no longer existed, it can easily be seen why the concept of the Dual State emerged at that time. It was perceived that administrative matters were settled, not in accordance with law, but according to considerations of political expediency and the conceptions of *raison d'état*.[468] When Franz Schnabel wrote that 'although the period of the reforms of Stein and Hardenberg sought to reduce the activities of the state and make the citizen self-reliant, it succeeded only in maintaining and renewing the old Police State,' [469] he approximated but did not completely grasp the significance of the period.

The conflict between the liberal individualistic economic legal order on the one hand, and the authoritarian absolute police state on the other, became all the more acute as the economic developments strengthened the bourgeoisie, since the chief aim of the police state of the Restoration was to prevent the political ascent of that very class. The Revolution of 1848 was an attempt to resolve this conflict. It was fought in the name of the Rule of Law under which the courts would reign supreme. The Frankfurter Constitution provided that all violations of law be dealt with by ordinary courts. The entire activity of the state was to be examined by the same types of judicial bodies and by the same legal methods which had been developed in the field of private law.

Would this attempt to permeate the entire legal system with the ideals of legal positivism be more successful than the previous attempt to permeate it with Natural Law? The Rule of Law for which the Revolution of 1848 strove represented another attempt to realize the ideal of the universality of law. But the effort was fruitless against the vitality of the feudal-bureaucratic groups which thought in political rather than in legal terms.

d. THE RECHTSSTAAT

The vigour of these political forces was amply demonstrated by the resistance they offered to the liberal democratic forces after the delay of the feudal forces and the defeat of absolutism. It is especially revealing that, during the conflict between Bismarck and the liberal opposition in the 'sixties, the groups demanding the rule of law and parliamentary system of government never succeeded in dominating the entire structure of the state. By retaining unlimited control of the military, the crown pre-

served the nucleus of political power. Thus, in constitutional monarchy, the control of military and foreign affairs and the power
to declare martial law remained 'Prerogatives of the Crown' independent of and separate from parliamentary constitutionalism
and the Rule of Law.

While to the free trade liberals of the 'sixties the political prerogatives of the Crown appeared as vestiges of a bygone age, the
protectionist National-Liberals of the Wilhelmian era strove to
strengthen the political and military power of the monarch.

At the beginning of the first world war Emil Lederer [470] already clearly saw that, within the dualistic Bismarckian state, the
monarchical power was greater than that of the parliamentary
Rule of Law. In discussing the martial law of the first years of
the war, Lederer stated the proposition that the modern state has
a dual nature. Lederer understood that the armed forces which
were then in charge of the administration of martial law were not
affected by the constitution and that for the modern power state
(*Machtstaat*), the constitution does not exist. 'The last trace of
Natural Law was erased.' [471] The military forces demonstrated
their absolute independence of the civil government and emerged
victorious whenever there was a conflict between the army command and the civil government. To our knowledge, Lederer's
article was the first to depict the co-existence of the Normative
State and the Prerogative State. Lederer's statement of 1915 to the
effect that these conflicts were really clashes between two types
of state was borne out in 1917, when the majority of the Reichstag
crossed swords with the *Vaterlandspartei*. The foes of parliamen-
tarism and democracy were represented both by monarchical
aristocratic groups and by imperialistic sections of the upper
bourgeoisie (Grand-Admiral Tirpitz was their most important
leader.) Both groups wanted to bring the dual nature of the state
to an end. Indeed, it seemed to have been definitely overcome
when the Reich became a parliamentary republic after the revolution of November 1918. The independence of the military prerogative was abolished. The previous victory of the conservative
forces seemed to have been reversed.

¶ The Weimar Republic aimed at organizing and regulating the totality of political activity within a framework of norms. Yet, one of the fatal illusions of the authors of the Weimar Constitution was the belief that the elimination of monarchical power meant the reduction to impotence of those groups which by propagating the idea of the *Machtstaat* (power state) sought only the aggrandizement of their own power. The case of the *Vaterlandspartei* should have furnished an adequate demonstration to the representatives of German democracy that the specifically political functions of the state were no longer an attribute of the Crown and that the Crown had become a façade hiding the real intentions of these power-oriented groups. The revolution of 1918 had permanently terminated the formal dual nature of the structure of the state, but the political influence of those imperialist, plutocratic, and protectionist circles which had been the proponents of *Machtpolitik* since Bismarck's time was not terminated.

The history of the Weimar Republic should serve as evidence that the constitutionally recognized political power of the monarchy was less dangerous to the existence of the Rule of Law than the legal negation of any specific political power whatsoever, as pronounced in the Weimar Constitution. The real political power, in its monarchical disguise, was legitimized by traditions which provided the justification of the monarchy itself. The traditional legitimation of the exercise of power limits not only the source of power but also its scope. When these traditionally legitimized bearers of power had been swept from the stage, groups which were primarily oriented towards power had to choose between the following alternatives: Either (a) to establish *praeter legem* a political power outside the legal order and to revise the constitution with the aim of establishing the authoritarian *Machtstaat*, or (b) to substitute *contra legem* a dictatorial state for the rational constitution of the *Rechtsstaat*. This dictatorship would have to be detached from the traditionalist limits of the monarchy and from the rational limits of the republic.

The attempt to make an authoritarian power-oriented revision of the Weimar Constitution was actually undertaken during Brüning's government. With the juxtaposition of the extraordinary presidential powers (permitted under Art. 48 of the Constitution) and the maintenance of a considerable part of the Rule of Law, there reappeared for a time the familiar picture of the dualistic state but the failure of the Brüning experiment paved the way for the complete annulment of the decision of 1918.

It was no accident that the National-Socialist Party was formed originally from a section of the *Vaterlandspartei*[472] nor is it less significant that the Third Reich endeavors to link itself directly to the Bismarckian era while trying to expunge the intervening fourteen years (1919-33) from German history. In a deeper historical sense, the National-Socialist Party is the continuation of the *Vaterlandspartei*. The latter had been founded by the plutocratic proponents of the power state in order to supplement the military and the economic with political mobilization. The National-Socialist Party, as the agent of political mobilization, has undertaken an economic mobilization (Four Year Plan) which in its turn has served as the indispensable basis of military mobilization.

Hitler's prototypes in German history are Friedrich Wilhelm, the Great Elector, and Hardenberg. Adolf Hitler not only restored the achievement of the Great Elector (*miles perpetuus*) and that of Hardenberg (military conscription); Adolf Hitler's achievement is total mobilization. Like the Great Elector and Hardenberg, he is the creator of a new form of absolutism. Monarchical and bureaucratic absolutism are followed by dictatorial absolutism.

We have indicated the groups which made the compromises which resulted in monarchical and bureaucratic absolutism — in the *miles perpetuus* and in the revival of universal military service. It is now our task to determine which social groups are entered into the formation of the present-day German Dual State.

CHAPTER II

THE ECONOMIC BACKGROUND OF
THE DUAL STATE

THOUGH the author is not an economist it is essential to discuss certain economic aspects of the present German system in order to understand some fundamental problems. Only against an economic background can we understand why it is that the state in Germany is neither completely 'prerogative' nor completely 'normative' but rather 'dual.' We must know the kind and the degree of historical 'necessity' involved in the emergence of the Dual State in Germany. For it is in the Dual State that we shall find the starting point towards a solution of the much debated problem: Is the German economic system capitalistic or non-capitalistic?

Although the German economic system has undergone many modifications it remains predominantly capitalistic. Until now at least the modifications which have been mainly towards *étatisme* and bureaucracy have been of less significance than the persistent capitalistic traits; but they have been sufficiently numerous to justify our considering the present German system as a new type or phase of capitalism. And this new type is so closely interwoven with the Dual State that neither would be possible in its present form without the other.

When the National-Socialists came into power the German economy, as far as its institutional structure was concerned, could be characterized as organized private capitalism with many monopolistic features and much state intervention. Liberal, competitive capitalism was no longer the order of the day; what prevailed was rather 'organized' quasi-monopolistic capitalism with huge concerns and many cartels which were, on the whole, subject to only slight governmental supervision. This system was supported by protective tariffs and government subsidies. Public ownership and partial control was of some significance in certain branches of industry but, in general, this control was restricted to 'overhead industries' (such as transportation and power) and to industries where state participation in ownership or control supported rather than modified the capitalistic system. During the great depression, the power of the government in the economic sphere sharply increased. In the field of banking and in the steel industry, bankruptcies were avoided by governmental intervention. The Reich extended its regulatory power to almost all aspects of economic activity, including wage-levels. As a leading trade-unionist put it, the democratic state and the groups which supported it intended to act as 'doctors at the sick-bed of capitalism.' [473]

In many aspects, the economic policy of the Dual State seems a mere continuation, a somewhat more developed phase, of the 'organized capitalism' of the Weimar period. This similarity becomes particularly clear if both phases are contrasted with 'liberal' capitalism on the one side and any consistent type of socialism on the other. However, the maintenance of these particular institutional features was accompanied by a modification of others. These modifications usually occurred along lines which had been visible for a long time. But they were sufficiently sharp to justify the characterization of National-Socialist economy as a distinct phase. The following pages will attempt to apply this twofold perspective to the institutional aspects of property control and the organization of group interests.

As far as the institution of private property in general and of private ownership in the means of production is concerned, we should note first that it was upheld by National-Socialists both in principle and in fact. Only Jewish property was attacked. One may note that the German Reich increased the sphere of private ownership as compared with 1932 by returning its controlling shares in the steel industry and in some of the biggest banks to

private corporations and owners. The principle of private ownership was upheld even for businesses towards which the National-
Socialist program had shown some degree of antipathy, e.g., department stores and banks. This preservation of the traditional
realm of private property is, however, accompanied by important
changes in specific property *rights*. The right to dispose of private property and the income derived from private property
is being modified in many directions, e.g., by investment control, by control of foreign trade and especially capital export,
by stock exchange control, by limitations on the distribution
of dividends, by decommercialization of a considerable area of
landed property, by control of prices and consumption, and
last but not least, by taxation. As far as the private property
in the means of production is concerned, there is general agreement that the small- and middle-capitalist entrepreneurs have suffered more than the bigger ones. With the intensification of the
re-armament campaign even the larger entrepreneurs and capitalists increased their complaints concerning the restrictions imposed upon private property. All known facts indicate, however,
that even now they enjoy at least a comparative advantage.

Even though private property rights have been somewhat qualified, they still exist and, with them, the differentiation of German
society into propertied and propertyless groups. It is also a significant fact that income from private property is now, on the
whole, much safer than it was before. These individual risks are,
so to speak, pooled into the general political risk necessarily involved in re-armament and war.

As to the importance of public control, it is obvious from the
foregoing summary of rather well-known facts that government
control, already considerable in the Weimar period, has been increased and is still increasing. However, the intensity and thoroughness of the present system of control suggest the presence of
additional causes, such as the requirements of a deliberate control
of business cycles. The present regime is determined to use all its
power to prevent the recurrence of a new depression. For this
determination, it has many reasons, partly economic and partly
political and military. Successful control or, rather, prevention of

depressions requires an especially high degree of government intervention. The justification of an increase in political control is also interwoven with military preparedness. In addition to these factors, we may mention another: in any developed bureaucracy, an inherent tendency exists to widen the sphere of governmental control. Historically this propensity has been checked by the constitution, legislation, parliamentary control and social and political influence of the objects of bureaucratic control. Of course, some specific controls will be required only for a temporary reason and will later be abolished. Furthermore, any intelligent bureaucracy will try to decrease possible resistance by emphasizing the merely temporary character of any imposed hardship even though it has no idea when the emergency will end and even if it knows that the new control, by its very existence and through the vested interests it creates, will tend to become permanent. There are also certain sectors in the bureaucracy which work in closer co-operation with important private interests. These will attempt to encourage and console private interests by pointing to future opportunities for private initiative. But, very probably, all this does not affect the general trend which, throughout the fluctuations in the degree of government control, points toward a permanent increase in the importance of public control in economic matters as well as in others.

As to the methods of central control, only some general remarks are necessary. They vary from direct command to more indirect forms of control. It is important to consider these variations in the degree of control because every step away from direct command implies the preservation of some sphere of private initiative. The most typical case seems to be a combination of a general regulation by means of law and more concrete decisions by an authority endowed with discretionary, but not arbitrary, power. Where necessary, state subsidies are given.

The general rule that the individual enterprises (if not all the individual investors) should earn a fair profit, suggests that some sphere of bargaining power and corresponding initiative has been left to the entrepreneur. There are two major developments in the sphere of private initiative and control. The first is the further growth of monopolistic associations under National-Socialism. Many cartels have been created which strengthen the bigger and more influential members of the cartel. The second development is the further growth of individual 'concerns and trusts' despite the ideological hostility of National-Socialism towards trusts. This development is partly the effect of anti-Semitism, partly the consequence of the increase in profits which were often used to buy up shares of other corporations, and partly due to the fact that the growth of the concern became imperative because of the difficulties of obtaining raw materials.

Finally one should inquire into the role of interest groups. The fundamental fact is, of course, that all labor organizations have been destroyed. Unlike Italy, Germany does not have even state syndicates for workers' organizations, towards which the introduction of compulsory arbitration and the corresponding tendency of the trade unions to become state organs during the Weimar period seemed to form a preliminary step. On the other hand, the interest organizations of other groups have not been destroyed. In industry and commerce not only the various 'estates' but also the many advisory committees and cartel organizations are used to promote the interests of particular groups.

After this description of the 'structural' aspects of the National-Socialist economic system, let us turn to a brief summary of the economic policies which the National-Socialist state pursues.

The chief objectives of National-Socialist economic policy may be summarized under three headings:

1. The establishing of the politico-economic *power* of the National-Socialist state.

2. The extension of employment and production.

3. The salvation and promotion of two main sectors of German economy: the 'heavy' industries and the grain-growers of the large East-German agricultural estates. Both of those were threatened with ruin by the great depression and — in spite of all their political influence — they were thought to be in political danger during the last phase of the Weimar Republic.

For an understanding of National-Socialist economic policy, it seems indispensable first to deal with each problem separately, although it will be found later that all three converge on and support each other.

1. Power as the aim of economic policy means the subjugation of all 'economic' policies to considerations of political necessity or expediency. In the present world situation, striving for an increase in power is identical with striving for economic nationalism and imperialism. This force always works both externally and internally. Characteristically, force applied internally was considered and justified as a means of increasing the strength of the group in its external relations. The main task became that of organizing the economic system as an instrument for the increase and preservation of the power of the state and of the groups which aspired to greater power in which this power has been invested and centralized. Correspondingly the direction of economic affairs had to aim chiefly at increasing the power of the state for protective and expansionist purposes even when such a policy involved considerable hardship for many producers and consumer groups.

The pursuit of the second and third policies listed above, also served the first and most important objective. The solution of the problem of unemployment and of the special slump in the heavy industry and in eastern agriculture helped greatly to strengthen the power of the regime in Germany. The expansion of production — particularly of foodstuffs and steel — strengthened the power of the regime externally. This aspect of the German economic system appeared increasingly in the foreground and, in its later phases, overshadowed all other considerations. Even in periods of 'peace,' the German economy was a war economy.

This supreme aim of making the German state as powerful as possible in a short time imposed several conditions upon the concrete policies to be pursued and upon the methods to be applied. In the light of the guiding objective, every waste of possibly employable resources is a failure from the point of view of providing the necessary war equipment. Resources must be exploited to an abnormally high degree — even if political pressure is necessary.

For an effective re-armament program not only a rapid increase in production, but also a permanently high level of production, was necessary. If for no other reasons than simply for military 'preparedness' any cyclical reaction or depression had to be prevented. The danger of a reaction is increased, however, by the very intensity of the 'recovery' brought about by public spending. Therefore a high degree of direct and indirect control is required. Such a degree of control has been more easily accepted in the German economic system than in most other countries since German capitalism was, from its inception, more closely connected with the state than most other capitalisms.

In addition to the two points discussed thus far — i.e., full and stable use of all resources — there is a third implication of extreme importance: economic preparation for expansionist power politics requires a definite direction of the economic process in reference to what should be produced and consumed. Two consequences may be distinguished, namely: (a) foreign trade, and (b) internal aspects.

a. Since Bismarck's famous change of policy in 1878, German capitalism has been more tied up with protectionism than the capitalism of any other country. Even in the Weimar period (since 1925) protectionist interests were supreme. Even in the time of Locarno and Geneva the most important argument behind the revival of German economic nationalism was the 'war' argument coupled with the fear that any serious attack upon the national branches of German economy (western heavy industries and eastern big estates) would completely disturb the social, political and economic structure of Germany. In the great depression, increased protectionism and other methods of strangling world trade were practiced in Germany in the same fashion as in every other country. With the arrival of Hitler, nationalistic protectionism or 'autarchy' was bound to increase sharply. The new regime favored those economic groups which were most important from a 'national' point of view: the steel and iron industry and the grain producing sector of German agriculture.

In the field of foreign economic policy the re-armament program demanded a sharp increase in the traditional protectionist policies and a combination of two somewhat antagonistic tendencies: as much autarchy as possible and, at the same time, the importation of raw materials vital for re-armament. This situation (rendered even more difficult by the lack of gold and foreign exchange) compelled the National-Socialist government to use and expand to an unheard degree all means of controlling imports which had been introduced by the Brüning government in 1931. This type of control proved to be perhaps the most outstanding encroachment upon the freedom of the enterprises. This control of imports was accompanied by many economic and political attempts to expand and redirect exports in order that new markets might be opened in countries which were considered especially important from the point of view of military and economic expansion.

b. In the field of internal economic policy, two main facts stand out:

1. The increase of investment was much greater than the total increase in production of consumers' goods.

2. In the sphere of consumption, the share of the state rose strongly as compared with the share allotted to private consumers for private purposes.

Taking 1928=100, the index of total industrial production rose from 54 in 1932 to 132,7 in the first quarter of 1939. The index for the production of all consumers' goods rose from 74 in 1932 to 118,1 in 1938; the index for the production of investment goods from 35,4 in 1932 to 140,5 in the first quarter of 1939. The production of consumers' goods rose by about 60 per cent, the production of investment goods by about 260 per cent.[474] The fact that in a recovery period investments should expand at a higher rate than consumption is in itself nothing unusual. However, there are four closely interrelated features of the German expansion which distinguish it from other expansions.

First, total production expanded more than one could have expected under normal conditions. This high degree of total expansion is all the more remarkable in view of the overcapacities in many industries which had developed during the rationalization period before 1929. The cause of this high degree of expansion after 1932 lies, of course, in the high rate of public investment financed by credit expansion.

A second particular feature of the Hitler prosperity was the degree to which investment, as compared with consumption, was expanded. This was certainly made possible by the fact that at the beginning of the process there existed huge unused productive capacities in these investment industries. But those capacities could be used only if some *new* fields of investment were opened up or created. This was done precisely by the re-armament program with its cumulatively increasing pace. However, ordinarily the expansion of the investment good's industries is checked by the expansion of the wage-earning with its consequent expenditure on consumers' goods and increase in interest rates. This reaction is highly undesirable from the point of view of any policy which is interested in the prevention of slump or even of a slowing down in the rate of expansion. The Hitler regime had to expect the emergence of such a situation when it embarked upon a policy of rapid expansion for the purpose of re-armament. Therefore especially strong checks upon the expansion of consumption had to be introduced. This became the major problem of German economic policy and almost all repressive and directive control measures in Germany served primarily this one purpose: to restrict consumption as far as possible and to put as many productive resources as possible in the service of war preparations. This was one of the major functions of the control of imports, of investments, of prices, of capital markets and interest rates, and finally of the most important means of all: the keeping down of the wage rates. On the whole, the policy of keeping down consumption was highly successful, although the intentions of the government could not be realized completely. There were important increases in prices, if only because of deteriorations in quality. It was imperative for the whole policy of investment expansion to prevent any considerable increase of nominal wage rates beyond their depression level. This wage policy implied a tremendous pressure upon the working class. Hitler would not have been able to carry through his policy with a working class whose economic organizations were still functioning. The fact that Hitler did not copy Mussolini at this particular point cannot be explained by the higher stage of development of the German labor organization in general; it must be explained by an examination of the implications of the whole re-armament and investment policy with respect to wage conditions.

A third special feature of the 'Hitler recovery' is the persistence of, and increase in, the proportion of public investment to total investment. In early Hitler Germany, the main function of public investment was thought to consist in 'pump-priming,' that is: in the stimulation of private investment (through an increase in total national income) until private investment could once more stand on its own feet. In present-day Germany, however, the role of public investment has proved to be quite different. When German economy approached the point of full employment, public and private investment clearly became rivals. But the Hitler government has maintained public investment at its very high level through its re-armament policy. As a consequence, restriction of private investment was added to the restriction of private consumption. Practically, only such private investments were permitted which directly or indirectly served the re-armament program.

There is one further feature of the German rearmament 'boom' closely related to the price and wage policies discussed above: though a large part of the public investments were financed out of additional credit there have been no significant indications of real inflation in Germany even during the stage of full employment. This can be explained chiefly by the deliberate policy of keeping prices down and the policy of maintaining nominal wage rates. In addition, the taxing of a part of the profits has time and again prevented the appearance of additional purchasing power on less controlled markets which would normally tend to push prices upward. The short time in which the Hitler regime has attempted to fulfil the tasks of re-armament was obviously qualified by one important limitation: it had to be performed without inflation. The German people, however, were forced to pay rather heavily for this protection against inflation: they had to submit to a whole set of controls which advanced far into the realm of production, consumption and other traditional forms of freedom like the freedom of movement and the freedom of occupational choice.

As compared to the situation at the beginning of the Hitler regime, most of those who had been employed at that time were faced with complete economic loss. Those who had been out of work gained in the absolute sense, but lost relatively in comparison with what would have been their lot under other regimes. This relative loss was subjectively balanced or overcompensated by the feeling of greater 'security.' Objectively speaking, the relative loss was aggravated by the increasing probability that this kind of re-armament policy would lead to war.

Most of these considerations hold true also for the propertied classes. The qualifications on property rights and on the freedom of enterprise were matched by a considerable increase in property incomes and in profits. The simple fact that their property rights and their social position had been saved at all was regarded as a positive value which was not to be outweighed by the sacrifices which they had to make, particularly in the field of politics.

This consideration leads to a last implication of the Hitler policy of rearmament. If the supreme task consists in using all available resources for the sake of war preparation in a minimum time, then major experiments in social reforms are out of the question. Such reforms, in the direction of socialism for example, require time and energy and would, for a rather long period, slow down total output. The decision to protect the institution of private property as the basis of the existing social order was not only politically necessary in view of the preferences of the supporters of the party, but was also an unavoidable consequence of the rearmament policy.

2. We must now consider the other possible major objective of National-Socialist economic policy: re-employment of the unemployed at all costs and the salvation of those politically and economically powerful but (before 1932) seriously threatened sectors of the German economy mentioned above, i.e. western heavy industry and eastern grain-producing estates.

First, to take the objective of re-employment, one may argue that in 1933 at least this was the most important, the almost only visible and the only professed aim of National-Socialist policy. This objective was emphasized in the beginning, because the other two objectives were either not useful for propaganda or not as yet ripe for realization. In order to stimulate re-employment, the Hitler government used many devices already utilized by former governments and put the pressure of the party machine behind this campaign. The first period was one of mere makeshift. For a time this system was reasonably successful, but when it reached its limit, the Hitler regime was ready to give the general program of re-employment a specific object: re-armament. From that time on, the aim of re-employment becomes practically indentical with the objective of war preparation. Under the conditions prevailing in Germany, the great difficulties of the program of re-employment pure and simple would have led the existing system in the direction of economic and political nationalism. After a period of makeshifts it would have become imperative either to wait until world economy recovered — a solution which from a political and psychological viewpoint was unbearable — or to organize all efforts of re-employment in some 'plan.' As soon as the regime decided to make a more systematic and co-ordinated attack upon the problem of unemployment, it became indispensable to give a clear direction to the 'plan': re-employment for what? Because of the hardship implicit in such a policy, the main objective had to be popular. The easiest way out was a nationalist policy. This choice was supported by the very implications of an independent policy of recovery itself.

In order to make the program for re-employment popular it was necessary only to point to the unused material resources which had to be re-employed as well as the unemployed workers. Unemployment of both men and equipment was especially serious in the heavy industries. Did not these industries and their allies, the large scale farms, utilize the resources of the 'national soil'? Thus the program of re-employment became dovetailed not only with re-armament but also with the salvation of those sectors of German economy which had been dominant for so many decades.

3. Within the scope of this chapter it is neither possible nor necessary to inquire whether the National-Socialist leaders deliberately shaped their economic policies to save eastern grain-producing agriculture and the coal, iron and steel industries in the west. There are many people who believe that National-Socialism is, so to speak, nothing but the house-servant of German monopoly capitalism. They point to the important role which representatives of both groups played in the decisive days which brought Hitler to power and to the benefits which these sectors of the nation received from the National-Socialist government. These oversimplified theories tend quite unnecessarily to discredit the economic interpretation of fascism. Such an interpretation should be formulated in terms of far more minute and deeper reaching categories.

A quotation from Schumpeter's paper '*Zur Soziologie der Imperialismen*,' seems especially pertinent to a description of the relationship between National-Socialism and private capitalism or between the politics and economics of the present German order.

'Nationalism and militarism are not created by capitalism. They become, however, capitalized and, finally they take their best strength out of capitalism. Capitalism is gradually drawing nationalism and militarism into its own circles, thereby maintaining and nourishing them. They again influence and modify capitalism.' [475]

The industrialists in the west and the landlords in the east supported Hitler in the hope that they would be able to remain masters, to use Hitler for their purposes: if necessary, to get rid of him and of his movement. It is true that those same groups received certain special favors from the government, that, thanks to the policy of the government, they actually were enabled to reap considerable profits and gains in capital values and to strengthen their position in the leading concerns. People who emphasize these benefits should not entirely overlook the price which had to be paid for them. At best, the former masters must now share power with the *élite* of the party and with the bureaucracy of the state and party. Their prosperity and control rights have also been considerably qualified. Actually they are not free

to change the National-Socialist leadership and they depend mainly on the chance that this leadership will not be interested in re-
moving them from their economic and social positions.

It has been shown by many theoretical and empirical investigations that 'monopoly capitalism' on the one side and the growth
of economic nationalism and imperialism on the other are closely
interrelated. Each of these phenomena reinforces the other.

The present National-Socialist government added many monopolistic organizations to those which had previously been created
and, so to speak, inherited from them the same type of foreign
policy they had always promoted, sharp nationalism and imperialism. With all this, however, the question is still open whether the
National-Socialist regime pursued its policies along the patterns
worked out by monopolistic interests or by continuous effects
of 'monopoly situations,' i.e., whether the favors given to the more
monopolistic sectors of the German economy are a by-product
of National-Socialist policy more than of its deliberate main objectives. Although the present author is inclined to attach considerable importance to the salvation of the mentioned capitalistic
interests in the whole complex of National-Socialist objectives, it
seems best to say that the National-Socialists have consistently
acted *as if* the protection of monopolistic interests and the salvation of the most endangered sectors of the German economy were
the most important objectives of their economic policy. It can
then be left for further investigation, to determine how much
historical truth is contained in the words 'as if.'

We may now sum up the result of our analysis of the present
German economic order:

1. Although the rights of the owners of private property have
been limited, the kinds and the extent of private property modified, and state control increased, the fundamental institutions of
capitalism have not been abolished.

2. All private activities, through the medium of state controls,
have been put to the service of political, chiefly military, expansion.

3. The total public investment is closely correlated with the
wage policy of the regime, which is based on the destruction of
all labor organizations.

4. There still exist: capitalistic enterprises, markets in which these enterprises sell and buy, markets for property titles, private credit transactions and all kinds of accompanying disputes over claims and obligations.

5. The system of private economic activities is surrounded, supported and limited by a vastly increased public bureaucracy which acts partly on the basis of generally clear, circumscribed laws and partly on the basis of more or less wide discretionary powers with the reservation that each matter may be regulated arbitrarily.

We must prove not only that a close relationship exists between political and economic events, but also that it exists between the economic and political structure. The problem to be dealt with is this: what is the precise function of the Normative State and what are the functions of the Prerogative State in the economic sphere? Which aspects of the political and economic order correspond with each other?

The Normative State functions clearly as the legal frame-work for private property, market activities of the individual business units, all other kinds of contractual relations, and for the regulations of the control relations between government and business. Even if the rules of the game are changed by the lawmaker, some are indispensable in order to secure a minimum of predictability of the probable consequences of given economic decisions. In order to avoid misunderstandings, it is important to note that the activities of the bureaucracy which interfere with the 'free enterprise system' are also regulated by the Normative State, even though its interference greatly reduces former spheres of freedom. To that extent, legal ways of defining and protecting individual rights against other members of the economy and against the encroachment of state authorities are still open and used.

Although the Normative State retains some powers in spheres that are not strictly economic, the field of economics remains the most important domain of the qualified 'Rule of Law' in present-day Germany. Not only private business, but also public enterprises are regulated and protected by the Normative State. The underlying fact is the necessity for decentralization of certain functions in any large-scale society with advanced technology.

This decentralization requires a stable and yet flexible framework of rules. In present-day Germany, this decentralization of socially vital functions is effected through a complex of institutions called private property, contract and private enterprise. Private business is protected by the Normative State even under National-Socialism because it happens to be accepted as the main form of decentralization of social economic functions.

When we suggest that the Normative State in the Third Reich is closely related to the existing (although modified) private property and enterprise system, we do so chiefly to indicate the striking difference between the treatment of property and labor interests. It is in the field of labor that the Prerogative State has advanced into the sphere of economic affairs, through the destruction of all genuine labor organizations and through the constant persecution of all former and all potential new labor leaders as 'enemies of the state.'

If our analysis of the relations between the world of business and the Normative State is correct, then it follows, that the Prerogative State cannot be a direct and positively controlling power, but rather a limiting and indirectly supporting power.

1. After the fundamental decision in favor of radical nationalism was made in 1933, this daring program required safeguards against political disturbances and premature interruptions. Such a guarantee was indispensable in view of the many sacrifices and pressures which this policy was to impose on almost all classes and especially on the working and lower middle classes. The activities of the agencies of the Prerogative State were therefore prerequisite to the continuous execution of the economic program of the government.

2. Because of the magnitude and intensity of the effort required of German society and because open class struggles arising from the continuance of relatively free class organizations would impair the efficiency of the regime, through waste of energy and deadlocks, the National-Socialists demanded the suppression at least of open class struggles.

3. The Prerogative State is also important to the success of the economic policies of the government because it can use direct

threats to enforce the more severe regulations of the Normative State. Because these threats cannot be calculated or predicted the Prerogative State is far more powerful than the Normative State: in fact the mere potentiality of such threats is, in doubtful cases, sufficient to keep men on the safe side, even though their too frequent use may upset the whole economic process. In this way the Prerogative State is able to influence the behavior of capitalists and enterprisers although they are nominally not only controlled but also protected by the Normative State.

The best analysis of the National-Socialist revolution which could be offered on the basis of the economic interpretation of history has been made before the *Reichstag* on May 21, 1935 by Adolf Hitler himself:

'In order to assure the functioning of the national economy it became necessary to arrest the movement of wages and prices. It was also necessary to stop all interferences which are not in accord with the higher interests of our national economy, i.e., it was imperative to eliminate all class organizations which pursued their own policies with regard to wages and prices. The destruction of the class-struggle organizations of employers as well as of employees required the analogous elimination of those political parties which were financed and supported by those interest groups. This process, in its turn, caused the introduction of a new constructive and effective "living constitution" and the refoundation of Reich and State.' [476]

CHAPTER III

THE SOCIOLOGY OF THE DUAL STATE

1. 'PLANT-COMMUNITY' AND 'SHOP TROOP'

ANY sociological analysis which involves the use of the concept of 'community' must make use of the work of Ferdinand Toennies.[477] The distinction between 'community' and 'society' is not primarily a distinction between two types of relationships. It is rather a distinction between structural types, the emergence, development and decline of which are bound to premises which can be definitely determined.[478] In spite of his own personal predilection for the community, which derives its coherence from kinship and traditional ties (as it still does in the village community), Toennies had no illusions about the course which Western civilization is traversing: from community to society.

Alfred von Martin raised a very significant question therefore when he asked 'whether and to what extent the re-establishment of a communal form of social organization is possible today.'[479] Von Martin uses sharp words against those for whom the longing for 'community' is nothing but romantic yearning. In this connection he cites Werner Sombart's perverse book on German Socialism.[480]

In comparison with the common mass of National-Socialist glorifications of the *Gemeinschaft*, Sombart's book has at least the virtue that in addition to wishing to erase the two hellish centuries which have disordered the world since the beginning of the Industrial Revolution, and to return to the conditions of 1750, he also has the courage to call for the restoration of the economic conditions which would make a communal form of organization possible. It is more important to recognize Sombart's consistency than to ridicule it. The vision of a communal organization established after certain necessary economic conditions have been created, is, at any rate, much less fantastic than the promotion of further industrialization while hoping for the re-establishment of the pre-capitalistic community.

It should not be forgotten that National-Socialism in its early stages contained elements who were interested in constructing the economic prerequisites for the existence of community. Those tendencies which were directed at the strengthening of the lower middle-classes, the demands for the abolition of department stores, the dissolution of the consumers' co-operatives and the elimination of trusts, as well as the anti-rationalization-laws of 1933, were representative of this aspect of the National-Socialist Program. But this section of the National-Socialist Program has long since been discarded. The National-Socialists who came to power as a result of middle class opposition to socialism are sacrificing to their aspiration of a new German empire the very substance of their *raison d'être*.[481]

Under the Four Year Plans, the industrialization of Germany, the modernization of its mills and factories, and the accumulation of capital have made rapid strides. Unwittingly, National-Socialism has corroborated Ferdinand Toennies' proposition that the trend from community to society cannot be stayed. This is especially true in the economic field.

The only German sociological study which has dealt with this problem — Heinz Marr's *Die Massenwelt im Kampf um ihre Form*[482]— is now of interest only for the history of National-Socialist ideologies, for Marr contended that labor problems were no longer of central importance in Germany. He stated that they had been replaced — by the problems involved in the situation of the peasant and small craftsman. Marr wrote under the inspiration of a kind of peasant socialism and all his expectations were built on the assumption that 'urban industrial society, though still comprising by far the larger part of the population, was steadily decreasing in relative importance.'[483] But the years 1934-9 have amply shown the fallacies in Marr's assumption. Since National-Socialism has associated its destiny with the remilitarization of the German economy, all idyllic schemes built around peasants and craftsmen have become impossible of realization. Gigantic factories are so to speak springing out of the ground, armies of specialized laborers are feverishly busy ten and more hours a day and, at least since 1935, the army demanded as a military necessity that industry be so mechanized that women and children would be able to replace skilled workers needed for the armed forces. Thus National-Socialism has not retraced the path of the Industrial Revolution of the nineteenth century. It has rather sought to accelerate it.

Is the type of rationalized, impersonal and complex system necessitated by industrialization compatible with a 'communal' ideology? And what are the causes and consequences of this experiment which National-Socialism has announced itself ready to carry out?

The National-Socialists are no academic theorists. In order to prove the correctness of their communal ideology, they point to their success. They claim that they have created new communal forms during their struggle for power. For them the SA (Storm Troopers) and the SS (Blackshirts), the Labor Service and the Hitler Youth are great manifestations of the new communal ideology. The National-Socialists claim to have proved (and this is one of their supreme dogmas) that a 'communal' ideology and a 'communal' social structure can be had if the real will to have it exists. If this was possible in the case of the SA, the SS and the HJ (Hitler Youth) why should it not also be possible outside of and beyond such political organizations? Thus the National-Socialists have tried to reorganize non-political groups — the family, the farm, the factory, the apartment house, the business and craftsmen groups along the lines of the militant political organizations.

Once the spirit of the SA has penetrated the workshops and factories with a 'communal sense,' the aims of National-Socialism will have been achieved. Every social group will then become a community and constitute as such a source of thinking according to the concrete theory of order. The above ideas form the nucleus of the social theory of National-Socialism. The most important academic interpreter of this theory of the 'totalitarian community,' designed after the model of the political formations, is Professor Reinhard Hoehn of the University of Berlin. This National-Socialist attitude is very prominent in the discussion between Koellreutter, Professor of Constitutional Law at the University of Munich, and Hoehn, Professor of Political Science at the University of Berlin. Koellreutter had claimed that it is the task of law to give a certain degree of calculability to acts of the state so that the people may have a certain degree of legal security. To this view, Hoehn responds that 'this problem does not exist for a communally oriented point of view.' [484]

In this connection the problem of ideology becomes particularly acute. If it is true that the processes of rationalization and impersonalization have been accelerated, what then is the significance of the diffusion of this communally oriented outlook? This apparent contradiction between the relationship involved in economic life and the National-Socialist *Weltanschauung* is dissolved once we grasp the falsity of the communally oriented ideology. Even if the entire population had become National-Socialist, the attitudes of the members of the various social groups (the workers of a factory, the inhabitants of an apartment-house, the people of a farm etc.) would not necessarily be communally oriented, and, as will be demonstrated, this was least so in those groups most exposed to the 'SA spirit.'

The extension of the communally oriented attitudes from the realm of politics to the field of non-political relations has been expressed by National-Socialist theorists in this syllogism: SA attitudes are communally oriented attitudes, attitudes of the factory groups are identical with SA attitudes, hence attitudes of factory groups are communally oriented.

If we examine the major premise the fallacy will immediately be obvious. We are not interested here in the correctness or falsity of National-Socialism's interpretation of its own history, but rather in the validity of the proposition that the attitudes of Storm Troopers are communally oriented. For, even if the whole legend of the period of struggle were actually true, there could still be no doubt that during its classical phase the SA was not a *Gemein-*

schaft (community) as modern sociologists understand the term. It formed rather, during the period of the 'struggle for power,' what might be called a 'fraternity' (*Bund*).

In one of the best sociological analyses by a National-Socialist, Andreas Pfenning's 'Gemeinschaft und Staatswissenschaft,' the term 'community' is used for the National-Socialist military associations; but when he characterizes these groups with the following words we see that he has something different in mind: 'The basic experience was not idealistic, it was not the will to fight for an ideal, for an idea which presides with eternal validity over the activities of mankind. The SA did not emerge in the struggle for an ideal, the True, the Good and the Beautiful. This basic experience came into existence in the course of the struggle.' [485] Reinhard Hoehn has a similar concept when he writes that 'the SA is not defined by a common set of beliefs.' [486]

These negative criteria justify our designation of the National-Socialist battle formations as fraternities (*Bünde*). The sociological category of the *Bund* was first developed by Hermann Schmalenbach. This notion has since been employed by numerous German sociologists, e.g. von Martin, Marr and Behrendt.

Hermann Schmalenbach's investigations [487] of the *Bund*, which are indispensable to the scientific analysis of National-Socialism, are somewhat influenced by Max Weber's theory of domination, especially by his distinctions between rational, traditional, and charismatic domination. Schmalenbach presents his own work as an extension of Toennies' treatment of community and society, and in the course of his discussion it becomes clear that the counterpart of community in the power sphere is what Weber called 'traditional domination,' while the counterpart of rationalized impersonal society is Max Weber's 'rational domination.' From this, Schmalenbach proceeded to the conclusion that the counterpart of charismatic domination is the 'fraternity' (*Bund*).

The followers of a charismatic leader (*Führer*) do not constitute a community (*Gemeinschaft*) but rather a fraternity (*Bund*). They are associated not on the basis of traditionally valid norms and habitual patterns of conduct but rather on the basis of common emotional experiences. The individual is born into the community but he enters the fraternity on his own decision. The community aims at the preservation of traditional values, while a fraternity unites those individuals who have been freed from all traditional norms. The community exists even when the individual member is not fully conscious of his membership in the group, but membership in the fraternity involves an act of self-conscious decision. The community lives by traditional values and transmits them to the next generation. The *Bund*, made up of the organized followers of a charismatic leader, is (like charism itself) transitory, and unstable. The community is a stable and continuous formation. Like charism, the fraternity stands in contrast to the matter-of-fact routines of daily life. As soon as the authority of the charismatic leader becomes routinized and continuous, the 'fraternity' ceases to be a fraternity. Routinization leads to the dissolution of the fraternity or to its transformation, either into society or community.

Friedrich Schiller's *Die Räuber* provides a classical description of the 'fraternity.' Around Karl Moor, the leader, whose career has been disrupted, equally uprooted comrades assemble in order to transform the world. But at bottom, they do not want a revolution in the structure of society. They do not attack the present order; rather they complain that other people and not they are in power within this order. They desire only the supplanting of the ruling *élite* by a new *élite* formed from their fraternity. Unfavorable circumstances compelled Karl Moor's fraternity to take refuge in the Bohemian forests and there to lead the life of robbers. Under more favorable circumstances, Moor would have attained political dominance; his followers would have become the new *élite*, divided up the spoils, but would have left the structure of society unchanged. The successful charismatic revolution is the ideal type of the *circulation des élites*.

Shortly after their accession to power, the National-Socialists made a genuine attempt to reorganize the factories in accordance with the model of the Storm Troops. By roll-calls, daily flag ceremonies and evenings of comradely entertainment, they attempted to engender the spirit of the SA in the factories. The experiment failed, however, after a short time. Werner Mansfeld,

the National-Socialist expert on labor law, has formulated the
effect of this transplanting of the fraternity ideology into other
social groups, affirming that 'even if no reference had been made
to his roll as leader, the dominant position of the employer would
legally have been the same.' [488] Heinz Marr, though an enthusiastic National-Socialist, is a sufficiently good sociologist to see the
serious difficulties to be overcome in any reconstruction of social
groups in order to bring them closer to the spirit of National-
Socialist battle formations. 'The fraternity may make very intense impressions on its members, but these impressions do not
last in their original forms.' And he continues 'purely economic
and legal relationships are incompatible with fraternity attitudes.' [489] But Marr touches only the real problem as to whether
it would be possible to implant communally oriented attitudes in
non-communal groups. 'One quickly realizes,' he says, 'how much
more difficult it is to transplant the attitudes of the fraternity
which now prevail in the political sphere of the state into the
sphere of business and particularly into big enterprises.' [490]

After the failure of the most diverse experiments, such as the
establishment and dissolution of the NSBO (*Nationalsozialistische
Betriebszellen-Organisation*), the National-Socialists realized that
their object could not be achieved in the plants. Hence, at present, they are trying a new mode of attack: the *Werkscharen*
(Shop Troops). In 1938 Dr. Ley, the leader of the German Labor
Front, remarked that 'without a firmly organized Shop Troop . . .
the factory community would ultimately degenerate into a yellow trade union.' [491] Thus Dr. Ley attests the fact that the destruction of the labor unions, the elimination of the factory council
and the violent suppression of all manifestations of proletarian
class consciousness had led exactly to the result which the foes of
National-Socialism always predicted: the yellow trade union. Having admitted failure, National-Socialism has adopted a new means
of transforming private capitalistic enterprises into 'communities'
— the Shop Troop. 'It is,' says Dr. Ley, 'the soldierlike nucleus of
the factory community which obeys the *Führer* blindly. Its mot-
to is: the Leader is always right.' [492] Thus the project to organize
the whole factory as a fraternity and then to call it a community

has been dropped. Instead the vanguard within the factory is formed to represent a fraternity. Dr. Ley left nothing unsaid when he outlined the tasks of the Shop Troops: 'Should Germany once more have to undergo a severe trial of strength and should this process lead to serious disturbances in the factories as it did during the last war . . . every factory must be organized so that it will itself be able to take the measures necessary for the creation of order.' [493] The 'soldierlike nucleus of the factory community' is intended to suppress any independent expression of the workers' demands and to 'create order.' Shop Troops are organizations for the suppression of strikes, but, says Dr. Ley, 'the Shop Troop must be prevented by all means from becoming — if not at present, then perhaps in fifty or a hundred years — a class-troop.' [494] Dr. Ley expressly rejects the possibility of organizing the Shop Troops of the different enterprises into large associations. On the contrary, 'the factory is the center of the Shop Troop. Hence the Shop Troops cannot constitute a hierarchical organization embracing all the Shop Troops in a city, or a district, or in the Reich as a whole.' [495]

In his description of the Shop Troops Dr. Ley stresses the differences between them and the other quasi-military organizations of the SA and SS. This structure of the Shop Troops differs also from those of the estate organization of the non-manual occupations. In the various entrepreneurial and professional groups, no objections have been raised against organizations transcending local boundaries. But Dr. Ley and the National-Socialist leadership have deliberately sought to prevent such translocal organization of the Shop Troops in order to avoid the danger of distracting these groups whose class homogeneity is pronounced from their proper tasks. The Shop Troops recruit a small group from within the whole force of the plant to counteract any defections on the part of the rest of the working force. Without this institution, Dr. Ley believes that the factories would remain a potential source of disorder. And the dangers would only be re-introduced if translocal organization of the Shop Troops were allowed. Thus all that Dr. Ley has done is to confer the honorable title of community on a strike-breaking agency. The Shop Troops are nothing but a factory police agency appropriating certain fraternal characteristics and veiled by the community ideology.

Meanwhile, even the National-Socialist Storm Troops, which had been genuine fraternities, continue to lose their fraternal character and become bureaucratized and rationalized. This evolution became most clear in the case of the SS, which had been transformed into a real police force. The unstable character of the fraternity is responsible for the continual failures of the efforts to impose fraternal character on rationalized social and economic structures. The incompatibility between the emotional and unspecific character of fraternal attitudes and the sober necessities of modern economic enterprise constitutes a further obstacle to the realization of the National-Socialist program.

These theoretical considerations are corroborated by experience. The social and economic organizations of the Third Reich have remained what they were before Hitler's seizure of power: rationalized and co-ordinated entities, governed by calculations of gain and loss. That these social structures are called 'communities' and that in unimportant matters concessions are made to communally oriented attitudes, changes nothing. They serve only to veil the true character of these structures and to reinforce the existing system of domination.

Mansfeld, giving the most explicit form to this aspect of National-Socialism, says: 'The faithfulness of the ethnic comrades (*Volksgenossen*) to the Leader and of the Leader to the ethnic comrades must not be confused with material considerations.' [496] The pseudo-'community' of present-day Germany is nothing but the capitalistic system of production incidentally modified, though fundamentally the same as before. The communally oriented concrete theory of order is nothing but the new legitimation of this capitalistic legal order. Romantic enthusiasm for the 'community' should not prevent our seeing the highly unromantic re-inforcement of certain aspects of modern capitalism.

'The political economist applies the conceptions of law and property of the pre-capitalistic era to this completed world of capital, and, the more the facts are at variance with his ideology, all the more anxious is his zeal and all the greater his function.' [497]

Pfenning has stated with unusual directness that the function of all Fascist undertakings is 'to galvanize with the aid of a strong state the tradition of bourgeois-capitalistic class society and to preserve this order by means of state interference at those points where difficulties arise.' [498] Pfenning's view is by no means rare in the National-Socialist literature. Neese goes so far as to infer a general law from this common tendency of all Fascist revolutions by saying that 'today every revolutionary movement must be concerned with preserving the integrity of the economic system.' [499] Theoretically competent National-Socialists are well aware of the social character of Fascism; they do not deny that it is the political structure appropriate to the imperialistic phase of capitalism. Pfenning remarks: 'Community is a cleverly designed necessity for the maintenance of certain social relationships.' [500] According to him, the German community, which is constituted by 'blood' and not by any rational concept has, thanks to its racial basis, a 'natural system of ranks' the nature of which entitles it to acceptance.

2. Ethnic Community and Armament Boom

The refutation of the opinion that certain economic and social structures have been permeated with communally oriented attitudes does not settle this question as to the extent to which National-Socialism has succeeded in fusing the German people into an ethnic community (*Volksgemeinschaft*).

At this point, we should recall what we said earlier about one of the primary conditions for the triumph of National-Socialism, namely, the successful refutation of utopian pacifism which the German parties of the Left espoused after the war. National-Socialists challenged the faith in salvation through international order as represented by the rational League of Nations and proposed instead the dogma that the resurrection of the Fatherland could be attained only by the union of all Germans against the common enemy. The idea of the ethnic community undoubtedly arose out of the defeat in the last war, and the subsequent misery, and out of the conscious opposition to foreign powers.

This connection between belief in an external threat and the awakening of domestic solidarity is not a chance phenomenon. 'Only in cases of a common danger can communal action be expected with some degree of probability.' [501] At the same time it should be remembered that 'no community is so strong as to be indissoluble.' [502] It is obvious that if belief in external threats is the principal source of communally oriented attitudes, internal cleavages will increase as this belief diminishes.

Communally oriented attitudes are accorded the status of absolute values in National-Socialist Germany. The National-Socialist Party views the preservation of these values as its chief task. However, if devotion to the community is immediately dependent on the magnitude of an actual or imagined threat, it is possible to explain the paradox which we will call the 'political scissors' of National-Socialism, i.e., the more successful the foreign policy of National-Socialism, the greater the contradiction between the National-Socialistic domestic policy and the international position of Germany.

If the ethnic community has an absolute value in itself, then it is dependent upon the existence of an enemy. If communally oriented attitudes are intensified by the existence of an actual or imagined enemy, then the preservation of the ethnic community is favored by the existence of an enemy whose hostility endures as long as the ethnic community itself. It does not matter whether this enemy is real or imaginary. Nor is it of much importance who the enemy is. The mere fact that an enemy exists is the important point. The continuous existence of an enemy is a substitute for rational goal.[503] 'War is the source of everything. The form of the state as a whole is determined by the nature of the total war . . . the total war, however, obtains its meaning from the total enemy.' [504]

Adolf Hitler expressed the same idea at the Nürnberg Party Congress in September 1935: 'Driven by savage impulses, peoples and races fight without knowing the objectives for which they fight.'[505] An editorial of the *Völkische Beobachter* of December 21, 1931 stated, in like vein:

'The *Rechtsstaat* (Rule of Law State) is the organization which unifies all the energies of the ethnical group for the protection of its right, both domestically and in the world at large. . . . This can only be accomplished by the concentrated force of the people as a whole, just as only concentrated explosives were able to stop the tanks which attacked the front line. This organized application of the concentrated energies of the people for the protection of its life represents our conception of the *Rechtsstaat*.'

It may be noted that it was not the author of this book who exhumed this editorial. The Secretary of the Ministry of Justice Freissler — the author of this article — thought it good enough to be reproduced in the *Handwörterbuch der Rechtswissenschaft*.[506] The fact that the opinion of a politically motivated lawyer during the period of the struggle for power has become the official opinion of a high state official and has been incorporated into the chief publication of National-Socialist legal theory is evidence enough that even the best-trained National-Socialist jurists are still living in the ideological atmosphere of the days before 1933. To define the *Rechtsstaat* as a concentrated explosive may have been effective during the period of preparation for the charismatic revolution. But that the figure should have been repeated three years after the National-Socialists had taken power reveals that the movement had no substantial aims. Once the restoration of regularity which followed the charismatic revolution had been consummated, nothing remained but recollections and the quest for enemies — old or new.

At this point we are able to perceive the significance of the Jewish problem for National-Socialist policy. The threat of racial danger which the Jews constitute (according to the National-Socialist theory) is intended to have an integrating influence. According to the National-Socialist conviction, the Jew is incessantly striving to undermine Germany in order to attain complete domination over the world. Hence Germany is faced by a lasting state of emergency which can be overcome only by establishing the ethnic community. National-Socialist propagandists have endeavored to present the Jew as a demon.[507] Any restriction on freedom and material well-being can be justified on the ground of its necessity for protection from this demon.

The ethnic community is the supreme value in the National-Socialist value system. Everything which might injure this community is considered a disintegrating element. In any discussion or any dispute over religious, ethical or social questions lies the possibility of disrupting the integrity of the community. Every type of group which is devoted to substantive values other than the ethnic community presents this danger. In the words of Professor Hoehn of the University of Berlin: 'From the standpoint of the ethnical community every association for which values other than the community itself are central is destructive of the community.' [508] Making a fetish of the ethnic community implies the refusal to tolerate associations based upon values other than its own, the rejection of the autonomy of the law, the repudiation of all norms of rational Natural Law, the identification of justice and convenience.

Belief in the reality of external threats contributed to the establishment of the ethnic community; its preservation necessitates the discovery or creation of external dangers. The myth of a 'permanent emergency' would not find credence if it could not be shown that a hostile army is permanently ready to attack. Thus, if there are no real enemies, they have to be created. Without enemies, there can be no danger, and without danger, there can be no communally oriented attitudes, and without communally oriented attitudes there could be no ethnic community. Were there no ethnic community then associations based on religious, ethical, social or political values could not be suppressed.

3. THE CONCEPT OF POLITICS IN NATIONAL-SOCIALIST THEORY

In National-Socialist thought the concept of politics is defined by reference to 'the enemy.' All deeper understanding of National-Socialist policies depends on our grasp of the nature of politics as interpreted by National-Socialism. Many misunderstandings of

National-Socialist policies arise from erroneous conceptions of the meaning of political activity for National-Socialism.

It would be well to open our discussion with an analysis of the conceptions of politics implicit in each of the major types of domination.

Traditional domination is characterized by the fact that neither the dominator nor the dominated gives evidence of having a notion of what we call politics. In the Middle Ages (the period par excellence of traditional domination), as F. Kern [509] once pointed out, social thought allowed no place for this specifically political aspect of the state. The realm of the state and politics was completely controlled by law. Actions which today would be viewed as political were regarded by the age of traditional domination as controversies over subjective rights.

Rational domination has been associated with the attempt to organize and canalize conflicts over values through political institutions. The late Austrian historian Ludo Moritz Hartmann, a rationalistic democratic-socialist, once defined politics as 'the art of canalizing social activity into legal form.' [510] This definition is as appropriate to the rational type of domination as it is foreign to the other types.

The special character of this definition becomes all the more clear when we contrast it with Carl Schmitt's [511] definition of politics as the 'friend-enemy' relationship. This definition of political activity has a rather interesting ancestry. It is based directly on Rudolf Smend's essay on political power in the constitutional state. Smend inquires into the distinguishing characteristics of government and administration. He concludes that the decisive criterion of government is its 'political' character and that the mark of administration is its 'technical' character. Smend claims that this distinction is equally applicable to both domestic and foreign politics. 'Contentlessness,' he says, 'is a characteristic of all foreign policy in so far as it has political and not technical objectives. . . . The political element which in domestic affairs distinguishes political statecraft from technical administration is exactly the same.' [512] In a footnote, Smend acknowledges, as his source for this idea, Josef Schumpeter's famous essay *Zur Soziologie der*

Imperialismen.[513] There Schumpeter asserted that the aimless quest for power is the central element in imperialistic expansionism.

From Smend's assertion that aimlessness is the essential characteristic of all political activity, Schmitt deduced the proposition that the existence of an enemy is the essential element in political activity. Thus, Schmitt furnished a legitimation for National-Socialism by showing that the absence of a positive content to political activity is not a shortcoming but rather a complete realization of the nature of political activity. Schmitt's definition of politics hypostatizes a political conception of fraternity (*Bund*). This kind of politics, in a situation in which traditional values have lost their binding power and rational values are not acceptable, is oriented towards the attainment of power for its own sake. In 1932 the American journalist Knickerbocker asked leading National-Socialists what the National-Socialist Party would do after it seized power. The reply was: 'Keep it!' [514]

This briefly was the National-Socialist conception of politics. To consider the fight for power neither as a struggle for subjective rights nor as a fight for the realization of objective ideas of justice, to gain and to hold power without legal title and without legal objective regardless of legal principles — all these are only corollaries of the central interest in power for the sake of power.[515]

A major element in the victory of the Rightist elements in postwar Germany was the fact that they were seized by the *furor politicus* in the debacle of 1918-19, and, impelled by its force, came to triumph over the largely depoliticized Leftist elements. The defeat of the Left was preceded by its renunciation of 'political politics' — expressed perhaps most characteristically by Walther Rathenau in the introduction to his book *Vom neuen Staate*, published in March 1919. 'The war and its aftermath, the peace,' he said, 'seem to have been the florescence of all the great questions of "political policy"; in reality, however, they have destroyed "political policy". . . . foreign and political policy will remain on the stage a little while longer but will soon be replaced by economic

and social policy.'[516] Contrary to Rathenau's expectations, economic and social policy were to remain on the stage for only a
short time, yielding their places to those men who realized that
political activity and not pure economic policy would be decisive.

It seems necessary repeatedly to point out the role of foreign
policy in the development of National-Socialism. It should not be
forgotten that faith in law in international relations had been
abused. The fact that war indemnities were called 'reparations'
and a predatory invasion like the occupation of the Ruhr Basin
was called a 'sanction' was a blow to those Leftist groups in Germany which believed in the validity of Natural Law programs.
They never recovered from this blow. The emergence of National-
Socialism cannot be understood without taking into account the
effects of Poincaré's foreign policy on the internal situation in
Germany.

National-Socialist negation of all universally valid values and
its suppression of all communities based upon such values, its
negation of an order sanctioned by Natural Law may be said to
be at least partially due to foreign threats; at the same time, it is
necessary to recognize that the relaxation of the international
threat was accompanied by an intensification of the war against
internal disintegration.

The international threat was seized upon by German capitalism as an opportunity to stabilize the social and economic order
and thus to facilitate the realization of its own interests. When
the threat declined, it became necessary to invent one. The de-
fenders of capitalism in post-war Germany were unable to con-
vince the masses of the German people that it was the best of all
economic systems. Capitalism had no chance in a democratic
struggle against proletarian socialism, in whose extirpation its
salvation lay. The violence of the German tyranny is indicative
not only of its power but also of its fear of losing that power, a
sign not only of its political strength but also of its social weakness. 'Early capitalism . . . as well as capitalism in its decadent
period, characterized by a highly unstable social equilibrium,
stands under the sign of state autocracy,'[517] as Hans Kelsen has
formulated this phenomenon.

In an ideologically distorted form, this proposition has been supported by Professor Herrfahrdt of Marburg University. To his own heretical question: 'May we assume the people to be united by the National-Socialist idea, or is a Leader necessary because the idea has no real unifying power?' he answers: 'The German people, because of their disunity, are united in their need of a Leader.' [518]

How spurious is the ethnic community of a people whose Leader finds it necessary to punish a few youths for hiking in unauthorized uniforms, because such an 'offence' might undermine national unity! How fundamentally different is this attitude from the one expressed by the English statesman Balfour: '. . . it is evident that our whole political machinery presupposes a people so fundamentally at one that they can safely afford to bicker; and so sure of their own moderation that they are not dangerously disturbed by the never-ending din of political conflict.' [519] How fundamentally different is it from the proud words of Thomas Jefferson's first Inaugural Address, written after one of the bitterest fights in American history:

'If there be any among us who would wish to dissolve this Union, or to change its Republican form, let them stand undisturbed as monuments of the safety with which error of opinion may be tolerated where reason is left free to combat it.' [520]

In present-day Germany, the forces which might create a real unity have been shattered. Hitler does not dare to follow Hegel's recommendations regarding the toleration of religious sects. A policy which cancels a peddler's permit if he is suspected of sympathy with Jehovah's Witnesses, regrets Hegel's plea for tolerance — and it should be remembered that Hegel has always been looked on as the most extreme idolator of the state. The toleration which Hegel demanded for the religious sects obviously did not involve a public danger in the Prussia of 1820.

Hegel mentions in this connection the Quakers and Anabaptists and characterizes both as members of civic society who are not citizens of the state. He proposes that the state shall exercise tolerance towards the members of these groups as long as the state may rely upon the 'inner reason' of its institutions. [521]

Adolf Hitler's Germany, however, cannot rely upon the 'reason of its institutions'; the social body of the people is, at bottom, not homogeneous enough.

German capitalism once sincerely believed that its own development would contribute to world peace, well-being and culture. Present-day German capitalism has lost this belief in its humanitarian mission. Having lost the belief in its own rationale, it elevates the cult of the irrational to the status of a modern religion. Both early capitalism and mature capitalism have faced crises and mastered them by economic means. The late-capitalism of the post-war Germany used only one method to overcome the crisis which threatened its existence, the armament boom. Early liberal capitalism sought to reduce the functions of the state to a minimum because it had faith in its own inherent laws. Contemporary German capitalism, however, needs a state which removes its socialist opponent, proves that 'private benefit is public benefit' and provides it with the external enemies against whom it must arm itself as a *sine qua non* for its preservation.

In 1653 the noble-estates were willing to tolerate the absolute rule of the Great Elector in exchange for absolute authority over the serfs. In the same manner the German business dealers recognized the rule of the National-Socialist Party in 1933 in exchange for the strengthening of their own power.

The National-Socialist Party promised that as far as possible interferences with business would be avoided, that the entrepreneur would again be master of his enterprise, and that free initiative would be preserved. Another important guarantee which the National-Socialist Party had to extend to German capitalism was (as Dr. Schacht[522] declared to the heavy applause of German business leaders) the preservation of an objective orderly legal system, the Normative State.

German capitalism today requires state aid in two respects:

(a) against the social enemies in order to guarantee its existence, and (b) in its role as guarantor of that legal order which is the pre-condition of exact calculability without which capitalist enterprise cannot exist. German capitalism requires for its salvation a dual, not a unitary state, based on arbitrariness in the political sphere and on rational law in the economic sphere. Contemporary German capitalism is dependent on the Dual State for its existence.

Alfred von Martin perceived the dual character of the contemporary German state and expressed his conclusions as directly as one is permitted to do so in Germany: 'When the masses are organized by means of irrational ideologies the real nature of the prevailing method of domination is tinged with a communal tone. This type of domination combines rational bureaucratic methods with irrational or — to use Max Weber's terminology — charismatic ones.' [523]

The only political scientist in National-Socialist Germany who has so much as caught a glimpse of this problem is Professsor Koettgen of the University of Greifswald. His debt to Max Weber is apparent: 'It is precisely the Leader-state which cannot dispense with charismatic forms of leadership, but at the same time the rulers of the modern state, in order to satisfy the diverse, numerous demands of the population, are inevitably forced to depend upon highly rationalized and bureaucratized forms of organization.' [524]

This integration of rational and irrational activities which is peculiar to the Dual State — this rational core within an irrational shell — brings us to the culmination of our investigation. The author accepts Karl Mannheim's distinction between substantial and functional rationality as particularly relevant to this problem. This distinction can perhaps be best examplified by reference to chess. When it is said that chess is too serious for a game and too much of a game to be serious, the word 'game' implies the lack of substantial rationality (characteristic of any game) whereas the word 'serious' represents the high degree of functional rationality which many consider 'too high.' [525]

The legal order of the Reich is thoroughly rationalized in a functional sense for the regulation of production and exchange in accordance with capitalistic methods. But late capitalistic economic activity is not substantially rational. For this reason, it has had recourse to political methods, while giving to these methods the contentlessness of irrational activity. Capitalism at its best was a system of substantial rationality which, relying on the pre-established harmony which guided its destinies, exerted itself to remove irrational obstacles. When the belief in the substantial rationality of capitalism disappeared its highly rationalized functional organizations still remained. What is the character of the tension which arises out of the juxtaposition of disappearing substantial rationality and an overdeveloped functional rationality?

Carl Schmitt, while writing still in the name of political Catholicism, described the incongruity between functional and substantial rationality with the acuteness and lucidity characteristic of his earlier writings: 'Our economic organization,' Schmitt wrote, 'represents a thoroughly non-rational consumption hand in hand with a highly rationalized production. A mechanism which is a marvel of technical achievement caters indifferently and with equal thoroughness and exactitude to any and every demand, whether it be for silk blouses or poison gas.' [526] As long as Carl Schmitt still believed that Roman-Catholicism would eventually be triumphant — that 'the inheritance will be hers' — he was profoundly disturbed by this incongruity. He wrote:

'This alarm felt by genuine Catholics arises from the knowledge that the notion of rationality has been distorted in an utterly fantastic manner; a mechanical system of production purporting to cater to any and every material requirement is described as "rational," though at the same time the rationality of the purpose served by this supremely rational machine (which purpose is the only essential point) is left wholly out of account.' [527]

After he had turned his back on the Catholic Church, Schmitt lost this 'genuine Catholic alarm' as well as the realization that the only essential rationality is the rationality of ends. He sought security in Sorel's theory of the myth, which an intelligent young National-Socialist, Heyne, once characterized as 'irrational, and therefore irrefutable and absolutely safe from the attack of rational criticism.' [528] Thus a myth proves to be the haven in which the capitalistic system in Germany seeks refuge. The 'myth of the twentieth century' is not only the title of the National-Socialist Bible; it is also one of the means by which there was established and maintained a state which defends itself against rational criticism by denying the validity of substantial rationality itself, as Heyne said: 'The correctness of an idea is of no interest to the political community and the political movement . . . ideas are only ideologies, they are exposed to criticism and hence subjected to decomposition. . . . Only that is true which works and which helps and supports man and his community in the struggle for existence.' [529]

Thus German capitalism, finally realizing the irrationality of its own existence, discards substantial rationality. The tension which arose from the interplay of the disappearance of substantial rationality and the high development of functional rationality is rendered more acute by the self-consciousness with which the two processes are fostered. In order to augment technical rationality, the irrationality of the ends in intensified; and the belt to attain these irrational ends, technical rationality, is heightened. For the sake of the armament industries, armaments pile up; for the sake of armaments, armament industries prosper.

Faced with the choice between substantial rationality and substantial irrationality, German capitalism casts its vote for the latter. It will accomodate itself to any substantial irrationality if only the necessary pre-requisites for its technically rational order are preserved. German capitalism has preferred an irrational ideology, which maintains the existing conditions of technical rationality, but at the same time destroys all forms of substantial rationality.[530] If such substantially irrational ideology is useful to capitalism, the latter is ready to accept the programmatic aims of this ideology. This symbiosis of capitalism and National-Socialism finds its institutional form in the Dual State. The conflict within society is expressed in the dual nature of the state. The Dual State is the necessary political outgrowth of a transitional period wrought with tension.

The solution of these tensions depends ultimately on ourselves.

ABBREVIATIONS

Akademie Ztschr.	Zeitschrift der Akademie für Deutsches Recht
ALR.	Preussisches Allgemeines Landrecht
Arbeitsr. Entsch.	Arbeitsrechtliche Entscheidungen
Arb. R. S.	Arbeitsrechtssammlung
Arch. f. öff. Recht	Archiv für öffentliches Recht
Arch. f. Rechts- u. Soz. Phil.	Archiv für Rechts- und Sozialphilosophie
Arch. f. Szw.	Archiv für Sozialwissenschaften und Sozialpolitik
Bad. Verw. Ztschr.	Badische Verwaltungszeitschrift
BGB.	Bürgerliches Gesetzbuch
BGBl.	Bundesgesetzblatt
Bl. f. Gefk.	Blätter für Gefängniskunde
D. A. Z.	Deutsche Allgemeine Zeitung
D. J. Z.	Deutsche Juristenzeitung
D. Jstz.	Deutsche Justiz
Dt. Bergw. Ztg.	Deutsche Bergwerks-Zeitung
Dtsch. Arb. R.	Deutsches Arbeitsrecht
Dtsch. Recht	Deutsches Recht
Dtsch. Rpfl.	Deutsche Rechtspflege
Dtsch. Rw.	Deutsche Rechtswissenschaft
Dtsch. R. Z.	Deutsche Richter-Zeitung
Dtsch. Str.	Deutsches Strafrecht
Dtsch. Verw.	Deutsche Verwaltung
Dtsch. Verw. R.	Deutsches Verwaltungsrecht
Entsch. des KG. und OLG. München	Entscheidungen des Kammergerichts und Oberlandesgerichts München
Fft. Ztg.	Frankfurter Zeitung
Hans. R. u. Ger. Ztg.	Hanseatische Rechts- und Gerichtszeitung

HGB.	Handelsgesetzbuch
Höchst. R. Rspr.	Höchstrichterliche Rechtsprechung
H. Z.	Historische Zeitschrift
Jahrb. f. Entsch. der freiw. Gbk.	Jahrbuch für Entscheidungen der freiwilligen Gerichtsbarkeit
Jgdr. u. Jgdwohlf.	Jugendrecht und Jugendwohlfahrt
J. W.	Juristische Wochenschrift
Kart. Rundsch.	Kartellrundschau
Mbl. f. i. Verw.	Ministerialblatt für innere Verwaltung
N. F.	Neue Folge (New Series)
OVG.	Entscheidungen des Preussischen Oberverwaltungsgerichts
PGS.	Preussische Gesetzessammlung
RAG.	Entscheidungen des Reichsarbeitsgerichts
Reger	Entscheidungen der Gerichte und Verwaltungsbehörden auf dem Gebiete des Verwaltungs- u. Polizeistrafrechts, begründet von Reger
RGBl.	Reichsgesetzblatt
RGSt.	Entscheidungen des Reichsgerichts in Strafsachen
RGZ.	Entscheidungen des Reichsgerichts in Zivilsachen
R. Verw. Bl.	Reichsverwaltungsblatt
Verkehrsr. Abh.	Verkehrsrechtliche Abhandlungen
V. B.	Völkischer Beobachter
Ztschr. f. ausl. öff. u. Völkerr.	Zeitschrift für ausländisches öffentliches und Völkerrecht
Ztschr. f. Beamtenr.	Zeitschrift für Beamtenrecht
Ztsch. f. dtsch. Kult. Philos.	Zeitschrift für deutsche Kulturphilosophie
Ztsch. f. d. ges. Staatsw.	Zeitschrift für die gesamte Staatswissenschaft

NOTES

NOTES

1 The decree is reproduced in the appendix.

2 The expression 'sphere' is not exact and is merely used provisionally.

3 Regarding the opportunities for revolutions and *coups d'état* in present-day society, see Max Weber, *Wirtschaft und Gesellschaft* (Tübingen, 1922), p. 670.

4 The distinction between 'mandatory' and 'absolute' dictatorship was created by Carl Schmitt in *Die Diktatur* (München, 1921). Our use of these terms is identical with that of Carl Schmitt.

5 RGSt 59, 187-8.

6 *Garde* v. *Strickland* (1921), quoted in D. L. Keir and F. H. Lawson, *Cases in Constitutional Law* (Oxford, 1928), p. 373.

7 The assassination of Röhm, Schleicher and many other opponents of the Hitler government.

8 Reinhard Heydrich, 'Die Bekämpfung der Staatsfeinde' *Dtsch. Rw.* Band I, Heft 2, p. 97.

9 Oberlandesgericht Karlsruhe, June 25, 1936 (*J. W.* 1936, p. 3268).

10 Oberlandesgericht Hamburg, March 31, 1936 (*D. J. Z.* 1936, p. 771).

11 Ib.

12 Ib.

13 Landesarbeitsgericht Berlin, November 17, 1934 (*D. Jstz.* 1935, p. 73).

14 *PGS.* 1933, pp. 122, 413; 1936, p. 21.

15 We find certain technical differences in various statutes, caused by the fact that the police law is state law (*Landesrecht*) and that it must be adjusted to the administrative laws of the states (*Länder*). The legal functions of the Gestapo are dependent on the police laws of the several states. The same is true with regard to the review of actions of the *Gestapo* by the administrative courts.

16 John Neville Figgis, *Studies of Political Thought from Gerson to Grotius*, 1414-1625 (Cambridge, 1907), p. 86.

17 Carl Schmitt, *Die Diktatur* (*Von den Anfängen des modernen Souveränitätsgedankens bis zum proletarischen Klassenkampf*) (2nd. ed. München 1928) p. 59, note 3. This book is the first of many scholarly and literary efforts to 'exploit' the practical possibilities of Art. 48 of the Weimar Constitution.

18 Samuel Rawson Gardiner, *The Constitutional Documents of the Puritan Revolution* (Oxford, 1899), p. 105.

19 J. R. Tanner, *English Constitutional Conflicts of the Seventeenth Century* (Cambridge, 1928), p. 78.

20 Cf. Justice Breese in *Johnson* v. *Jones* (44 Ill. 166) who characterized

emergency as something that 'placed the dearest rights of the citizen at the mercy of a dominant party who have only to declare the "emergency" which they can readily create, pretext for which, bad men are keen to find and eager to act upon.'

[21] Mittermaier, 'Die Gesetzgebung über Belagerungszustand, Kriegsrecht, Standrecht und Suspension der Gesetze über persönliche Freiheit,' *Archiv für Criminalrecht,* 1849, p. 29.

[22] Ib.

[23] Ruthardt, *Entwurf eines Gesetzes über das Verfahren in Strafsachen* (Regensburg, 1849), p. 211.

[24] 'In order to cope with rebellion, sabotage and similar politically sterile outbreaks...any government would have resort to martial law.... The firm traditions of politically more mature nations which are less easily intimidated have been maintained in such a situation. In such nations the people have kept their heads overcoming violence by violence while remaining sensible enough to seek to eliminate the tensions which resulted in the outburst, above all restoring all guarantees of liberty as soon as the emergency is over and remaining uninfluenced by the revolutionary events in their approach to other questions of government. We (Germans) may expect with certainty that the representatives of the old order of the unchecked bureaucracy...will exploit every syndicalist *Putsch*...however insignificant, to exert pressure on the "weak nerves" of the lower middle classes. The reaction to this will show whether the German nation has achieved political maturity. We may well despair of our political future if they should be successful, although unfortunately past experience indicates that such a success is entirely in the realm of possibility.' (Max Weber, 'Parlament und Regierung im neugeordneten Deutschland' in *Gesammelte politische Schriften,* München, 1921, p. 223).

[25] Walther Hamel, in Frank, *Deutsches Verwaltungsrecht* (München, 1937), pp. 387, 394.

[26] Ib.

[27] Walther Hamel, 'Die Polizei im neuen Reich,' *Dtsch. Recht,* 1935, p. 414.

[28] See note 25.

[29] Sondergericht Hamburg, March 15, 1935 (*Dtsch. R. Z.* 1935, p. 553).

[30] *The Eighteenth Brumaire of Louis Napoleon* (translated by Daniel De Leon), 3rd edition (Chicago, 1913) p. 61.

[31] Carl Schmitt, *Legalität und Legitimität* (München, 1932), pp. 93-4.

[32] A historically correct analysis of the events of 1933 is to be found only in one National-Socialist document. A decision of the Appellate Court of Berlin of November 1, 1933 (*D. Jstz.* 1934 p. 64) stated that 'the Decree of February 28, 1933, by suspending fundamental rights, deliberately creates an emergency situation for the purpose of realizing the National-Socialist state.'

[33] Reichsgericht, October 22, 1934 (*RGZ.* 145, p. 367).

34 Ernst Huber, in a comment on a decision of the Sondergericht Darmstadt, March 26, 1934 (*J. W.* 1934, p. 1747).

35 Sondergericht Darmstadt, March 26, 1934 (*J. W.* 1934, p. 1747).

36 Landgericht Dresden, March 18, 1935 (*J. W.* 1935, p. 1949).

37 Reichsgericht, September 24, 1935 (*J. W.* 1935, p. 3377).

38 Preussisches Oberverwaltungsgericht, May 27, 1936 (*J. W.* 1936, p. 2277). [Cf. Preussisches Oberverwaltungsgericht, April 17, 1935 (*J. W.* 1935, p. 2676)].

39 Ib.

40 Published in *Mbl. f. i. Verw.* 1933, p. 233.

41 Kammergericht, May 31, 1935 (*Dtsch. R. Z.* 1935, p. 624).

42 Reichsarbeitsgericht, October 17, 1934 (*J. W.* 1935, p. 378). It is of considerable interest to note that at about the same time the Supreme Court of the United States was called upon to decide whether, in dealing with a great national crisis, a constitutional agency can lay claim to extra-constitutional powers owing to the existence of an emergency. Chief Justice Hughes denied this in the Schlechter case in words which have already become classical: 'Extraordinary conditions may call for extraordinary remedies. But the argument necessarily stops short of an attempt to justify action which lies outside the sphere of constitutional authority. Extraordinary conditions do not create or enlarge constitutional powers.' *Schlechter* v. *United States*, 295 US 495, 528; May 27, 1935.

43 Walther Hamel, in Frank, *Deutsches Verwaltungsrecht* (München, 1937), pp. 386-7.

44 Sondergericht Hamburg, March 15, 1935 (*Dtsch. R. Z.* 1935, p. 553; also quoted in *J. W.* 1935, p. 2988).

45 Kammergericht, July 12, 1935 (*R. Verw. Bl.* 1936, p. 61).

46 Ib.

47 Kammergericht, March 5, 1935 (*D. Jstz,* 1935, p. 1831).

48 Ib.

49 Reichsgericht, August 6, 1936 (*Dtsch. Str.* 1936, p. 429).

50 Carl Schmitt, *Die Diktatur,* (2d ed., München, 1928), p. 94.

51 Württembergischer Verwaltungsgerichtshof, September 9, 1936 (*Dtsch. Verw.* 1936, p. 385).

52 Landgericht Berlin, November 1, 1933 (*D. Jstz.* 1934, p. 64).

53 Ullrich Scheuner, 'Die Neugestaltung des Vereins-und Verbandsrechts' *D. J. Z.* 1935, p. 666.

54 The limitations of the police power are set forth in § 14 of *Preussisches Polizeiverwaltungsgesetz* (*PGS.* 1931, p. 77). They are taken over almost literally from the *Allgemeines Preussisches Landrecht* of 1794 and, owing to their acceptance by the courts and by custom, have prevailed in Germany for many decades.

55 Preussisches Oberverwaltungsgericht, January 10, 1935 (*R. Verw. Bl.* 1935, p. 923).

216 NOTES

56 *Mbl. f. i. Verw.* 1933, p. 233.

57 See Reichsgericht, January 23, 1934 (*J. W.* 1934, p. 767).

58 Ludwig Eickhoff, 'Die Preussische Geheime Staatspolizei,' *Dtsch. Verw.* 1936, p. 91.

59 See note 51.

60 Ib.

61 Ib.

62 Ernst Swoboda, 'Das Protektorat in Böhmen und Mähren,' *R. Verw. Bl.* April 2, 1939, pp. 281-4.

63 Badischer Verwaltungsgerichtshof, January 11, 1938 (*Bad. Verw. Ztschr.* 1938, p. 87). Inasmuch as the courts of Baden at this time still claimed competence in reviewing the actions of the police, the decision of the administrative court has a definite historical significance, for it is the last decision in which a German administrative court reviewed political acts by the police authorities. (Since that time Baden has followed the example of Prussia and of the other German states).

64 Ib.

65 Ib.

66 Dannebeck deals with this question in Frank, *Deutsches Verwaltungsrecht* (München, 1937), p. 307. He condemns the review of political measures with reference to abuse or arbitrariness. (Cf. Lauer in *J. W.* 1934, p. 2833).

67 Oberlandesgericht Braunschweig, May 29, 1935 (*Höchst. R. Rspr.* 36, 98).

68 *Regina* v. *Nelson & Brand.* (Charge of the Lord Chief Justice of England to the Grand Jury at the Central Criminal Court in the case of the Queen against Nelson & Brand. 2nd ed., London, 1867, p. 86.)

69 Field in '*ex parte* Milligan' 1864, 4 Wallace 2,35.

70 Carl Schmitt, *Politische Theologie* (München, 1922), p. 13.

71 Ministerialdirigent und SS-Oberführer Dr. Werner Best in *D. A. Z.* July 1, 1937, (reprinted in Frank, *Deutsches Verwaltungsrecht*, München, 1937).

72 Preussisches Oberverwaltungsgericht, October 25, 1934 (*R. Verw. Bl.* 1935, p. 458).

73 Preussisches Oberverwaltungsgericht, May 2, 1935 (*R. Verw. Bl.* 1935, p. 577).

74 *PGS.* 1933, p. 41.

75 This view has been upheld by the Supreme Administrative Court of Prussia in its decision of May 23, 1935 (*J. W.* 1935, p. 2670), which explicitly denied that the political character of a police order was in itself sufficient to exclude review. The Prussian Supreme Court (Kammergericht) in decisions of May 3, 1935, and January 9, 1936, expressed the same view. (*D. Jstz.* 1935, p. 1831; *J. W.* 1936, p. 3187).

76 Gesetz über die Freizügigkeit, November 1, 1867 (BGBl. 1867, p. 55).

77 Preussisches Oberverwaltungsgericht, December 5, 1935 (*OVG.* 97, 103).

[78] Gesetz über die Geheime Staatspolizei, February 10, 1936 (*PGS.* 1936, 21).
[79] Preussisches Oberverwaltungsgericht, March 19, 1936 (*J. W.* 1936 p. 2189).
[80] *PGS.* 1936, No. 6.
[81] See note 79.
[82] Cf. *Dtsch. Verw.* 1936, p. 318 and *R. Verw. Bl.* 1936, p. 549.
[83] Preussisches Oberverwaltungsgericht, November 10, 1938 (*J. W.* 1939, p. 382).
[84] Ib.
[85] See Preussisches Oberverwaltungsgericht, December 15, 1938 (*R. Verw. Bl.* 1939, p. 544).
[86] The first decision of this type was rendered by the District Court (Landgericht) of Tübingen on January 25, 1934 (*J. W.* 1934, p. 627) which refused to invoke the provisions of the poor law in the case of a man wanting to sue the state for unjust imprisonment in a concentration camp. It held 'that the state cannot set aside actions which it has found politically necessary.' Of greater significance is the decision of the Supreme Administrative Court of Hamburg (Hamburger Oberverwaltungsgericht) of October 7, 1934 (*R. Verw. Bl.* 1935, p. 1045). The political police had dissolved a *Bürgerverein* of mixed Aryan and Jewish membership. The court refused to hear the appeal of the association, declaring that its dissolution was a political act and, accordingly, not subject to review.
[87] See note 78.
[88] Gesetz über die Zulassung zur Rechtsanwaltschaft, April 7, 1933 (*RGBl,* 1933, p. 188).
[89] Reichsgericht, May 6, 1936 (*J. W.* 1936, p. 2982).
[90] *BGB.* §839; *Reichsverfassung* Art. 131.
[91] Reichsgericht, March 3, 1937 (*J. W.* 1937, p. 1723).
[92] Ib.
[93] Deutsches Beamtengesetz, January 26, 1937 (*RGBl.* 1937, p. 39).
[94] This interpretation of the importance of the *Konflikt* is opposed to the opinion of the *Reichsgericht,* which interprets §147 only as a shift in jurisdiction and not as a change in substantive law. Needless to say, we cannot regard this interpretation as correct.
[95] Gesetz über den Ausgleich bürgerlich-rechtlicher Ansprüche, December 13, 1934 (*RGBl.* 1934, p. 1235).
[96] Reichsgericht, September 7, 1937 (*RGZ.* 155, p. 296).
[97] Ib.
[98] Oberlandesgericht München, November 4, 1937 (*Entsch. des KG. und OLG. München* 17, p. 273).
[99] Ib.
[100] Dr. Best, 'Werdendes Polizeirecht' *Dtsch. Recht,* 1938, p. 224.
[101] *V. B.,* July 5, 1935.
[102] Landesarbeitsgericht Gleiwitz (*Dtsch. Rpfl.* 1936, p. 59).

[103] Reichsarbeitsgericht, April 14, 1937 (*J. W.* 1937, p. 2311).
Cf. Landesarbeitsgericht München, July 31, 1937 (*D. Jstz.* 1937, p. 1159).
[104] In a decision of the Supreme Administrative Court of Prussia (Preussischer Oberverwaltungsgerichtshof) of June 29, 1937 (*R. Verw. Bl.* 1937, p. 762), a parallel case dealt with the exclusion of a civil servant from the National-Socialist Party on his continued service as an official. The prosecuting attorney contended that the exclusion of an official from the National-Socialist Party necessitated his dismissal from the public service. The Supreme Administrative Court did not, however, share the view, but held that actions of the party cannot have such far-reaching consequences unless they are supported by legislation.
[105] The Appellate Court (*Oberlandesgericht*) of Stettin, on March 25, 1936, had granted damages to a plaintiff who had been injured by an automobile owned by the National-Socialist Party, although the defendant argued that since the party was an institution the funds and purposes of which were devoted to the public weal, it could not be ordered to make payments to private persons (*J. W.* 1937, p. 241). A parallel case was decided by the *Reichsgericht* on February 17, 1939 (*R. Verw. Bl.* 1939, p. 727).
[106] Reichsarbeitsgericht, February 10, 1937 (*RAG.* 18, p. 170).
[107] Carl Schmitt commenting on a decision of the Kammergericht of March 22, 1935 (*D. Jstz.* 1935, p. 686) in *D. J. Z.* 1935, p. 618.
[108] Oberlandesgericht Düsseldorf, July 10, 1935 (*D. J. Z.* 1935, p. 1123).
[109] Reichsgericht February 28, 1936 (*Höchst. R. Rspr.* 1936, p. 900). This decision was followed by several courts regarding various branches of the National-Socialist Party [Hitler Youth Movement Decision, Appellate Court of Dresden, January 31, 1935 (*D. J. Z.* 1935, p. 439); National-Socialist Party Decision, Appellate Court of Zweibrücken, December 24, 1934 (*D. J. Z.* 1935, p. 442)]. All these decisions indicate that this theory has become an established rule.
[110] Kompetenzgerichtshof June 27, 1936 (*R. Verw. Bl.* 1936 p. 860).
[111] See note 93.
[112] Preussisches Oberverwaltungsgericht, December 5, 1935 (*OVG.* 97, p. 117).
[113] 'The *Gestapo* protect the community rather than the individuals and are therefore exempt from the restraint imposed by the ordinary police law.' Lauer, 'Die richterliche Nachprüfung polizeilicher Massnahmen,' *J. W.* 1934, p. 832.
[114] 'The compelling and supreme necessity of strengthening the new state requires the widest possible extension of discretion in political cases.' Preussisches Oberverwaltungsgericht, October 24, 1934 (*OVG.* 94, p. 138).
[115] Wilhelm Frick, 'Auf dem Wege zum Einheitsstaat' *Dtsch. Verw.* 1936, p. 334.
[115a] James I, Works (ed. of 1616) pp. 553 ff.

[116] Quoted in J. R. Tanner, *Constitutional Documents of the Reign of James I* (Cambridge, 1930), p. 19.

[117] Reichsgericht, September 22, 1938 (*J. W.* 1938, p. 2955).

[118] Ib.

[119] Ib.

[120] Heinrich Himmler, 'Aufgaben und Aufbau der Polizei' *Festschrift für Dr. Frick,* edited by Pfundtner, Berlin, 1937, reviewed in *Fft. Ztg.,* March 12, 1937; Hans Frank, 'Strafrechts — und Strafvollzugs-Probleme' *Bl. f. Gefk.* 1937, Band 68, p. 259.

[121] Ministerialdirigent und SS-Oberführer Dr. Werner Best (Gestapo) in *D. A. Z.,* June 22, 1938.

[122] At this point we will not discuss whether this form of state may be called a 'Justice State' (*Gerechtigkeitsstaat*) as suggested by Carl Schmitt (see Frank, *Nationalsozialistisches Handbuch für Recht und Gesetzgebung,* München, 1935, p. 6). It is, however, of interest that Schmitt derives his concept from the Czarist Russian Gosudarstwo Prwady.

[123] HansThieme, 'Nationalsozialistisches Arbeitsrecht' *Dtsch. Recht,* 1935, p. 215.

[124] Weimar, Attorney in Cologne in *R. Verw. Bl.* 1937, p. 479.

[125] Hans Franzen, *Gesetz und Richter; eine Abgrenzung nach den Grundsätzen des nationalsozialistischen Staates* (Hamburg, 1935), p. 11.

[126] It may be noted that Franzen supplements Carl Schmitt's concept of 'politics' with the propositions that the 'friend-enemy' dichotomy has nothing to do with the 'just-unjust' dichotomy.

[127] Preussisches Oberverwaltungsgericht, January 28, 1937 (*Verkehrsr. Abh.* 1937, p. 319).

[128] Gesetz gegen heimtückische Angriffe auf Staat und Partei und zum Schutz der Parteiuniformen, December 20, 1934 (*RGBl.* 1934, p. 1269).

[129] Dr. Crohne, 'Die Strafrechtspflege 1936' *D. Jstz.* 1937, p. 7-12.

[130] Kammergericht, May 3, 1935 (*D. Jstz.* 1935 p. 1831).

[131] See note 37.

[132] Oberlandesgericht Kiel, November 25, 1935 (*Höchst. R. Rspr.* 1936, p. 592).

[133] Ib.

[134] Oberlandesgericht München, January 27, 1937 (*Jahrb. f. Entsch. der freiw. Gbk.,* Band 15, p. 58).

[135] See note 127.

[136] Ib.

[137] Oberlandesgericht Stettin, April 14, 1937 (*J. W.* 1937, p. 2212).

[138] Criminal proceedings for tax evasion were instituted against the attorney.

[139] February 6, 1875 (*RGBl.* 1875, p. 23).

[140] Reichsgericht, November 2, 1936 (*J. W.* 1937, p. 98).

[141] Massfeller, *Akademie Ztschr.* 1937, p. 119.

[142] See note 134.

[143] Rudolf Sohm, *Kirchenrecht* (*Systematisches Handbuch der Dt. Rechtswissenschaft, Band VIII*) (München, 1923), p. 1.

[144] Cf. Max Weber, *Wirtschaft und Gesellschaft*, (Tübingen, 1922), p. 59, 396.

[145] Ernst Forsthoff, *Der totale Staat* (Hamburg, 1933), p. 30.

[146] Hermann Heller, *Rechtsstaat und Diktatur* (Tübingen, 1930), p. 19.

[147] *V. B.*, July 5, 1935; also formulated by Huber, 'Die Verwirkung der rechtsgenössischen Rechtsstellung im Verwaltungsrecht' *Akademie Ztschr.* 1937, p. 368, insofar as administrative law is concerned: 'The administrative authorities are not only entitled to act when explicitly empowered to do so by statute but also upon demand of the unwritten principle of the ethnic community.'

[148] Reichsdienststrafhof, June 15, 1937 *Ztschr. f. Beamtenr.* 1937, p. 104.

[149] Ib.

[150] R. H. Tawney, *Religion and the Rise of Capitalism* (New York, 1926), p. 161.

[151] This relationship has been pointed out by Max Weber, *General Economic History* (translation by Frank H. Knight, New York, 1927), p. 342, and by George Jellinek, *Allgemeine Staatslehre* (Berlin, 1900), p. 89.

[152] The concept of the 'agnostic state' has been elaborated by the Fascist theory of the state. In German theory it was developed by Carl Schmitt, *Staatsethik und pluralistischer Staat* (*Kant-Studien*, 1931, Band XXXV), pp. 28-42, especially p. 31.

[153] Georg Dahm, 'Verrat und Verbrechen' *Ztschr. f. d. ges. Staatsw.* Band 95, p. 283, 288.

[154] Dr. Diener, 'System des Staatsverbrechens,' *Dtsch. Recht*, Band IV, pp. 322-29.

[155] Reichsstrafgesetzbuch, May 15, 1871, *RGBl.* 1876, p. 40.

[156] Sondergericht Hamburg, May 5, 1935 (*J. W.* 1935, p. 2988).

[157] Roland Freissler, 'Der Volksverrat (Hoch-und Landesverrat) im Lichte des National-Sozialismus,' *D. J. Z.* 1935, p. 907.

[158] Georg Dahm, in a comment on a decision of the *Reichsgericht*. (*J. W.* 1934, p. 904).

[159] Reichsgericht, September 8, 1938, (*J. W.* 1938, p. 2899) and October 27, 1938 (*J. W.* 1939, p. 29).

[160] Oberlandesgericht München, August 12, 1937 (*D. Jstz.* 1938, p. 724).

[161] Ib.

[162] Volksgerichtshof, May 6, 1938 (*D. Jstz.* 1938, p. 1193); Kammergericht, March 26, 1938 (*D. Jstz.* 1938, p. 1752). Detailed discussion of the problem by Mittelsbach (*J. W.* 1938, p. 3155), and Niederreuther (*D. Jstz.* 1938, p. 1752). The decision of the Kammergericht is not published. Parts of the decision are quoted in Niederreuther's article.

[163] Carl Schmitt, 'Die Diktatur des Reichspräsidenten nach Artikel 48 der Weimarer Verfassung'; appendix to *Die Diktatur*, (2d ed., München, 1928)

p. 248 (paper read on the meeting of the Vereinigung deutscher Staatsrechtslehrer, 1924). This distinction goes back to Robespierre's speech in the *Convention Nationale* on December 3, 1792, when he indicted Louis XVI with these famous words: '*Vous n'avez point une sentence à rendre pour ou contre un homme mais une mésure de salut public à prendre, une acte de providence nationale à exercer.*'

164 Joint opinion of James and Stephen on Martial Law with reference to the Jamaica Insurrection 1866, quoted in William Forsyth, *Constitutional Law*, (London, 1869), appendix, pp. 551-563, especially pp. 560-1.

165 Ib., especially p. 561.

166 Ib., especially p. 552.

167 One high-treason decision of the Oberlandesgericht Hamburg of April 15, 1937 was apparently published by accident in *Funkarchiv*, 1937, p. 257.

168 Bayerischer Verwaltungsgerichtshof, May 8, 1936 (*Reger*, Band 37, p. 533).

169 Sächsisches Oberverwaltungsgericht, December 4, 1936 (*J. W.* 1937, p. 1368).

170 Reichsdienststrafhof, February 11, 1935 (*Ztschr. f. Beamtenr.* 1936, p. 104).

171 Reichsgericht, February 17, 1938 (*J. W.* 1938, p. 1018).

172 Alfred Rosenberg, 'Die nationalsozialistische Weltanschauung und das Recht,' *D. Jstz.* 1938, p. 358.

173 Sermon on King James' birthday, 1621: *The Works of William Laud, D. D.*, ed. Wm. Scott, vol. I, London 1847, p. 28.

174 Landgericht Hamburg, May 6, 1936 (*Jgdr. u. Jgdwohlf.* 1936, p. 281). The above-mentioned matters belong to the jurisdiction of the lower courts. We quote therefore decisions of the district and municipal courts concerning the relations of children and parent.

175 Amtsgericht Berlin-Lichterfelde, April 15, 1935 (*Das Recht*, 1935, No. 8015).

176 Amtsgericht Hamburg, April 15, 1935 (*Das Recht*, 1935, No. 8016).

177 Amtsgericht Frankfurt Main-Höchst, May 4, 1937 (*Dtsch. Recht*, 1937, p. 466).

178 Amtsgericht Wilsen, February 26, 1938 (*J. W.* 1938, p. 1264).

179 Landgericht Zwickau, March 14, 1937 (*J. W.* 1938, p. 2145).

180 Sondergericht Breslau (*Dtsch. R. Z.* 1935, p. 554).

181 Carl Schmitt, *Politische Theologie* (2d. ed., München, 1934), p. 1.

182 Hermann Reuss, in a comment on a decision of the Prussian Supreme Administrative Courts (*Preussischer Oberverwaltungsgerichtshof*) of June 30, 1936 (*J. W.* 1937, pp. 422-3).

183 At this point the American reader will probably recall the famous passage of Justice Stone's dissenting opinion in *United States* v. *Butler* (297, US 79). Justice Stone defined the supremacy of the courts over legislative and administrative actions as follows: '...the other is that while unconstitutional exercise of power by the executive and legislative branches

of the government is subject to judicial restraint, the only check upon our exercise of power is our own sense of self-restraint.' Underlying this statement is the insight that in every legal and constitutional system the old problem, *quis custodiet custodem?* can be answered only by an appeal to conscience. The parallel with the problem of the Dual State should not be extended further, since the question discussed in the American decision deals with the relationship of governmental bodies within the framework of legal order, while the line which separates the Normative and the Prerogative States is the borderline between legal order and lawlessness.

[184] Sächsisches Oberverwaltungsgericht, November 25, 1938 (*R. Verw. Bl.* 1939, p. 103).

[185] Ib.

[186] Bürgerliches Gesetzbuch, August 18, 1896. *RGBl.* 1898, p. 195.

[187] Preussisches Oberverwaltungsgericht, December 15, 1938 (*R. Verw. Bl.* 1939, p. 544).

[188] Heinrich Herrfahrdt, 'Politische Verfassungslehre,' *Arch. f. Rechts — u. Soz. Phil.*, Band XXX, p. 110.

[189] Roland Freissler, 'Totaler Staat? Nationalsozialistischer Staat!' *D. Jstz.* 1934, p. 44; Cf. Otto Koellreutter, 'Leviathan und totaler Staat,' *R. Verw. Bl.* 1938, pp. 803-7; Alfred Rosenberg in *V. B.* of January 9 & 10, 1934, and Ernst Huber, 'Die Totalität des völkischen Staates,' *Die Tat*, 1934, p. 60.

[190] Jacob Burckhardt. *Weltgeschichtliche Betrachtungen* (Kröner's Taschenausgabe, Band 55, Leipzig), p. 197. Cf. Hegel, *Die Verfassung Deutschlands* (Lasson, *Hegels Schriften zur Politik und Rechtsphilosophie*, Leipzig, 1913), p. 28.

[191] Erich Kaufmann, *Die clausula rebus sic stantibus und das Völkerrecht* (Tübingen, 1911), p. 136.

[192] Carl Schmitt, *Der Hüter der Verfassung* (Tübingen, 1931), p. 79.

[193] Ernst Jünger, 'Die totale Mobilmachung,' in *Krieg und Krieger* (edited by Ernst Jünger, Berlin 1930).

[194] *Dt. Bergw. Ztg.*, November 24, 1932 (partly reprinted in *Europäische Revue*, February 1933).

[195] Ib.

[196] Ernst Huber, 'Die Rechtsstellung des Volksgenossen erläutert am Beispiel der Eigentumsordnung,' *Ztschr. f. d. ges. Staatsw.* 1936, p. 452.

[197] Werner Best, *Jahrbuch der Akademie für deutsches Recht*, 1937, p. 133.

[198] Ib.

[199] Carl Bilfinger, 'Betrachtungen über politisches Recht,' *Ztschr. f. ausl. öff. u. Völkerr.*, Band I, pp. 57-76.

[200] Bilfinger demonstrated that the international arbitration treaties of the post-war period considered the political element insofar as they excluded questions touching on the existence of states from their scope. Those questions were segregated and relegated to the extra-legal field. Wherever existential questions were made the object of normative regulations, Bilfinger

argued that such treaties were made among unequal parties and involved the renunciation of the principle of equality.

201 Carl Schmitt, *Nationalsozialismus und Völkerrecht* (*Schriften der Hochschule für Politik*, Heft ix, Berlin 1934).

202 Carl Schmitt, '*Die Kernfrage des Völkerbunds*,' *Schmoller's Jahrbücher*, Band 48, p. 25.

203 This structural identity between National-Socialist domestic law and international law abolished the dualism which had existed in pre-war Germany between the domestic legal system, dominated by the Rule of Law, and the system of international relations which was completely governed by power politics. Cf. Hermann Heller, 'Staat,' in *Handwörterbuch der Soziologie* (Stuttgart, 1931), Band II, p. 610; Karl Mannheim, Rational and Irrational Elements in Contemporary Society. *L. T. Hobhouse Memorial Trust Lectures No. 4, delivered on 7 March 1934* (London, 1934), p. 34.

204 Hans Kelsen always opposed this doctrine and pointed out the dangers connected with this concept of government. [*Allgemeine Staatslehre* (Berlin, 1925), p. 254].

205 Otto Mayer, *Deutsches Verwaltungsrecht* (*Systematisches Handbuch der Deutschen Rechtswissenschaft*, Teil VI,) 3rd ed. (München, 1924) Band 1, p. 8.

206 Carl J. Friedrich, 'Separation of Powers,' in *Encyclopaedia of the Social Sciences*, ed. by Seligman and Johnson, vol. 13 (New York, 1934), pp. 663-6.

207 John Locke, *Two treatises of civil government*, §158.

208 Ernst Wolgast, 'Die auswärtige Gewalt des Deutschen Reiches unter besonderer Berücksichtigung des Auswärtigen Amtes' (*Arch. f. öff. Recht*, N. F. Band V, p. 96); Friedmann 'Geschichte und Struktur der Notstandsverordnungen,' *Kirchenrechtliche Abhandlungen*, 1905, p. 41.

209 'A speech in behalf of the Constitution against the Suspending and Dispensing Prerogative. House of Lords, Dec. 10, 1766.' (Published in Hansard, *Parliamentary History of England*, (London 1813) vol. XVI, pp. 251-313, especially pp. 265-6.)

210 'By executive power we mean no reference to those powers exercised under our former government by the Crown as of its prerogative.' The executive power, according to Jefferson, comprises 'those powers which are necessary to execute the laws (and administer the government) and which are not in their nature either legislative or judiciary.' (Thomas Jefferson, *Notes on the State of Virginia*, Richmond, 1853, p. 230, appendix).

211 Ib., p. 137.

212 Metternich, *Nachgelassene Schriften*, Band VIII, p. 114. This letter is extremely significant because its author had wielded tremendous political powers during more than forty years as Chancellor of Austria and had been overthrown by a political revolution only a few weeks previously.

213 Rudolf Smend, *Verfassung und Verfassungsrecht* (München, 1928); *Die politische Gewalt im Verfassungsstaat und das Problem der Staatsform (Festgabe für Wilhelm Kahl)* (Tübingen, 1923).

[214] Rudolf Smend, *Verfassung und Verfassungsrecht*, pp. 97-98.

[215] Carl Schmitt, *Verfassungslehre* (München, 1928), p. 131.

[216] We are now able to correct our preliminary formulation to the effect that the political sphere is a 'sector of the state.' Cf. note 2, and Ernst Huber, 'Die Einheit der Staatsgewalt,' *D. J. Z.* 1934, pp. 954-5.

[217] See note 215.

[218] A. V. Dicey's statement (*Law of the Constitution*, 8th ed., p. 198, London, 1926) that 'the predominance of regular law is opposed to the influence of arbitrary power and excludes the existence of arbitrariness of prerogative or even wide discretionary authority' insofar as it referred to discretionary authority, was never accepted in Germany. Cf. Harold J. Laski, 'Discretionary Power,' *Politica* vol. I, pp. 284-5.

[219] Supreme Court of the U. S.: *Myers v. United States* 272 US 52, 293.

[220] Hermann Reuss, in a comment on a decision of the Prussian Supreme Administrative Court (Preussisches Oberverwaltungsgericht) of June 30, 1936, *J. W.* 1937, p. 423.

[221] Ib.

[222] *Festschrift zum 60. Geburtstag des Staatssekretärs Schlegelberger* (Berlin, 1937), p. 43.

[223] Hermann Goering, 'Die Rechtssicherheit als Grundlage der Volksgemeinschaft,' *D. Jstz.* 1934, p. 1427.

[224] Entrepreneurial freedom has always been restricted by exceptional decrees introduced into the *Gewerbeordnung* of June 21, 1869 *RGBl.* 1900, p. 87.

[225] Preussisches Oberverwaltungsgericht, August 10, 1936 (*J. W.* 1937, p. 1032).

[226] Ib.

[227] Ib.

[228] Ib.

[229] Carl Schmitt, 'Staatsethik und pluralistischer Staat,' (*Kant-Studien*, Band XXXV, p. 41).

[230] Bayerischer Verwaltungsgerichtshof, June 5, 1936 (*R. Verw. Bl.* 1938, p. 17).

[231] Ib.

[232] Ib.

[233] August 18, 1896 (*RGBl.* 1898, 195).

[234] Kammergericht, June 25, 1937 (*Recht des Nährstandes* 1938, No. 63 of the decisions).

[235] Reichsdisziplinarhof, August 30, 1938 (*Dtsch. Verw.* 1939, p. 281).

[236] Ib.

[237] Ib.

[238] Oberlandesgericht Köln, February 1, 1935 (*J. W.* 1935, p. 1106).

[239] June 7, 1909 (*RGBl.* 1909, 499).

[240] Oberlandesgericht Hamburg, May 12, 1937 (*D. Jstz.* 1937, p. 1712).

[241] Ib.

[242] Reichsarbeitsgericht, April 25, 1936 (*J. W.* 1936, p. 2945).

[243] January 20, 1934 (*RGBl.* 1934, 45).

[244] This question is especially significant because one of the most important features of the new penal law introduced by National-Socialism is the authority granted to punish acts, not mentioned in the code, by analogy with acts specified by the court as punishable. This change in penal law does not apply to labor law.

[245] Reichsehrengerichtshof, September 30, 1935 (*Arb. R. S.* Band 25, p. 89).

[246] Werner Mansfeld, 'Die soziale Ehre,' *Dtsch. Recht* 1934, p. 125.

[247] Reichsgericht, November 14, 1936 (*D. Jstz.* 1936, p. 1941).

[248] Reichsgericht, December 2, 1936 (*RGZ.* 153, p. 71).

[249] Cf. below, 'The Legal Status of the Jews,' pp. 89-96.

[250] The discrepancy between the 'authoritarian leader state' and the 'sovereign central parliament' as proposed in the program is obvious. Nor have the trusts been abolished, etc.

[251] Reichsgericht, March 10, 1934 (*RGZ.* 144, p. 106 [112]).

[252] Zivilprozessordnung, May 17, 1898 (*RGBl.* 1933, 821).

[253] Reichsstrafgesetzbuch, May 15, 1871 (*RGBl.* 1876, 40).

[254] Reichsgericht, July 6, 1934 (*RGZ.* 144, p. 306 [310]).

[255] Landgericht Breslau, November 18, 1934 (*D. Jstz.* 1935, p. 413).

[256] As a matter of fact the Breslau decision was an exceptional one and was reversed by the next higher court.

[257] Paetzold, in a comment on the decision of the Landgericht Breslau. (*D. Jstz.* 1935, p. 413).

[258] Reichsgericht (Plenarentscheidung), November 16, 1937 (*RGZ.* 156, p. 305).

[259] Landgericht Hamburg (*Dtsch. R. Z.* 1935, No. 631).

[260] Ib.

[261] Oberlandesgericht München, August 10, 1936 (*Reger* 1937, p. 571).

[262] Amtsgericht Berlin, August 12, 1936 (*Jgdr. u. Jgdwohlf.* 1936, p. 283).

[263] Ib.

[264] A closer examination of the decision shows that the 'self-interest' of the Jewish parents consisted in the fact that even after they knew the racial laws 'the father still clung to the child.' Actually the father had no choice in the matter under the German Civil Code. In the name of 'public interest,' the court held that the father had to give up the child while continuing to provide for its support.

[265] Reichsgericht, July 12, 1934 (*RGZ.* 145, p. 1).

[266] Gesetz zum Schutz des deutschen Blutes und der deutschen Ehre, September 15, 1935 (*RGBl.* 1935, 1146). (So-called 'Nürnberger Gesetze.')

[267] Bürgerliches Gesetzbuch, August 18, 1896 (*RGBl.* 1898, 195).

[268] This short period was set to prevent upsetting the family status of the child and disturbance of the family peace over a long period of time.

269 Reichsgericht, November 23, 1937 (*RGZ.* 152, p. 390).

270 Ib.

271 Oberlandesgericht Naumburg, April 20, 1937 (*Akademie Ztschr.* 1937, p. 587).

272 Massfeller, in a comment on the decision of the Oberlandesgericht Naumburg (*Akademie Ztschr.* 1937, p. 587).

273 See p. 62 of this book.

274 This was a consequence of Dr. Schacht's policy.

275 June 7, 1909, (*RGBl.* 1909, 499).

276 Reichsgericht, February 25, 1936 (*RGZ.* 150, p. 299). This decision was overruled by the Reichsgericht on February 4, 1939 (*J. W.* 1939, p. 437).

277 Preussisches Oberverwaltungsgericht, November 21, 1935 (*R. Verw. Bl.* 1936, p. 553; see *Jugend und Recht,* October 1936).

278 Ib.

279 Hamburger (Hanseatisches) Oberlandesgericht, May 4, 1937 (*Hans. R. u. Ger. Ztg.* 1937, p. 216).

280 Ib.

281 Reichsgericht, March 30, 1938 (*J. W.* 1938, p. 1826).

282 Ib.

283 Reichsarbeitsgericht, June 2, 1937 (*Arbeitsr. Entsch.* 30, p. 153).

284 Reichsarbeitsgericht, March 20, 1937 (*J. W.* 1937, p. 2310).

285 Arbeitsgericht Saalfeld, July 13, 1937 (*J. W.* 1937, p. 2851).

286 Ib.

287 Gesetz über Mieterschutz und Mieteinigungsämter, June 29, 1926 (*RGBl.* 1926, 347).

288 Cf. Adami in *J. W.* 1938, p. 3217 and the official declaration of the Reich Ministry of Justice: 'Veröffentlichungen der Zeitschrift "Das Schwarze Korps,"' (item 7) published in *D. Jstz.* 1939, p. 175.

289 Amtsgericht Berlin-Charlottenburg, March 9, 1938 (*J. W.* 1938, p. 3173).

290 Amtsgericht Berlin-Schöneberg, September 16, 1938 (*J. W.* 1938, p. 3045).

291 Landgericht Berlin, November 7, 1938 (*J. W.* 1938, p. 3242).

292 Ib.

293 Friedrich Schiller, 'Letters upon the Aesthetic Education of Man,' in *Literary and Philosophical Essays* (ed. by C. W. Eliot, New York, 1910), p. 229. *'Der Mensch kann sich aber auf eine doppelte Weise entgegengesetzt sein: entweder als Wilder, wenn seine Gefühle über seine Grundsätze herrschen; oder als Barbar, wenn seine Grundsätze seine Gefühle zerstören.'*

294 Professor Kohlrausch, 'Rassenverrat im Ausland' *Akademie Ztschr.* 1938, p. 336, discussing a decision of the *Grosser Strafsenat des Reichsgerichts* of February 23, 1938 (*Akademie Ztschr.* 1938, p. 349).

295 Reichsgericht, June 27, 1936 (*Seufferts Archiv,* Band 91, p. 65).

296 Ib.

297 *Erlass des Reichswirtschaftsministers, Kart. Rundsch.* 1936, p. 754.

298 *Handwörterbuch der Rechtswissenschaft*, Band VIII (Berlin, 1936), article: 'Stand,' p. 683.

299 Dr. Knauth, 'Die Aufgaben der Polizei im nationalsozialistischen Staat,' *D. J. Z.* 1936, p. 1206, 1210.

300 Georg Schmidt, 'Zu einem Reichspolizeigesetz,' *R. Verw. Bl.* 1935, p. 838.

301 Reinhard Hoehn, 'Die Wandlungen im Polizeirecht,' *Dtsch. Rw.* 1936, p. 100.

302 Walther Hamel, in Frank, *Deutsches Verwaltungsrecht* (München, 1937), p. 391.

303 Ludwig von Koehler, *Grundlehren des Verwaltungsrechts* (Berlin und Stuttgart, 1935), pp. 347-8.

304 Arnold Koettgen, *Deutsche Verwaltung* (2nd ed., Berlin, 1937), p. 143.

305 Reinhard Hoehn, 'Das Führerprinzip in der Verwaltung,' *Dtsch. Recht*, 1936, p. 306.

306 Schriftleitergesetz of October 4, 1933 (*RGBl.* 1933, 713).

307 Reichsgericht, April 28, 1936 (*D. Jstz.* 1936, p. 1131). The author of the rumor that there was no freedom of the press in the Third Reich was not unconditionally acquitted. The court decided to investigate whether by 'freedom' he meant the freedom of the Weimar System or the regulated freedom of the Third Reich. Had it been determined that he meant the latter, he would have been found guilty and sentenced to the penitentiary for a maximum of five years.

308 Franz Wieacker, 'Der Stand der Rechtserneuerung auf dem Gebiet des bürgerlichen Rechts,' *Dtsch. Rw.* 1937, p. 7.

309 Werner Mansfeld, 'Die Deutsche Arbeitsfront,' *Dtsch. Arb. R.* 1933, p. 139.

310 Arnold Koettgen, 'Polizei und Gesetz,' *R. Verw. Bl.* 1938, p. 173.

311 At this point in our discussion, the justification of our undifferentiated treatment of state and party authorities is quite evident. A purely juristic analysis of the situation would treat the Labor Front and the Estates as public corporations. But this would only obscure the real situation.

312 Gesetz über Änderung einiger Vorschriften der Reichsversicherungsordnung, December 23, 1936 (*RGBl.* 1936, 1128); Reichsversicherungsordnung of July 19, 1911 (*RGBl.* 1926, 9, originally published *RGBl.* 1911, 509).

313 Gustav Radbruch, *Rechtsphilosophie* (3rd ed., Leipzig, 1932), pp. 182 ff.

314 The fact that, historically viewed, the principle of inviolability of law originated in Natural Law is purposely stressed by Radbruch, who in the preface of his book announces his opposition to certain more fashionable currents of thought and identifies himself with an epoch which the National-Socialist legal philosopher Larenz had ridiculed as the 'Night of the Enlightenment.'

315 The authoritative character of these utterances is indicated by their conspicuous publication in most law reviews.

316 Hans Gerber, 'Volk und Staat (Grundlinien einer deutschen Staatsphi-

losophie),' *Ztschr. f. dtsch. Kult. Philos.*, N. F. 1936, Band III pp. 15-56, especially p. 24.

317 Ib., p. 23.

318 Ib., p. 42.

319 Ib., p. 41.

320 Alfred Rosenberg, 'Lebensrecht, nicht Formalrecht,' *Dtsch. Recht* 1934, p. 233.

321 Alfred Rosenberg, *Der Mythos des 20. Jahrhunderts* (53rd-4th ed., München, 1934), pp. 571-2.

322 Gustav Walz, 'Der Führerstaat,' *D. Jstz.*, 1936, p. 814-15.

323 Rudolf Smend, *Verfassung und Verfassungsrecht* (München, 1928), p. 102.

324 See note 321.

325 Carl Schmitt, 'Nationalsozialistiches Rechtsdenken,' *Dtsch. Recht*, 1934, p. 225.

326 Leuner, 'Spekulatives und Lebensgesundes Staatsrecht,' *Jugend und Recht*, 1937, p. 49.

327 Hitler proclaimed this principle on the meeting of German lawyers in Leipzig in a famous speech (October 1933). This dogma, incidentally, completely denies the Kantian distinction between legality and morality. Cf. Georg Rusche and Otto Kirchheimer, *Punishment and Social Structure* (New York 1939) p. 179.

328 Carl Dernedde, 'Gesetz und Einzelanordnung,' *Ztschr. f. d. ges. Staatsw.*, vol. 97, p. 377.

329 See note 16.

330 Hermann Heller, 'Bürger und Bourgeois,' *Neue Rundschau* 1932, p. 725.

331 Speech delivered before the conference on legal and social philosophy April 11, 1914 (Chicago University); published in *The Philosophical Review*, vol. XXV, 1916. pp. 761-777, especially p. 761.

332 Carl L. Becker, 'Afterthoughts on Constitutions,' in C. J. Read, *The Constitution Reconsidered* (New York, 1938), p. 396. Cf. Otto von Gierke, *Johannes Althusius und die Entwicklung der naturrechtlichen Staatstheorien* (4th ed., Breslau 1929) pp. 318, 366, 391.

333 T. Werner Jaeger, *Paideia, the Ideals of Greek Culture* (translated by Gilbert Highet) (New York, 1939), p. 323. Smend was partly correct when, in his praise of Carl Schmitt's earlier writings (especially *Die Diktatur*), he wrote: 'The attitude of antiquity towards the state and the antiquarian approach are beautifully combined in this book.' (Smend: *Verfassung und Verfassungsrecht*, München, 1928, p. 104).

334 Reinhard Hoehn, *Otto von Gierke's Staatslehre und unsere Zeit* (Hamburg, 1936).

335 Alfred Manigk, 'Rechtsfindung im neuen Staat,' *Arch. f. Rechts-u. Soz. Phil.* 1936, p. 176.

[336] A. J. Carlyle, *A History of Medieval Political Theory in the West* (Edinburgh and London, 1903), vol. I, p. 8.

[337] Ib.

[338] Charles H. McIlwain, *The Growth of Political Thought in the West* (New York, 1932), pp. 364-5.

[339] Gesetz zur Behebung der Not von Volk und Reich (Ermächtigungs-gesetz), March 24, 1933 (*RGBl.* 1933, 141).

[340] Charles H. McIlwain, 'The Fundamental Law behind the Constitution of the United States,' in C. J. Read, *The Constitution Reconsidered* (New York, 1938), pp. 5, 7, and McIlwain, *Constitutionalism and the Changing World* (*Collected Papers*), article 'Liberalism and the Totalitarian Ideals' (New York, 1939), p. 263.

[341] Ernst Troeltsch, *Die Soziallehren der christlichen Kirchen und Gruppen*, 3rd ed. (Tübingen, 1923), English translation by Olive Wyon, *The Social Teachings of the Christian Churches* (London, 1931).

[342] Eduard Zeller, *Die Philosophie der Griechen* (5th ed., Leipzig 1909), English translation by Alleyne, *A History of Greek Philosophy* (London, 1881).

[343] See note 341.

[344] Martin Luther's *Sämtliche Werke* (*Deutsch*), Band 50 (Frankfurt a. M. – Erlangen, 1851), p. 349. Cf. Erich Brandenburg, *Martin Luther's Anschauung vom Staate und der Gesellschaft* (Halle, 1901), p. 5, note 6.

[345] Martin Luther, *Von weltlicher Obrigkeit, Sämtliche Werke, Band* 27, (Frankfurt a. M. – Erlangen, 1851), p. 83. In his latest work, *Der Leviathan in der Staatslehre des Thomas Hobbes* (Hamburg 1938), Carl Schmitt tries to prove that modern freedom of thought and conscience did not have its historical origin, as ordinarily assumed, in Protestantism. Schmitt argues that, according to Hobbes, the individual is free to believe what he desires to believe, provided he submits to the religious cult prescribed by the state. Thus the undermining of the omnipotent Leviathan was started by Hobbes himself. 'A few years after the publication of the Leviathan the first liberal Jew came across this ordinarily unperceivable inconsistency' (Schmitt, op. cit. p. 86.) This 'first liberal Jew,' by a 'simple logical maneuver' characteristic of 'Jewish mentality,' managed to pervert Hobbes' line of reasoning. Whereas Hobbes speaks of a sphere of reservation which the omnipotent state graciously grants to the individual regarding his religion, Spinoza (for Schmitt refers to no-one else by the application 'first liberal Jew') postulates the principle of the freedom of belief in a manner which makes it the duty of the state to respect all opinions in the sphere of religion except when they undermine public safety. Spinoza, according to Schmitt, thus took the decisive step in developing the conception of the neutral and agnostic state of the nineteenth and twentieth centuries, i. e., the conception of the very state which evokes the deepest contempt on the part of National-Socialist Germany.

It is not difficult to detect the political purpose of this novel historical interpretation. By declaring the doctrine of freedom of conscience to be a product of Jewish thought, Schmitt attempts to denounce the fight of the Confessional Church for this doctrine as a Jewish affair.

Schmitt, however, overlooks two things. First: the principle of tolerance as developed by Spinoza in his *Tractatus Politicus* had been realized by Roger Williams in Rhode Island at a time when Spinoza was only two years old. Secondly: Spinoza's conception that the freedom of thought must be granted to everyone and that the right of intervention is limited only to the public manifestation, not to the private creed, is in no way a product of 'Jewish mentality.' It was a German of pure Aryan origin who developed the same idea in his doctoral dissertation: Johann Wolfgang Goethe (cf. *Dichtung und Wahrheit*, 3. Band 11. Buch; English translation by John Oxenford: *The Autobiography of Goethe, 'From my own Life, Truth and Poetry.'* London, 1891, p. 408).

[346] Published in *D. Jstz.* 1937, p. 873.

[347] Niccolo Machiavelli, 'Discourses on the first ten Books of Titus Livius, Book II, Chap. 2,' in *The Historical, Political, and Diplomatic Writings of Niccolo Machiavelli* (translated from the Italian by Christian E. Detmold, Boston 1882), vol. II, p. 232.

[348] Op. cit., Book I, Chap. 11 (vol. II, p. 127).

[349] Hermann Heller, *Staatslehre* (Leyden, 1934), p. 218.

[350] Norbert Gürke, 'Der Stand der Völkerrechtswissenschaft,' *Dtsch. Rw.* Band II, p. 75.

[351] Otto von Gierke, *Johannes Althusius und die Entwicklung der naturrechtlichen Staatstheorien* (2nd ed., Breslau, 1902), p. 73.

[352] Hugo Preuss, *Verfassungspolitische Entwicklungen in Deutschland und Westeuropa (Historische Grundlegung zu einem Staatsrecht der Deutschen Republik).* (Aus dem Nachlass von Dr. Hugo Preuss herausgegeben und eingeleitet von Dr. Hedwig Hintze, Berlin, 1925), pp. 400-1; Alfred Vierkandt, *Der Geistig-sittliche Gehalt des neueren Naturrechts* (Wien, 1927), p. 17.

[353] Hans Kelsen, *Die philosophischen Grundlagen der Naturrechtslehre und des Rechtspositivismus* (Charlottenburg, 1928), pp. 39-40.

[354] Hermann Heller, 'Political Science,' in *Encyclopaedia of Social Sciences,* ed. by Seligman and Johnson, vol. 12 (New York, 1934) p. 218.

[355] Roscoe Pound, in *Interpretation of Legal History* (New York, 1923, p. 19), has shown that the Historical School of Law was based upon an irrational conception of Natural Law. Cf. Rexius, 'Studien zur Staatslehre der historischen Schule,' *H. Z.* Band 107, pp. 513-15.

[356] Carl Larenz, 'Volksgeist und Recht, zur Revision der Rechtsanschauung der historischen Schule,' *Ztschr. f. dtsch. Kult. Philos.* Band I, p. 40, especially p. 52.

357 Hegel, 'Die Verfassung Deutschlands.' *Sämtliche Werke* (herausgegeben von Lasson), Band VII (Leipzig, 1913) pp. 3-149.

358 Hegel, *Grundlinien der Philosophie des Rechts* (herausgegeben von Lasson) 3rd ed. (Leipzig, 1930), §182, Zusatz, p. 334, English translation by S. W. Deyde, *Philosophy of Right* (London, 1896), p. 186.

359 Ib. §324, Zusatz, p. 369. English translation, p. 332.

360 Hegel, 'Über die wissenschaftlichen Behandlungsarten des Naturrechts.' *Sämtliche Werke* (herausgegeben von Lasson), Band VII (Leipzig, 1913), pp. 329-416, especially p. 371.

361 Friedrich Meinecke, *Die Idee der Staatsraison* (München, 1924), p. 435.

362 Hans Frank, 'Die Aufgaben des Rechts,' *Akademie Ztschr.* 1938, p. 4.

363 Alfred Rosenberg, *Der Mythos des 20. Jahrhunderts* (München, 1934), p. 525.

364 Otto Koellreutter, *Grundfragen des völkischen und staatlichen Lebens im deutschen Volksstaat* (Berlin-Charlottenburg, 1935), p. 14, and Koellreutter, *Volk und Staat in der Weltanschauung des Nationalsozialismus* (Berlin, 1935), pp. 12 ff.

365 Carl Larenz, 'Die Rechts— und Staatsphilosophie des deutschen Idealismus und ihre Gegenwartsbedeutung' in *Handbuch der Philosophie*, (herausgegeben von A. Baeumler und M. Schröter), Abteilung IV, (München and Berlin, 1934), pp. 153, 187-8.

366 Julius Loewenstein, *Hegels Staatsidee; ihr Doppelgesicht und ihr Einfluss im 19. Jahrhundert* (Berlin, 1927), note 45.

367 Hegel, *Grundlinien der Philosophie des Rechts* (herausgegeben von Lasson), 3rd ed. (Leipzig, 1930), §270, p. 212; English translation by S. W. Deyde, *Philosophy of Right* (London, 1896), p. 263.

368 *Verhandlungen des Ersten Deutschen Soziologentages* (Tübingen, 1911), p. 187.

369 Ernst Troeltsch, 'Das stoisch-christliche Naturrecht und das moderne profane Naturrecht' in *Gesammelte Werke*, Band IV (Tübingen, 1921-25), pp. 166-91, especially p. 186.

370 Ernst Troeltsch, 'Das christliche Naturrecht (Überblick), in *Gesammelte Werke*, Band IV (op. cit.), pp. 156-66, especially p. 165.

371 Max Weber in *Wirtschaft und Gesellschaft* (Tübingen 1921 pp. 499-501) saw that beginnings of a proletarian Natural Law had been checked by the Marxian hostility to Natural Law.

372 Friedrich Engels, *The Housing Question*, (Moscow — Leningrad 1935), p. 88.

373 *Critique of the Gotha Programme*, edited by C. P. Dutt (New York, 1937), p. 17.

374 Karl Marx, *Capital*, Vol. I (translated by Samuel Moore and Edward Aveling, Chicago, 1912), pp. 258-9.

375 Ib., vol. III (translated by Ernest Untermann, Chicago, 1909), p. 399.

[376] Hellmuth Plessner, *Grenzen der Gemeinschaft* (*Eine Kritik des sozialen Radikalismus*) (Bonn, 1924), p. 36.

[377] Karl Marx, op. cit. vol. III. p. 954.

[378] Marx and Engels, *Gesamtausgabe*, vol. I, p. 325.

[379] Michael Freund, *George Sorel* (*Der revolutionäre Konservativismus*) (Frankfurt a. M. 1932).

[380] Quoted in Waldemar Gurian, *Der integrale Nationalismus in Frankreich* (*Charles Maurras und die Action française*) (Frankfurt a. M., 1931) p. 84.

[381] Ernst Jünger, *Der Kampf als inneres Erlebnis* (5th ed., Berlin, 1933) p. 78 and Ernst Jünger, 'Die totale Mobilmachung' in *Krieg und Krieger* (ed. by Ernst Jünger, Berlin, 1930).

[382] Carl Schmitt, '*Nationalsozialistisches Rechtsdenken*' Dtsch. Recht, 1934, p. 225.

[383] Even more characteristic than Carl Schmitt's well-known essay on the nature of political activity is a book by Richard Behrendt: *Politischer Aktivismus* (Berlin, 1932).

[384] Alfred Meusel, 'Der klassische Sozialismus,' *Arch. f. Rechts. u. Soz. Phil.* Band XXIV, 1930-1, pp. 125-168, especially 148.

[385] Carl L. Becker, *The Declaration of Independence* (New York, 1922) pp. 57, 60, 265, 274, 278. In the National-Socialist literature the problem is discussed by Max Mikorey: 'Naturgesetz und Staatsgesetz,' *Akademie Ztschr.* 1936, p. 932 especially p. 942). Cf. Friedrich Nietzsche, *Beyond Good and Evil, Prelude to a Philosophy of the Future* (1st ed. London, 1901), p. 32.

[386] The materialistic interpretation of history endeavors to derive the changing problem of natural science from the change in productive relations. Cf. Otto Bauer, 'Das Weltbild des Kapitalismus,' in *Der lebendige Marxismus, Festgabe zum 70. Geburtstag von Karl Kautsky* (ed. by Otto Jennssen, Jena 1924). Yet the sociology of the natural sciences is still an almost entirely unexplored territory.

[387] Otto von Gierke, *Das deutsche Genossenschaftsrecht*, Band IV (Berlin 1913), p. 391, note 47.

[388] Ib., p. 392, note 49; p. 491.

[389] Leibniz, *Deutsche Schriften* (Berlin, 1838) Band I, p. 414.

[390] George Gurvitch, article 'Natural Law' in *Encyclopaedia of the Social Sciences*, ed. by Johnson and Seligman (New York, 1933), vol. XI, pp. 284-90.

[391] The above references to the history of communal Natural Law are necessitated by the fact that National-Socialist propagandists of this theory —Professor Wolgast of Würzburg and his disciple Dietze—omit reference to it. Since National-Socialism is supposed to be the original creation of Adolf Hitler, such historical references are unfavorably viewed in the Third Reich. Dietze's 'Naturrecht aus Blut und Boden' (*Akademie Ztschr.* 1936, p. 818)

represents the best summary of the National-Socialist theory of communal Natural Law.

392 252 US 416, 433.

393 Adolf Hitler, *Mein Kampf* (42nd ed., München, 1933) p. 433.

394 Th. Buddeberg, 'Descartes und der politische Absolutismus,' *Arch. f. Rechts. u. Soz. Phil.* Band XXX, 1937, p. 544.

395 Andreas Pfenning, 'Gemeinschaft und Staatswissenschaft (Versuch einer systematischen Bestimmung des Gemeinschaftsbegriffes),' *Ztschr. f. d. ges. Staatsw.*, Band 96, pp. 312 ff.

396 Konrad Heiden, *History of National-Socialism* (translated from the German, London, 1934), has emphasized the influence of the Russian emigration upon the development of National-Socialism. In the early stages of the National-Socialist movement, Munich was the 'Coblenz' of the White Russian *émigrés*. It was from these circles that National-Socialists also borrowed this particular form of anti-Semitism.

397 Max Weber, *Wirtschaft und Gesellschaft* (Tübingen, 1921), p. 631.

398 Hellmuth Dietze, *Naturrecht der Gegenwart* (Bonn, 1936)

399 The work of Professor Wolgast of the University of Würzburg ('*Völkerrecht*' in *Das gesamte Deutsche Recht in systematischer Darstellung*, Teil XIII, pp. 698-993, Berlin 1934) is of importance in this connection. Wolgast acknowledges his indebtedness to Adolf Hitler, the Leader, and to Toennies, the Seer of the Third Reich.

400 Norbert Gürke, *Grundzüge des Völkerrechts* (Berlin, 1936).

401 Ferdinand Toennies, *Einführung in die Soziologie* (Stuttgart, 1931).

402 Henry Maine, *Ancient Law* (London and Toronto, 1917), pp. 67-100, especially p. 100. Cf. Ferdinand Toennies, *Gemeinschaft und Gesellschaft* (6th ed., Berlin, 1926), Buch III, §7, p. 182, and Toennies, *Soziologische Studien und Kritiken* (Jena, 1925), Band I, p. 54.

403 Karl Landauer, 'Zum Niedergang des Fascismus,' *Gesellschaft*, 1925, p. 168.

404 Hans Freyer, *Soziologie als Wirklichkeitswissenschaft* (Leipzig, 1930), p. 240.

405 Cf. Ernest Barker, Introduction to Otto Gierke, *Natural Law and the Theory of Society 1500-1800* (Cambridge, 1934), p. 17.

406 In the light of this claim it is of interest to note that during the post-war period the concept of *Gemeinschaft* was also used for a time in the Marxist labor movement in Germany. Though this appropriation of the *Gemeinschaft* concept never got very far in the socialist movement, it was not an isolated phenomenon. A somewhat similar *Gemeinschaft* theory is to be found in Friedrich Engels' *Origin of the Family*. The primitive conditions 'which preceded alienation,' as sketched by Engels, had many communal Natural Law traits.

Plessner's contention that the Marxian theory is intelligible to the proletariat only as a theory of liberation from the machine is correct. But when he continues to say that 'Socialism abolishes society for the sake of community' he is generalizing tendencies which existed in the German socialist youth movement at the time the book was written. These tendencies never became important in the policies of the German working class parties. (Hellmuth Plessner, *Grenzen der Gemeinschaft; eine Kritik des sozialen Radikalismus.* Bonn 1924, p. 36.)

[407] Johannes Heckel, 'Der Einbruch des jüdischen Geistes in das deutsche Staats– und Kirchenrecht durch F. J. Stahl,' *H. Z.* 155, 529.

[408] The present author, in spite of his complete skepticism regarding the proposition that there is a close association between an author's race and his political theory, thinks it is not without interest to present at least one example of a genuine 'Aryan' who has dealt with political theory and who has not arrived at the theory of the *Gemeinschaft.* Justus Möser, concerning whose Germanism National-Socialist authors have never raised any questions, wrote: 'Any civil society is like a stock company. Every citizen is a stockholder. A serf is a member of the state who has no shares and hence is without assets and liabilities. This is no more contrary to religion than it is to be an employee of the East India Company without possessing shares in it. At bottom there is an explicit or tacit social contract among all landowners who turned in their farms against shares.' (Justus Möser, *Patriotische Phantasien*, III, 3rd. ed., Berlin, 1804, No. 62).

[409] Carl Dernedde, 'Werdendes Staatsrecht,' *Ztschr f. d. ges. Staatsw.* 1935, Band 95, p. 349.

[410] Hans Gerber, 'Volk und Staat (Grundlinien einer deutschen Staatsphilosophie),' *Ztschr. f. dtsch. Kult. Philos.*, Band III, 1936, p. 47.

[411] Heinrich Herrfahrdt, 'Politische Verfassungslehre,' *Arch. f. Rechts. u. Soz. Phil.* Band XXX, 1936, p. 109.

[412] Carl Schmitt, *Über die drei Arten des rechtswissenschaftlichen Denkens*, (Schriften der Akademie für Deutsches Recht; Hamburg, 1934), p. 13.

[413] Theodor Maunz, in Frank *Deutsches Verwaltungsrecht* (München, 1937).

[414] Carl Schmitt, *Über die drei Arten des rechtswissenschaftlichen Denkens* (Hamburg, 1934), p. 52.

[415] Hegel, *Philosophie der Weltgeschichte. Sämtliche Werke* (herausgegeben von Lasson), Band VIII (Leipzig, 1923), p. 925; English translation by J. Sibree, *Lectures on the Philosophy of History* (London, 1890), pp. 470-1.

[416] Carl Schmitt, *Legalität und Legitimität* (München, 1932), p. 13.

[417] Georg Dahm, 'Die drei Arten des rechtswissenschaftlichen Denkens,' *Ztschr. f. d. ges. Staatsw.*, Band 95, p. 181.

[418] Friedrich Völtzer, 'Vom Werden des deutschen Sozialismus,' *Ztschr. f. d. ges. Staatsw.*, Band 96, p. 1.

[419] Friedrich Kühn, 'Der vorläufige Aufbau der gewerblichen Wirtschaft,' *Arch. f. öff. Recht*, Band 27, p. 334.

[420] Ib., p. 360.

[421] Friedrich Völtzer, op. cit., p. 9.

[422] Georg Havestädt, 'Grundverhältnisse des Eigentums,' Verwaltungsarchiv, Band 42, pp. 337-68.

[423] Ib., p. 365.

[424] Ernst Huber, 'Die Rechtsstellung des Volksgenossen (erläutert am Beispiel der Eigentumsordnung),' Ztschr. f. d. ges. Staatsw. 1935, p. 449.

[425] Hans Peter Ipsen, Politik und Justiz (Das Problem der justizlosen Hoheitsakte), (Hamburg, 1937).

[426] Ib., p. 276.

[427] He says that they refer 'not to heteronomous but to homogeneous spheres of a state in which justice rules.' (Ib, p. 239.)

[428] Ib., p. 12.

[429] Ib., p. 12.

[430] Max Weber, 'Der Sinn der Wertfreiheit der soziologischen und ökonomischen Wissenschaften,' (Gesammelte Aufsätze zur Wissenschaftslehre). (Tübingen, 1922), p. 458.

[431] Hans Frank, 'Der Nationalsozialismus und die Wissenschaft der Wirtschaftslehre,' Schmoller's Jahrbuch, Band 58, pp. 641-50, especially p. 643.

[432] Cf. Heinrich Rickert, Kant als Philosoph der modernen Kultur (ein geschichtsphilosophischer Versuch) (Tübingen, 1924), pp. 50, 125.

[433] See: Ferdinand Toennies, Gemeinschaft und Gesellschaft (6th and 7th eds., Berlin, 1926), p. 227, and Werner Sombart, Das Wirtschaftsleben im Zeitalter des Hochkapitalismus (München and Leipzig 1927) Band I, p. 48.

[434] Otto Hintze, 'Preussens Entwicklung zum Rechtsstaat,' Forschungen zur Brandenburgisch-Preussischen Geschichte, Band 32, p. 394.

[435] Ib., Staatsverfassung und Heeresverfassung (Dresden, 1906), p. 43.

[436] Michael Freund, 'Zur Deutung der Utopia des Thomas Morus (Ein Beitrag zur Geschichte der Staatsraison in England),' H. Z. Band 142, p. 255.

[437] Quoted in John Rushworth, Historical Collections (London, 1721), vol. II, p. 323.

[438] The Autobiography and Correspondence of Sir Simonds D'Ewes (edited by James Orchard Halliwell), (London, 1845), vol. II, p. 130.

[439] 4 Wallace 2 (121, 127).

[440] F. Morstein-Marx, 'Roosevelt's New Deal und das Dilemma amerikanischer Staatsführung,' Verwaltungsarchiv, Band 40, 1935, pp. 155-213.

[441] Reinhard Hoehn, 'Parlamentarische Demokratie und das neue deutsche Verfassungsrecht,' Dtsch. Rw. 1938, pp. 24-54.

[442] A. V. Dicey, Introduction to the Study of the Law of the Constitution, 8th ed. (London, 1926), pp. 198-9.

[443] Cf. William Ebenstein, 'Rule of Law im Lichte der reinen Rechtslehre,' Revue internationale de la théorie du droit, 1938, p. 316.

[444] The document is reprinted in Altmann, Ausgewählte Urkunden zur Brandenburgisch-Preussischen Verfassungs— und Verwaltungsgeschichte, 2nd ed. (Berlin, 1914).

445 Carl Brinkmann, in *Landeskunde der Provinz Brandenburg* (Berlin, 1910), Band II, p. 398, 'Wirtschaftsgeschichte.'

446 Bernhard Erdmannsdörfer, *Deutsche Geschichte im Zeitalter des Absolutismus* (Berlin, 1892-3), Band I, p. 423.

447 On the occasion of the 500th anniversary of the Hohenzollern Dynasty in 1915, Otto Hintze had to admit that the Prussian nobility had indeed known how to exploit the situation. (*Die Hohenzollern und ihr Werk* [Berlin, 1916], p. 206.)

448 Otto Hintze, 'Preussens Entwicklung zum Rechtsstaat,' *Forschungen zur Brandenburgisch-Preussischen Geschichte*, Band 32, p. 429.

449 Dr. Spatz in *Landeskunde der Provinz Brandenburg* (Berlin, 1910), Band II, p. 275, 'Zur Verwaltungsgeschichte der Städte und Dörfer, Marken und Kreise.'

450 Edgar Loening, *Gerichte und Verwaltungsbehörden in Brandenburg-Preussen* (Halle, 1914), p. 332.

451 Max Weber, *Wirtschaft und Gesellschaft* (Tübingen, 1922), p. 703.

452 Otto Hintze, 'Preussens Entwicklung zum Rechtsstaat,' *Forschungen zur Brandenburgisch-Preussischen Geschichte*, Band 32, p. 379.

453 Hugo Preuss, *Verfassungspolitische Entwicklungen in Deutschland und Westeuropa* (*Historische Grundlagen zu einem Staatsrecht der Deutschen Republik*), (Berlin, 1925), p. 401.

454 Friedrich II., König von Preussen: *Gesammelte Werke*, Band 9, p. 205.

455 Otto Hintze, '*Zur Agrarpolitik Friedrichs des Grossen,*' *Forschungen zur Brandenburgisch-Preussischen Geschichte*, Band 10, p. 287.

456 Cf. Karl Brinkmann, op. cit. Band II, p. 298.

457 The delimitation of this procedure was related to the concept of *status oeconomicus*, which came more and more to refer to questions connected with the royal domains.

458 Cf. A. Wagner, *Der Kampf der Justiz gegen die Verwaltung in Preussen* (*dargelegt an der rechtsgeschichtlichen Entwicklung des Konfliktgesetzes von 1844*), (Hamburg, 1936).

459 G. F. Knapp, *Die Bauernbefreiung und der Ursprung der Landarbeiter in den älteren Teilen Preussens* (2d ed., München, 1927). The decree provided for the cession of land by the liberated peasants as compensation to the *Junkers* for their losses. Hereditary copyholders had to give up one third of their land, non-hereditary ones one half and peasants without horses were entirely excluded from the soil.

460 Otto Hintze, *Die Hohenzollern und ihr Werk*, (Berlin, 1916), p. 495.

461 Gustav Schmoller made the following tabulation of the distribution of the rural population under the absolute monarchy in Brandenburg (*Zur*

NOTES

Verfassungs-, Verwaltungs- und Wirtschaftsgeschichte, Leipzig 1898, p. 623):

1618	1746	1774	1804	
18558	16646	18842	18097	peasants
13644	12709	17063	21045	cotters
2659	18456	28925	33228	attached to large estates.

(Cotters (*Kossäten*) tilled land but without regular holding in the village fields and without cattle.)

[462] Marie Dumler, 'Die Bestrebungen zur Befreiung der Privatbauern in Preussen,' *Forschungen zur Brandenburgisch-Preussischen Geschichte*, Band 33, p. 187.

[463] Rudolf Hilferding, *Das Finanzkapital* (Marx-Studien, Band II), (Wien, 1923), p. 432.

[464] Friese, quoted in Edgar Loening, *Gerichte und Verwaltungsbehörden in Brandenburg-Preussen*, (Halle, 1914), p. 133. Walter Hamel (*Dtsch. Recht* 1936, p. 413) has described this important development of police law. He proposes to substitute the Prussian Police Law of 1931 for Friese's decree of 1808.

[465] Eckhart Kehr, 'Zur Genesis der preussischen Bürokratie und des Rechtsstaats (Ein Beitrag zum Diktaturproblem),' *Gesellschaft*, 1932, p. 109.

[466] Rudolf Hilferding, op. cit., p. 432.

[467] In contrast with the monarchy of Frederic the Great, in which the leadership of the army and the upper hierarchy of the administration was staffed exclusively by the nobility, while the state was directed politically by the king and his bourgeois councillors, in post-Napoleonic Germany political leadership too fell into the hands of the aristocratic higher bureaucracy. Prince von Hardenberg in Prussia, Prince von Metternich in Austria were its most famous representatives.

[468] Ludwig Waldecker, *Von Brandenburg über Preussen zum Reich*. (Berlin 1935), p. 114.

[469] Franz Schnabel, *Deutsche Geschichte im 19. Jahrhundert* (Freiburg, 1929), Band II, p. 110.

[470] Emil Lederer, 'Zur Soziologie des Weltkrieges,' *Arch. f. Szw.* Band 39, p. 359.

[471] Ib., p. 373.

[472] Konrad Heiden, *History of National-Socialism* (translated from the German, London, 1934), p. 1.

[473] Fritz Tarnow, *Parteitag der Sozialdemokratischen Partei Deutschlands zu Leipzig 1931* (Berlin, 1931), p. 45.

[474] See *Deutschlands wirtschaftliche Lage in der Jahresmitte 1939* (published by the Reichskreditgesellschaft, Berlin, 1939).

475 Joseph Schumpeter, 'Zur Soziologie der Imperialismen,' (*Arch. f. Szw.* Band 46, p. 309).

476 *Fft. Ztg.* May 22, 1935.

477 Ferdinand Toennies, *Gemeinschaft und Gesellschaft* (Berlin, 1926).

478 Cf. Hans Freyer, *Soziologie als Wirklichkeitswissenschaft* (Leipzig 1930).

479 Alfred von Martin, 'Zur Soziologie der Gegenwart,' *Zeitschrift für Kulturgeschichte*, Band 27, pp. 94-119, especially p. 97.

480 Werner Sombart, *A New Social Philosophy* (Princeton, 1937).

481 See 'Germany's Economic War Preparations' in *The Banker*, vol. 41, 1937, p. 138.

482 Heinz Marr, *Die Massenwelt im Kampf um ihre Form* (*Zur Soziologie der deutschen Gegenwart*) (Hamburg, 1934), pp. 549, 564.

483 Ib., p. 550.

484 Reinhard Hoehn, review of Koellreutter, *Grundriss der Allgemeinen Staatslehre* (*J.W.* 1936, p. 1653).

485 Andreas Pfenning, 'Gemeinschaft und Staatswissenschaft (Versuch einer systematischen Bestimmung des Gemeinschaftsbegriffs),' *Ztschr. f. d. ges. Staatsw.* Band 96, p. 314.

486 Reinhard Hoehn, *Rechtsgemeinschaft und Volksgemeinschaft* (Hamburg, 1935), p. 81.

487 Hermann Schmalenbach, 'Die soziologische Kategorie des Bundes,' *Die Dioskuren*, Band 1, p. 35-105.

488 Werner Mansfeld, 'Der Führer des Betriebes,' *J. W.* 1934, p. 1005. Till 1933 Mansfeld was counsel for the mining industry. 'Whenever the legislature attempts to regulate the differences between masters and workmen, its counsellors are always the masters.' (Adam Smith, *Wealth of Nations*, Chap. X.)

489 Heinz Marr, op. cit. pp. 466, 7, 8.

490 Ib.

491 *D. A. Z.*, April 28, 1938.

492 Ib.

493 Ib.

494 Ib.

495 Ib.

496 Werner Mansfeld, 'Vom Arbeitsvertrag,' *Dtsch. Arb. R.* 1936, p. 124.

497 Karl Marx, *Capital*, vol. I, (translated by Samuel Moore and Edward Aveling, Chicago, 1912) p. 692.

498 Andreas Pfenning, 'Gemeinschaft und Staatswissenschaft,' *Ztschr. f. d. ges. Staatsw.* Band 96, p. 302.

499 Gottfried Neese, 'Die verfassungsrechtliche Gestaltung der "Einpartei," ' *Ztschr. f d. ges. Staatsw.* Band 98, p. 680.

500 See note 498.

501 Max Weber, *Wirtschaft und Gesellschaft*, (Tübingen, 1922) p. 198.

502 Hellmuth Plessner, *Grenzen der Gemeinschaft*, (*Eine Kritik des sozialen Radikalismus*), (Bonn, 1924) p. 54.

503 Hence, it is interesting to recall that more than 130 years ago the Federalists realized the same point when they were fighting Jeffersonian democracy. One of their leaders, Fisher Ames, wrote in 1802 to Rufus King: 'We need, as all nations do, the compression on the outside of our circle of a formidable neighbour, whose presence shall at all times excite stronger fears than demagogues can inspire the people with towards their government.' (Quoted in Raymond Gettell, *History of American Political Thought* (New York, 1928), p. 185.) This letter of Fisher Ames draws its meaning from the dread of Jacobinism which swept the western world after the French Revolution.

504 Carl Schmitt, 'Totaler Feind, totaler Krieg, totaler Staat,' *Völkerrecht und Völkerbund*, Band IV, 1937, pp. 139-145.

505 Quoted in *Rasse und Recht*, 1935, p. 29.

506 Article 'Rechtsstaat' in '*Handwörterbuch der Rechtswissenschaft*,' Band VIII, pp. 572-3.

507 Carl Schmitt (*Geistesgeschichtliche Lage des Parlamentarismus*, 2nd ed., München, 1926, p. 87) once pointed out quite aptly that the history of the stereotype of the bourgeoisie is as important as the history of the bourgeoisie itself. However, Schmitt accused Marxism unjustly of having given an almost supernatural aura to this stereotype. 'A synthesis of all that is hateful with which one does not discuss — but which one annihilates.' The racial problem has a bogey function in National-Socialist theory of the community. [On the 'bogey' cf. Paul Szende, 'Eine soziologische Theorie der Abstraktion,' *Arch.f. Szw.* Band 50, p. 469].

508 Reinhard Hoehn, *Rechtsgemeinschaft und Volksgemeinschaft* (Hamburg, 1935) p. 83. ('Vom Standpunkt der Volksgemeinschaft ist jede Wertgemeinschaft eine Zersetzungsgemeinschaft.')

509 Fritz Kern, 'Über die mittelalterliche Anschauung von Staat, Recht und Verfassung,' *H. Z.* Band 120, pp. 63-4.

510 Ludo Moritz Hartmann, 'Der Begriff des Politischen,' (*Festgabe für Lujo Brentano zu dessen 70. Geburtstag*, München 1916, p. 220.)

511 Carl Schmitt, 'Der Begriff des Politischen' *Arch. f. Szw* Band 58, p. 1.

512 Rudolf Smend, *Die politische Gewalt im Verfassungsstaat und das Problem der Staatsform*, (*Festgabe für Wilhelm Kahl*), (Tübingen, 1923), p. 17.

513 Joseph Schumpeter, 'Zur Soziologie der Imperialismen,' *Arch. f. Szw.* Band 46, pp. 1-39, 275-310.

514 Hubert R. Knickerbocker, *The German Crisis* (New York, 1932).

515 On September 20, 1922, Mussolini said in a speech at Udine: 'Our program is very simple — we want to rule Italy!'

516 Walther Rathenau, *Gesammelte Schriften*, Band V, p. 272.

517 Hans Kelsen, 'The Party Dictatorship,' *Politica*, vol. II, p. 31.

240 NOTES

518 Heinrich Herrfahrdt, 'Politische Verfassungslehre,' *Arch. f. Rechts- u. Soz. Phil.*,' Band XXX p. 107.

519 The Earl of Balfour, introduction to Walter Bagehot, *The English Constitution* (Oxford, 1928), p. xxiv.

520 'First Inaugural Address, March 4, 1801,' in *A Compilation of the Messages and Papers of the Presidents*, vol. I, (New York, 1897), p. 310.

521 Hegel, *Grundlinien der Philosophie des Rechts* (herausgegeben von Lasson), 3rd ed. (Leipzig, 1930), §270, p. 212; English translation by S. W. Deyde, *Philosophy of Right* (London, 1896), p. 263.

522 *Fft. Ztg.*, January 22, 1937.

523 Alfred von Martin, 'Zur Soziologie der Gegenwart,' *Zeitschrift für Kulturgeschichte*, Band 27, pp. 94-117.

524 Arnold Koettgen, 'Die Gesetzmässigkeit der Verwaltung im Führerstaat,' *R. Verw. Bl.* 1936, pp. 457-62.

525 See Karl Mannheim, *Mensch und Gesellschaft im Zeitalter des Umbaus* (Leyden, 1935), p. 27 and ib., 'Rational and Irrational Elements in Contemporary Society,' L. T. Hobhouse Memorial Trust Lectures No. 4, delivered on 7 March 1934 (London, 1934), p. 14.

526 Carl Schmitt, *Römischer Katholizismus und politische Form* (Hellerau, 1923), p. 31. This book was later withdrawn from circulation by Schmitt himself.

527 Ib., p. 30

528 Rainer Heyne, 'George Sorel und der autoritäre Staat des 20. Jahrhunderts,' *Arch. d. öff. Rechts*, N. F., Band 29, p. 129.

529 Ib.

530 Er nennt's Vernunft und braucht's allein,
Nur tierischer als jedes Tier zu sein.

(Goethe, *Faust.*)

REICHSGESETZBLATT

(Official Statute Book)

Teil I

1933   Issued at Berlin, February 28, 1933   No. 17

CONTENTS: Decree of the President of the Reich for the Protection of the People and the State. February 28, 1933, p. 83.

DECREE OF THE PRESIDENT OF THE REICH FOR THE PROTECTION OF THE PEOPLE AND THE STATE . . . OF FEBRUARY 28, 1933.

On account of the Article 48, paragraph 2 of the Constitution of the Reich, the following decree is issued for the defence against Communistic, state-endangering acts of violence:

§ 1.

The Articles 114, 115, 117, 118, 123, 124, and 153 of the Constitution of the German Reich are put out of force until further notice. Restrictions of personal freedom, the right of free expression of opinion, including the right of the press, the right of associations and meetings, interference with the secrets of letters, of the post, the telegraph and the telephone, the issue of search warrants, as well as of orders for confiscation or restriction of property — all these restrictions are therefore also admissable beyond the otherwise legally fixed limitations.

§ 2.

If the necessary measures for the re-establishment of public security and order are not taken the Government of the Reich may then temporarily exercise the authority of the supreme Government of the land.

§ 3.

The authorities of the lands and municipalities (Municipal Associations) have to comply with the orders of the Government of the Reich issued on account of 2 within the framework of their competence.

INDEX